T0305114

The State and the Economic Process

The State and the Economic Process

Edited by

C.W.M. Naastepad and Servaas Storm
Centre for Development Planning
Erasmus University Rotterdam

Edward Elgar
Cheltenham, UK • Brookfield, US

Published by
Edward Elgar Publishing Limited
8 Lansdown Place
Cheltenham
Glos GL50 2HU
UK

Edward Elgar Publishing Company
Old Post Road
Brookfield
Vermont 05036
US

British Library Cataloguing in Publication Data
The state and the economic process
   1. Keynesian economics 2. Economics
I. Naastepad, C.W.M. II. Storm, Servaas
330.1'56

Library of Congress Cataloguing in Publication Data
The state and the economic process / edited by C.W.M. Naastepad and
Servaas Storm.
   Most of the papers were discussed at an international conference
on The State and the Economic Process in Nov. 1993.
   Includes bibliographical references
   1. Developing countries—Economic policy—Congresses. 2. Economic
policy—Congresses. 3. Developing countries—Economic conditions-
–Congresses. 4. Economic history—1945- —Congresses.
I. Naastepad, C.W.M., 1961- . II. Storm, Servaas.
HC59.7.S757 1996
338.9—dc20   95–42421
                                              CIP

ISBN 1 85898 168 9

Printed and bound in Great Britain by
Hartnolls Limited, Bodmin, Cornwall

Contents

Figures

Tables

Contributors

Alice H. Amsden, Massachusetts Institute of Technology, Cambridge MA

Amit Bhaduri, Jawaharlal Nehru University, New Delhi

Serguey Braguinsky, Yokohama City University, Yokohama

Andrew Glyn, Corpus Christi College, Oxford

Alain Lipietz, CEPREMAP, Paris

C.W.M. Naastepad, Centre for Development Planning, Erasmus University Rotterdam, Rotterdam

Domenico Mario Nuti, University of Rome 'La Sapienza', Rome, and London Business School, London

Annemieke Roobeek, University of Amsterdam, Amsterdam, and University of Nijenrode, Breukelen

Ignacy Sachs, Ecole des Hautes Etudes en Sciences Sociales, Paris

Abhijit Sen, Jawaharlal Nehru University, New Delhi

Servaas Storm, Centre for Development Planning, Erasmus University Rotterdam, Rotterdam

Lance Taylor, New School for Social Research, New York

Piet Terhal, Centre for Development Planning, Erasmus University Rotterdam, Rotterdam

Dirk J. Wolfson, Scientific Council for Government Policy Making, Den Haag, and Erasmus University Rotterdam, Rotterdam

Acknowledgement

The editors would like to thank Dennis H. Arends for his enormous patience, meticulousness and dedication in preparing a camera-ready copy of the original manuscript of this book.

Preface

In November 1993, on the occasion of the 25th anniversary of the Centre for Development Planning of the Erasmus University Rotterdam, the Centre and the Dutch–Belgian Association of Post-Keynesian Economics joined hands in organising an international conference on *The State and the Economic Process*, which was at the same time the 14th annual conference of the Association. Most of the chapters in this book were discussed at the conference and reworked in the light of the discussions. The two editors, young scholars at the Centre, who are also active on the board of the Association, added a thorough introduction as a background to the chapters and did, in my view, a highly commendable job.

For several reasons, I think this collection is a valuable contribution to the literature on the subject. Firstly, it goes beyond the usual, rather superficial advocacy of the market as the institution that can deal adequately with most economic problems, nor does it stop at the microeconomic and largely static 'state or market' discussion in which the state is requested to pick up the pieces of market failures. It addresses some central elements of the economic process, first of all in a macroeconomic perspective which inevitably encompasses the important role which the modern state and its institutions play in this process.

Secondly, this book deals with developing economies, transitional economies, and so-called developed economies, giving each their own rightful place, in a broad global perspective. It does not suggest that the problems of any of these groups are just a minor variation of those of another, but invites the reader to think of each of them thoroughly and without bias taking advantage of some rather universal conceptualisations of economics. Thus the reader will discover rather than assume similarities in the problems of these groups. That this book is meant to encourage such analyses, which can help to understand the problems better and deal constructively with them, is signalled by the inclusion of chapters directed at environmental and sustainability issues.

Thirdly and finally, on several occasions the book takes a long-term view of several decades, which opens a proper and illuminating perspective. In this it calls to mind the book published on the occasion of the 20th anniversary of the Centre and the ninth annual conference of the Association on *A Dual World Economy, Forty Years of Development Experience*, to which the present book can be considered a deepened sequel, standing on its own feet. As a former director of the Centre and former chairman of the Association I congratulate both of them on this volume. The insights we gained at the conference are now available to a wider public of interested readers, who can also become beneficiaries of this serious endeavour.

J. George Waardenburg

1. The global 'crisis' of the 1990s: origins, dimensions and policy implications

C.W.M. Naastepad and Servaas Storm

'In the course of history, reason sometimes wins out.
This is called progress.'[1]

Introduction

In 1993, world output increased by little more than one per cent after two years of practically no growth. Hence, for the third year in succession, the rate of growth of world output was below that of world population. Poor growth and high unemployment levels characterise the developed market economies of the OECD in the 1990s. Economic decline continues to be a feature of the so-called economies in transition; as a result, open unemployment, virtually unknown in these countries for decades, rose sharply. The slowdown in the OECD and the former Comecon has reduced the growth of exports and output in the developing economies, but its impact varied widely among countries. The world recession hinders some of the Latin American countries, still burdened by debt, in the process of structural reform and adjustment. Many (not all) African economies remain locked in a pattern of stagnation and decline. It is only in South and East Asia that a number of economies, including some of the most populous countries, continue to expand their exports and output almost as vigorously as in the 1980s. Nonetheless, the economic situation in virtually all regions of the world has been and still is far from satisfactory and the prospect that the situation will not be radically improved soon raises a number of disturbing questions. How can the widespread unemployment in the OECD countries be reduced? Did the contraction of output and employment in the economies in transition have to be so deep and protracted? Why, after all

1

these years of 'structural adjustment', are many developing economies still suffering from stagnation and high inflation? Why, on the other hand, are more than ten Asian economies, both large and small, able to continue growing rapidly? Clearly, these questions take different forms, but they have one common theme: how to design and redesign economic policies in order to increase growth and bring down unemployment. The papers in this volume offer a critical examination of this important issue.

Chapter 2 by Amit Bhaduri is concerned with the role of the state in developing economies, drawing out the main long-term policy lessons of post-war economic history and policy in large, predominantly agrarian economies. Avoiding the sterile debate on 'market failure' versus 'government failure', Bhaduri draws the major lesson that, in contrast to more conventional thinking emphasising supply-side linkages, the sequence of investment decisions should be determined primarily by considerations of final demand. To be successful, however, the management of this demand-led industrialisation strategy must also focus on 'structural' factors, in particular the improvement of agricultural productivity. State intervention through public investment and a reorientation of property rights in land is essential, because of the nature of property rights in land as well as the 'free rider' problem. Bhaduri argues that public investment programmes and land reforms have to be supplemented by adequate price incentives aimed at maintaining a steady expansion of the domestic market for industrial goods.

Chapters 3 and 4 deal with the OECD economies. In Chapter 3, Andrew Glyn analyses the evolution of labour–capital relations during the OECD's 'golden age' and its aftermath. Glyn describes the post-war period as a succession of stages characterised by a particular balance of power between labour and capital. Glyn argues how a period of sustained rapid growth based on high investment – the so-called golden age (1952–68) – emerged from a period (1944–1948/49) in which tensions between labour and capital had ended in a balance of power satisfactory to employers (1948/49 – 1952/53). The golden age in turn collapsed into a period of slower growth (1968–79), because, as a result of the long boom, increasingly 'conflicting claims' led through rising relative prices of labour and raw materials to a fall in industrial profitability, investment, and growth. Only after 1979, the balance of power was restored in favour of capital, marked by a recovery of profits, a decline in inflation, increased unemployment, the scaling down of the Welfare State, and increased inequality.

Glyn's 'full employment profit squeeze' theory is complemented, in

Chapter 4, by Alain Lipietz's paper which argues that the fall in OECD profitability in the 1970s and early 1980s was caused by the declining efficiency of the 'Taylorist' model of the labour process. Lipietz identifies two historical responses to this supply-side crisis: labour–capital relations based on 'liberal flexibility' (prevailing in most OECD countries) and relations based on 'negotiated involvement'. The existence of the latter model is no longer obvious now that competition from East Asian and Latin American countries seems capable to impose on the whole world a single 'liberal' standard of ever lower wages and ever more flexible wage contracts. Lipietz addresses the question whether these different forms of labour–capital relations can coexist in a world which is more and more internationalised. He argues that the world will organise itself into three continental blocs (Asia and the Pacific around Japan, the Americas around the USA, and Europe around Germany) and that within each bloc there will be a division of labour between a centre (a country with skill-intensive, innovative industries, high wages, the highest internal flexibility based on negotiated involvement of all workers, but less flexible labour markets) and a periphery including countries with standard industries most sensitive to low cost, low wages, very flexible labour markets, and 'Taylorist' labour-capital relations within firms. Lipietz concludes that the coexistence of centre and periphery within one bloc is based on a socially constructed comparative advantage, *namely* the suitability of a country's labour force for the flexible 'Taylorist' paradigm.

The focus of Chapters 5 and 6 is on the post-communist countries of Eastern Europe and the former Soviet Union. Mario Nuti, in Chapter 5, reasons that the reforms in which the role of the state was drastically reduced, succeeded in activating some private sector supply response, but to a much smaller extent to date than originally expected and even that primarily due to real wage falls so large that 'arguably they would have led to some recovery and growth in any economic system' (Nuti, this volume). Nuti identifies a number of mitigating factors which constrain and possibly reverse the decline of the state, including the fact that the assistance of the international institutions is conditional on the adoption of conventional policies assigning an important role to the state, and the pursuit of association with the EC. With the rapprochement of institutions and policies to Western European standards, the post-communist countries are now facing a policy dilemma hitherto typical of 'capitalist countries': how to reduce high rates of (open) unemployment. Nuti observes that the pursuit of full (or fuller) employment and higher growth demand an enhanced role of the state, involving – domestically – the negotiation and validation of 'social pacts' and – internationally – the negotiation of improved reciprocal trade access.

In Chapter 6, Serguey Braguinsky analyses the evolution of the planned economy, from its inception in the 1920s to its breakdown in 1989, in terms of the conflict between planners (the principal) and the state-owned enterprises (SOEs or the agents). He argues that, in its initial stage, the planned economy based on a strict ('stalinist') police regime was highly effective in raising GDP growth because of its ability to mobilise formerly unutilised (or inadequately utilised) resources for investment purposes. However, with the sources of 'extensive' economic growth drying up, the system's inability to create incentives for technological progress forced planners to set milder targets allowing SOE managers some freedom of choice in the use of productive resources. This freedom was used, however, by the managers of the SOEs to divert resources away from their enterprises to the black market. The liberalisation thus failed to raise output growth and productivity. In response to this, the planning authorities tried to harden the planning constraint, but only temporarily, because after some time growth and investment began to stagnate, and further liberalisation became necessary. This resulted in the widely observed 'liberalisation-screwdriving' cycle, which through time led to the development of a large shadow economy, used by the SEOs to deploy their accumulated black-market proceeds for various purposes. *Perestroika* and the ensuing collapse of the socialist state finally resolved the conflict between planners and SOEs in favour of the latter. Braguinsky emphasises that, because of 'institutional hysteresis' and the very high inflation, basic elements of the old structure and its rules persist in the post-socialist system: the collapse of the state and the rise of the black economy have created a highly segmented market structure, with only a limited number of insider participants, providing ample motivation for opportunistic, often illegal, behaviour. Governments can counter these tendencies only by changing 'the rules of the game' while at the same time forging coalitions – necessary to support these changes – with those groups that are hurt by the prevailing 'free-for-all' situation. In this context, Braguinsky points to the priority of making the tax system less reliant on flow (income and profit) taxation and more on stock (wealth) taxation.

The two final chapters of the book by Lance Taylor and Ignacy Sachs explicitly consider the environmental aspects of economic growth and structural change. In Chapter 7, Taylor presents an analytical categorisation of possible interactions between the environment and the macroeconomic system, in terms of flows, stocks and policy and/or exogenous variables. Using two-dimensional phase diagrams, Taylor highlights the theoretical differences of opinion between 'technological and market optimists' such as the World Bank, who mainly think in terms of 'win–win' situations in which the environmental capital stock is 'crowded-in' by increases in the economy's physical capital stock and *vice versa*, and 'pessimists' who emphasise the potentially harmful effect of environmental degradation on economic performance and *vice versa*. Taylor argues that, although the feedback on the economic system of shifts in environmental flow and stock variables is often unclear, the economic costs of environmental policies (such as biodiversity protection and global warming control) could potentially be quite substantial, depending, of course, on the causal structure of the macroeconomic model. Towards the end of his chapter, however, using his analytical framework, Taylor portrays a low level environmental–economic equilibrium trap, characteristic of many low-income countries, in which the environment is exploited by a poor population, and a situation in which slow environmental degradation leads the macroeconomic system to crash – an outcome earlier stressed by the Club of Rome.

At a more general level, in Chapter 8, Sachs analyses the national and international consequences of the so-called three 'decouplings': between output growth and employment; between OECD output growth and the demand for raw materials (exported by both the developing and post-communist countries); and between the real trade flows and international financial flows (following the increased globalisation of financial markets so far escaping reasonable regulation). Domestically, the decoupling of output and employment will create an economically and social 'dual society', reminiscent of the 'dualism' that tends to characterise developing countries. Internationally, the other two decouplings will instigate a return to more protectionism and discrimination against exports from the developing and post-communist countries. Underlying these decouplings is an indiscriminate pursuit of competitiveness at the enterprise level which often entails labour-displacing investment, generating un- and underemployment, social exclusion and environmental disruption. As a possible remedy, Sachs proposes a labour-augmenting sustainable development strategy (a 'win–win' strategy in Taylor's terms) requiring little additional investment and involving a 'war against wastefulness'; a second green revolution (blending peasant know-how and advanced science), biomass-based industrialisation; a shift to 'flexible specialisation'; and infrastructural public works.

The chapter at hand introduces the volume by providing an overview of the historical and theoretical arguments of the book. We will first discuss the origins of the recent economic crisis in conjunction with a changing role of the state, which necessitates a look back at the 1980s.

The OECD economies: stabilisation, reform and no growth.

For most developed market economies, a slow-down in growth began in 1989 (Table 1.1). Recessionary tendencies were reinforced by the uncertainties caused by the Gulf war, which was widely expected to reproduce conditions in world oil markets similar to those of the early 1970s (UNCTAD 1993). In continental Europe, recession was delayed by the increase in business investment in anticipation of the 'single EC market' and, more especially, by the sharp increase in demand due to the German unification. However, the expansionary effect of German unification provided only short-lived relief, while leading to tight monetary conditions which in turn led to a slowdown in EC growth, rising unemployment, and falling government revenue. The crisis became acute after the private sector had joined governments in cutting expenditure (see Glyn 1992).[2] Private consumption and investment spending dropped because of the rising unemployment (and the threat of it), the high debt levels of both households and firms and a sharp deflation of asset prices.

The steady rise in unemployment, in combination with moderate GDP growth, is one of the most prominent features of OECD performance in the 1980s, or in the terminology used by Sachs (this volume) the first of the three 'decouplings'. The unemployment rate averaged nearly 7.5 per cent in the 1980s for the OECD as a whole, a substantial increase compared to the period 1974–79. In the first half of the 1990s, unemployment increased even further to reach 35 million persons or 8.5 per cent of the labour force by the end of 1994. These figures do not include discouraged workers who drop out of the labour force because of the poor job opportunities nor workers who are forced into part-time employment (see Glyn and Gregg 1994); if these are included, unemployment is estimated at over 50 million persons or 12.5 per cent of the labour force (OECD 1994). The increase in (long-term) unemployment has not been an isolated phenomenom, but is – as documented by Glyn (this volume) – the reflection of a much more general trend towards an increasingly unequal distribution of work in terms of availability, security and remuneration. Unskilled workers in particular bear a disproportionate share of rising unemployment: unemployment rates for manual workers in the 1980s and early 1990s typically were two to three times higher than those for non-manual workers (OECD 1994). Earnings inequality rose in most countries, sharply in some (UK, USA, and Canada), reversing the previous pattern of stable or falling inequality (Glyn, this volume). Conventional employment in manufacturing and services was replaced at an accelerated tempo by part-time or temporary, non-unionised labour or increased self-employment. Frequently, this represented a serious deterioration of working conditions and a reduction in employment security (Glyn and Gregg 1994). Where employment growth was relatively high, as in the USA, data show that it was accompanied by a weak average productivity growth, a widening of wage differentials, and an absolute fall in real wages for the low paid, resulting in growing in-work poverty. In that context, Schor (1991) shows that, to reach the same standard of living as in 1973, the production and non-supervisory employees, who make up 80 per cent of the US labour force, are required to work 245 hours (equivalent to six working weeks) more in a year. US employment increased particularly in low-skill jobs, where – according to the OECD (1994, p. 30) – workers 'had no option but to accept low wages, precarious conditions and few health and other benefits, because they lacked the skills needed for higher-paid jobs, and did not have the alternative of European-style social support.' To some extent, the same phenomenon can be observed in the UK, where – in the 1980s – structural reforms to raise labour market flexibility were enforced on industrial relations: papers in a recent volume edited by Glyn and Miliband (1994) provide detailed evidence of increasing inequality in income, employment, education, housing, and health in the UK as well as of its considerable (macroeconomic) costs in terms of the waste of economic potential due to high unemployment, low average educational attainments, increased crime, and ill-health. The cutback in permanent employees not only introduces flexibility and reduces costs, but – according to Glyn (this volume) – no less important is that it provides for a higher degree of socio-political control over the labour force. In his view, the increase in inequality is the outcome of state policy (for instance regressive tax reforms, declining welfare expenditure, deregulation of labour markets, and high interest rates) to diminish labour's capacity to frustrate managerial prerogatives and prevent it from exerting its bargaining power to the point where firms' profitability is threatened.[3] The combination of rising unemployment, falling real wages, and increased

Table 1.1 Developed market economies, economies in transition, and developing countries: rates of growth of real GDP, 1985–93 (annual percentage change)

	1985	1986	1987	1988	1989
All developed market countries	3.3	2.8	3.2	4.4	3.3
EC	2.5	2.8	2.8	4.1	3.4
France	1.9	2.5	2.3	4.5	4.1
Germany	1.9	2.2	1.4	3.7	3.3
Italy	2.7	2.8	3.1	4.1	3.1
UK	3.9	4.1	4.8	4.4	2.1
Japan	5.0	2.6	4.1	6.2	4.7
USA	3.2	2.9	3.1	3.9	2.5
Economies in transition	2.0	3.5	2.6	4.5	2.1
Eastern Europe	2.6	3.1	2.3	2.7	0.0
Bulgaria	2.7	4.2	6.1	2.6	−1.4
former Czechoslovakia	2.2	1.8	0.8	2.6	1.3
Hungary	−0.3	1.5	3.8	2.7	3.8
Poland	3.6	4.2	2.0	4.4	0.2
Romania	−0.1	2.3	0.8	−0.5	−5.8
former USSR	1.7	3.6	2.8	5.3	3.0
Developing countries	3.5	3.8	4.0	4.4	3.5
Latin America	3.6	4.2	3.0	0.7	1.1
Africa	5.0	1.9	0.2	2.3	3.0
West Asia	−3.6	−3.1	−0.8	0.0	3.2
South and East Asia	3.6	6.2	6.9	8.5	6.1
Mediterranean	2.8	5.5	1.1	0.8	0.3
China	13.3	7.8	9.4	10.9	3.6

Source: UN (1993).

Table 1.1
(continued)

	1990	1991	1992	1993
All developed market countries	2.3	0.7	1.5	1.5
EC	2.7	0.9	1.2	0.5
France	2.3	1.2	1.6	0.0
Germany	4.7	1.2	2.0	-0.5
Italy	2.0	1.6	0.9	0.5
UK	0.6	-2.3	-0.5	1.5
Japan	4.8	4.0	1.3	1.5
USA	0.8	-1.2	2.1	3.0
Economies in transition	-6.3	-9.0	-16.8	-10.0
Eastern Europe	-11.8	-12.0	-6.2	-1.0
Bulgaria	-9.1	-16.7	-13.0	-8.0
former Czechoslovakia		-15.9	-7.2	-2.0
Hungary	-4.0	-11.9	-5.0	1.5
Poland	-12.0	-7.6	0.0	2.0
Romania	-7.4	-13.7	-15.0	-6.0
former USSR	-4.0	-8.0	-20.0	-13.5
Developing countries	3.4	3.4	4.9	5.0
Latin America	0.1	2.9	2.2	3.0
Africa	2.9	2.0	1.4	3.0
West Asia	1.9	-0.1	6.6	6.0
South and East Asia	6.4	5.3	4.9	5.5
Mediterranean	1.1	-7.9	-5.2	3.0
China	5.2	7.7	12.8	11.0

inequality has severely curtailed domestic consumption in the OECD.

A second factor contributing to falling domestic consumption is the increase in households' saving rates in order to repay debts. Easier access to credit in the 1980s (in a situation of limited growth of real incomes) had encouraged rapid increases in consumer borrowing. The easier access to credit was the result of a policy of financial deregulation, which was adopted in most OECD countries as part of the turn towards free-market policies. Pressed by low real returns from productive investment and released from some regulatory restraints, financial institutions in many OECD countries enthusiastically went into new forms and/or higher levels of lending. Private debt levels increased sharply and although the details and scale of the debt problem varied from country to country, its main causes and results were broadly similar. Expectations of long-run increases in asset prices associated with rising demand fuelled a surge of financial activities that was released by the financial liberalisation. The rapid increase in credit drove up house and property prices as well as the values of financial assets, thereby adding to personal and corporate wealth. The prospects for further gains provided even more incentives for new borrowing and lending and the higher-valued assets provided increased collateral. Accordingly, for some time, the debt build-up fed on itself. However, by the end of the 1980s, inflation started to rise and, in several countries, monetary policy was tightened in response. High real interest rates stalled the process of debt-led growth and made the mismatch between debt-service costs, on the one hand, and profits and incomes, on the other, unsustainable. Personal income growth lagged far behind mounting debt-servicing payments, while corporations lost some of the ability to pass on cost increases (due to higher interest costs) to final buyers. Profitability was squeezed and in the absence of new credit injections, assets values tumbled. The rise in the share of income devoted to interest payments began to restrain private sector spending. Thus the private sector was forced to modify its borrowing and lending strategies and repair its balance sheet as a result of the debt explosion (Glyn 1992). Limits on the ability to expand private credit are subsiding only gradually, thus constraining the potential pace of economic recovery (UN 1993).

Finally, falling business investment, which declined by seven per cent in the USA in 1991 (the greatest decline since 1975), and 12 per cent in the UK, played a very important role in the slowdown. Even in Japan, where investment had grown very fast in the later 1980s, business investment declined in 1992 (the first fall since 1975). Besides, Germany's investment boom of 1989–91 (the strongest since the 1960s) petered out in 1992. Two factors contributed to the investment decline. Firstly, the easy credit conditions of the later 1980s were reversed as banks restricted their lending in order to restore their balance sheets and make good their mounting bad debts (see OECD 1992, p. 17). Secondly, in the international sphere, the abolition of controls, and a retreat from official interventions in exchange markets increased the volatility of major currencies and made less certain the returns from investments dependent on export revenues. Probably the particularly weak investment in manufacturing, the sector where international competition is strong, is partly due to the rise in international financial instability (Glyn 1992).

The length of the economic downturn and the weakness of the recovery, where it is taking place at all, have recently induced a modest shift of policy towards greater government involvement to stimulate growth and reduce unemployment. Macroeconomic policy in Japan, the UK, and the USA (and also the EC) now includes a package of fiscal stimulus, but the ability of governments to provide an adequate fiscal stimulus to aggregate demand is constrained both by the size and by the nature of the fiscal imbalances. The persistence of high real interest rates, due firstly to the USA's internal policies, and secondly to Japan's efforts to quell the 'bubble economy' and Germany's attempts to dampen inflationary pressures arising from the unification boom, has meant that in many countries it is the cost of interest on outstanding debt rather than inappropriate tax or expenditure policies that has become a major cause of budgetary imbalances. The reduction in interest costs of debt required budget surpluses to reduce the stock of outstanding debt – an aspect which is reinforced by the convergence conditions contained in the Maastricht treaty as the precondition for European monetary union. The 'structural' nature of the budget imbalances makes it difficult to employ expansionary fiscal policies to combat cyclical downturns. To reduce the debt service burden by means of interest rate reductions would be an important option, but any unilateral decision to do so automatically risks producing exchange rate instability (UNCTAD 1993, pp. 74–75). As the turmoil in exchange rate markets in the second half of 1992 showed, the deregulation and globalisation of the financial markets have eroded the governments' ability to control key parameters. Accordingly, the few actions OECD governments took appeared to be more of a 'hesitant response to accumulated evidence than a conscious effort to anticipate events' (UN 1993, p. 1).

Post-socialist economies: shock rather than therapy

For the economies in transition from state ownership and central planning to a market system with private ownership and enterprise, the results of the reform efforts so far, whether of the 'shock therapy' type as applied in Poland or of a more 'gradualist' type as in Hungary, include severe economic recession, very high inflation, and substantial unemployment without an adequate social security system to cushion the loss of earnings. In less than three years, enthusiasm and optimism about the transition turned into disappointment and pessimism. What went wrong? Initially, for most Eastern European economies and the Soviet Union, the governments' commitment to change was thoroughgoing, notably in their rejection of any 'Third Way' or 'market socialism' which would perpetuate the economic functions of a discredited state (Nuti, this volume). To overcome the crisis of communism, market reforms were believed necessary, but, it was argued, since many attempts had been made in the past at creating 'market socialism' and had failed, to give effect to market incentives and to ensure the irreversibility of the reform it was necessary to dismantle fully the structures of central planning and abandon state ownership. This required, it was further argued, a 'big-bang' rather than piecemeal reform, since distortions and imbalances were so pervasive and interrelated that to obtain positive results in one area required success in many others. Hence, there were primarily two roles for the state: to restore macroeconomic stability and to create a market economy based on private property.

The need for macroeconomic stabilisation was obvious. All the economies at the outset of their transition were characterised – as is documented by Fry and Nuti (1992) – by acute external and internal (though often repressed) imbalances. Most countries suffered from large government deficits, which were automatically funded by monetary expansion, given the absence of a market for state bonds (no other financial assets existed). With profits of state enterprises as its main source of revenue (income taxation being low or absent), the fiscal deficit was strongly dependent on wage discipline and, given the administered output price policy, vulnerable to demands by state enterprise workers (see Lipietz, this volume, for an analysis of labour relations in the 'Iron Age'). Fry and Nuti (1992, p. 31) argue that, owing to overambition, overoptimism, and the inability to adjust to external shocks, budgetary balance was the exception, while 'the rule everywhere turned out to be an increasingly frequent and diffuse state of excess demand'. One reason for this unhealthy state of affairs, as is emphasised by Braguinsky (this volume), was that by the 1980s the control by central planning authorities over the state-owned enterprises had been replaced by a system of actual insider control by the management, linked to the black economy and to organised crime. Endemic inflationary gaps, repressed by public price controls, cumulated through time to form large-scale monetary overhangs. The domestic imbalance spilt over into external imbalances, mounting foreign indebtedness, and serious debt-service problems. These problems became acute after the collapse of the CMEA and the Warsaw Pact – both disappeared in July 1991 but had been moribund from January 1990 – disrupted established trade and payments relationships and almost annihilated military procurement.[4] Hence, internal and external stability – prerequisites for the viability of any system – were given priority in the transition process. The stabilisation programmes concentrated on the control of the budget deficit and on eliminating the monetary overhang, the latter to be achieved through so-called corrective open inflation, which is tantamount to a tax on liquid assets (Gotz-Kozierkiewicz and Kolodko 1992; Kaser and Allsopp 1992).

Corrective inflation was the essence of the Polish stabilisation programme of January 1990, which was, by and large, followed by other countries (see Fry and Nuti 1992). Its major assumption was that inflation and market disequilibria stemmed from accelerating excess supply of money, fuelled by a rising government deficit used to pay rising wages and excessive subsidies and grant unjustifiable credit. This was held to result in excess demand for goods and hence in inflation – whether repressed or open. The state budget was to be balanced by a radical limitation – in many cases a complete abolition – of subsidies (for details, see Gotz-Kozierkiewicz and Kolodko 1992). Furthermore, the authorities imposed a ceiling on wage increases, enforced financial rules on firms (making bankruptcy a real possibility), raised interest rates, devalued the zloty, deregulated numerous prices, and introduced currency convertibility. The programme made it clear that the fulfilment of the monetary goals might cause some moderate output losses (loosely estimated as totalling up to five per cent of GDP), some temporary unemployment, and bankruptcies. The stabilisation was to be achieved quickly through radical actions ('shock therapy'), so that the transitional stage, so hard on society, be cut as short as possible. As is well-known, actual events took a different course. Consumer price inflation rose to almost 600 per cent in 1990. Partly because of this price jump and the fall in real wages (by 30 per cent), the decline in GDP of about 12 per cent (Table 1.1) and in industrial production by 25 per cent was much larger than expected. The government finances deteriorated: owing to the fall in GDP and industrial output, there was an automatic reduction in tax revenues; government revenue from state-owned enterprises was eroded by privatisation and the decline in profitability of what remained of the state sector, while the budget became charged with a 'safety net' for the newly unemployed and the other losers from the transition process.

In contrast to Poland, Hungary opted for a more gradual approach to price reform, believing that lasting improvements in the effectiveness of monetary policy were dependent on prior changes in the economic system. Hungary had an early start (1968) in the reform process: it developed a thriving market in government and state enterprise bonds in the second half of the 1980s, which – according to Fry and Nuti (1992) – decoupled wage formation, the budget deficit, and monetary expansion, allowing the country more freedom in the conduct of its monetary and fiscal policies as well as greater flexibility in responding to exogenous (external) shocks. Hungary had also avoided a large-scale monetary overhang by the gradual relaxation of price control, and the fostering of the private sector in consumer goods and services had brought about 'household equilibrium' (with tolerable inflation) well in advance of the political turnaround of October 1989 (see Kornai 1993). Yet, the systemic problems took the form of a severe 'transformational recession': GDP declined by 19 per cent and industrial production by 36 per cent in the 1990–92 period (Kornai 1993, p. 185). On the side of demand, public investment (because of the fiscal adjustment) and private investment declined dramatically. Exports declined as a the result of the serious decline in trade with the former Comecon countries, and with declining real wages, personal consumption also fell. However, because – at the macro level – supply fell even faster than demand, inflation remained high. As in Poland, private production was pulled down mainly because of several unfavourable circumstances (Nuti, this volume; Kornai 1993): the uncertainty, which in fact is much greater than in a market economy, regarding the future legal situation, property rights, taxation and other public levies and not the least regarding the general state of the economy; the financial sector's backwardness and its reluctance to lend to private firms; the weakness of the (emerging) capital market; and the high level of interest rates. These problems are due – in Nuti's (this volume) words – to the 'systemic vacuum' in which bureaucratic coordination through the central planning system no longer applies and market coordination does not yet apply. Nuti stresses that governments need to act not only to dismantle the old structures of central planning, but also to intervene in new ways to give shape to the market system, and to cushion the transition process. Those tasks have not figured prominently on the reform agenda.

Market reforms in Russia have resulted in a process of decumulation of capital – large-scale disinvestment on an unprecedented basis. Overall output, industrial production, investment and consumption declined. The decline accelerated sharply following the Yeltsin restoration of January 1992 (see Table 1.1), which involved the liberalisation of prices, thus releasing powerful inflationary forces which were expected to absorb the monetary overhang of unspent cash from earlier monetary expansion. Braguinsky (this volume) argues that the freeing of prices, which was tantamount to the imposition of an 'inflation tax', was nothing more than survival tactics by the Russian state, which was otherwise facing bankruptcy because of its inability to collect taxes. Braguinsky points out that, under strong inflation, the effective tax rate on profits will be substantially higher than the nominal tax rate, which will negatively affect profits and investments in industries with a long production cycle, forcing many firms to underreport profits, evade taxes, borrow in the black markets, use only foreign exchange as medium of exchange *etc.*. This in turn reduces tax collection by the state, making it more dependent on revenues from the 'inflation tax'. As a result, in 1992–94, output levels continued to fall and one reason was the macroeconomic strategy itself, because it severely curtailed aggregate demand as well as supply. On the supply side, under the new policy, enterprises found themselves in a severe liquidity squeeze as a result of the fact that credit became very tight, while at the same time inflation rapidly depreciated the value of their financial assets. On the side of demand, purchasers of intermediate goods were caught in a credit squeeze, domestic buyers of consumer goods were experiencing a fall in real income (and felt great concern about future incomes), and buyers of investment goods were hesitant as they did not know who would own or control the enterprises when potential investments reach fruition. Within this pattern of a generalised industrial slump across sectors, the (exporting) raw-material sectors were hit less hard than producers of finished products. As a result, low value-added primary products (mostly fuel) are accounting for an increasing share of GDP and exports. This indicates that, so far, the restructuring of Russia has diminished its capacity to participate gainfully in the world economy. The market reforms have lessened its ability to export non-primary products and to grow at a time when it severed long-established links to regional trading partners and even diminished trade with formerly constituent parts of the Soviet Union. Internally, the guarantees of employment, welfare provision and price stability enjoyed by the working class before the collapse of the Soviet Union are disappearing. According to one estimate (UN 1993), total unemployment, hidden and official, is of the order of seven to 10 per cent. The surge of inflation has reduced real wages by more than 50 per cent, wiped out household savings and pensions and diminished the ability of the existing social security system to meet the demands of the population. To fight inflation, households withdraw their money from regular savings banks to engage in – what Braguinsky (this volume) calls – high-risk 'money gambles'. Education and health services have been drastically cut down. Hence, Russia is experiencing what Petras and Vieux (1993, p. 2718) have called 'a reversion to a less industrialised economy, highly polarised society, dependent on a few specialised exports and a cheap labour force'.

One common experience of all post-socialist countries is that the control of the budget was greatly weakened with the onset of the transition process: deficits increased considerably following the reform, largely owing to falling revenue rather than increased spending. These deficits are now financed by borrowing from the commercial banks (in Poland, Hungary, and Bulgaria) and by selling government paper to the public (Czech Republic). These ways of deficit financing have reinforced the sharp increases in interest rates resulting from the financial liberalisation. Monetary conditions have tightened further because, in the (virtual) absence of other (fiscal) instruments, governments have had to rely almost exclusively on monetary policy to control demand and reduce inflation. In practice, this meant containing credit expansion to the private sector through the banking sector through such measures as direct credit ceilings (Bulgaria, Czechoslovakia, Hungary, Poland, and Romania) and increased reserve requirements (Russia). As a result, credit availability fell sharply, restricting supply (since enterprises were highly dependent on credit-in-advance). The credit squeeze, by reducing capacity utilisation in the same way as a shortage of energy or any other physical input, was both contractionary and inflationary, creating shortages of output rather than of effective demand (UNCTAD 1993, p. 159). Besides, the world economy outside the states in transition have not offered conditions particularly propitious for the reforms, either in terms of short-term balance of payments relief or of aid meant for long-term restructuring. Although better access to OECD markets has been afforded – *through* the EC's association agreements with Czechoslovakia, Hungary and Poland and the USA's according of 'Most Favoured Nation' treatment – recession in the OECD and the domestication of the German export surplus offered little OECD incremental demand at a time when buoyant markets and capital outflow could have helped to offset transition-induced recession in Eastern Europe (Kaser and Allsopp 1992).

In effect, the reforms resulted in a drop in economic activity, the worst decline since the period of stabilisation after World War II. Inflation remains high and real wages continue to decrease sharply almost everywhere. Open unemployment has increased dramatically, because the newly autonomous management of firms and farms has used its freedom to reduce its labour force to match its needs, given the potential productivity of existing installations and the level of demand; 'flexibility' in the labour relations was introduced widely (see Lipietz, this volume). Early optimism about the transformation process diminished with experience and already in the winter of 1991–92, the shock therapies were toned down in Albania, Poland, and Russia to allay public dissatisfaction, and by 1993, most countries were pursuing more gradualist reform policies to minimise political strains. The prolonged recession, which resulted in a dramatic fall in per capita output in the region, has led to widespread political disillusion about the (possible) achievements of the market-oriented reforms. In fact, as is argued by Nuti (this volume), in many countries it was gradually recognised that the reduction in the role of the state had gone too far and had led to 'capitalism sauvage'. Nuti concludes that the mode of transition might have been more orderly and less costly with less dogmatism and haste, entrusting government with a much greater role.

The developing economies: adjustment, stagnation and growth

The high growth rate of about five per cent in the developing countries as a whole contrasts with the stagnation in the OECD area and the continuing output decline in the economies in transition (Table 1.1). However, the growth that has been achieved has not been uniform and across the board. In fact, within the group of developing countries, an increasing differentiation between regions and countries has taken place.

Output growth for Africa as a whole decelerated to less than two per cent a year; with population growing at some three per cent a year, per capita income in the region suffered an absolute decline. Four out of five African countries still depend on only two commodities for half of their export earnings – the major export commodities (cocoa, coffee, cotton, sugar, tea, and tobacco) being primary products which account for almost 90 per cent of exports (UNCTAD 1993). Given their heavy dependence on demand from the industrialised countries, the poor performance of many African exports is largely the result of the OECD recession and the changes in the post-communist countries. The latter factor has had two profound consequences. First, because of declining real incomes and foreign exchange shortages, the economies in transition drastically reduced their imports of food and industrial raw materials in spite of falling world prices (UNCTAD 1993). This sudden decline in demand augments the longer-run decline in world demand for many of the raw materials produced by the African economies – the third 'decoupling' emphasised by Sachs (this volume). Second, because of the pressing need to earn foreign exchange at a time of sharply declining domestic demand, the post-socialist countries have greatly increased their exports of primary products, most evidently of aluminium, copper, and cotton. This unfavourable external environment is reflected in sharply declining world commodity prices. UNCTAD (1993, p. 93) estimates show that the prices of commodities exported by the sub-Saharan countries declined by almost 15 per cent during 1990–92. As a result, the overall balance of trade of the region worsened, leading to a further widening of the region's payments deficit – all this happening despite substantially lower interest payments, due to various refinancing programmes. The (sub-Saharan) African economies performed poorly in the face of intense policy efforts and market-oriented reforms which many of them adopted in the past years; UNCTAD (1993, p. 94) figures show that since 1980 more than 35 countries in this region have been under IMF and/or World Bank sponsored adjustment programmes. The rate of discontinuation has been very low: of the countries which engaged in structural reforms during the 1980s, only Mauritius ended its adjustment programme as a result of success in improving its economic conditions; all other countries which severed links with the IMF and World Bank did so either because they could not meet performance criteria or repayment obligations (Congo in 1988–89 and Côte d'Ivoire in 1987–88) or because of domestic political pressures (Zambia in 1986 and Kenya in 1993). Taylor (1993) argues that the poor performance of these economies is related to the structural adjustment policies themselves. First, adjustment programmes typically comprise cuts in public investment which negatively affects (rather than stimulates) private investment. The resulting decline in overall investment has been a major factor underlying the stagnation in output. It also appears to be a major reason why there has been so little diversification of production and exports. Second, currency devaluation, aimed at switching goods from domestic absorption to exports, is the most frequently used policy instrument in African adjustment programmes. However, for some countries (such as Ghana and Côte d'Ivoire), the attempts to raise the volume of traditional (primary) exports by aggressive exchange rate policies and outward-oriented trade strategies turned out to be self-defeating, as they served to depress world prices because of low price elasticities of world demand. Accordingly, Sachs (this volume) reasons that these countries cannot rely on export-led growth unless they modify their export-mix through an overall diversification of their economies. Without such diversification, UNCTAD (1993, p. 7) foresees that growth in most African countries will continue to depend on 'the evolution of the terms of trade, external aid, and the weather.'

Since the beginning of the 1990s, growth has accelerated in Latin America, averaging 2.3 per cent annually for 1990–92 (Table 1.1). Moreover, inflation fell drastically after peaking in the late 1980s: for the region as a whole, excluding hyperinflationary Brazil, inflation dropped to 49 per cent in 1991 and to 22 per cent in 1992 (UNCTAD 1993). The region's recovery took place at a time when the OECD countries, particularly the USA, its main trading partner, entered into a deep and prolonged recession and world trade slowed down significantly. While export purchasing power declined owing to the fall in export prices and stagnating export volumes, due to the sluggish growth in the OECD countries, import capacity in the region was considerably enhanced as a result of lower debt service payments (due to lower interest rates) and of substantial net capital inflows. For the region as a whole, in 1991, the net transfer of resources (that is, net capital inflows less payments of profits and interest) was positive for the first time since 1981. By substantially relaxing the region's external constraint, increased foreign capital inflows allowed imports and domestic absorption to increase substantially. The reversal in capital flows occurred so abruptly and significantly that in many countries foreign exchange reserves accumulated as Central Banks intervened to relieve pressure on their currencies to appreciate. However, none of them succeeded in avoiding an appreciation in real terms, which in turn reinforced the rise in imports. The currency appreciation had two important effects. First, by keeping import costs down, it contributed to the steep fall in inflation, despite the expansion of domestic aggregate demand. This impact was particularly strong in countries (notably Argentina) which used the exchange rate as a nominal anchor to dampen inflationary expectations at the cost of further real appreciations of their currency; in these countries, real wages increased, leading to a significant expansion of consumer demand. Private investment also recovered, though hesitantly. Second, since it was accompanied by tariff reductions and liberalisation of trade, the appreciation put considerable squeeze on domestic industry in some countries, particularly Argentina and Venezuela, by raising import demand and reducing export demand. The improvement in economic activity and price stability thus had clear weaknesses and risks. First, with very few exceptions, growth is still slow compared to the postwar average of the continent. Besides, growth is generally driven by increased consumption rather than by investment. Investment levels are still considerably below pre-crisis levels. In particular, public investment was reduced to extremely low levels during the fiscal adjustment and – given the complementarity between public and private investment – this has led to the slow recovery of the latter. Second, many countries in the region achieved price stability at the cost of international competitiveness, because of currency appreciations brought about by the inflow of foreign capital. Equally important, there is a risk of a sharp drop in private capital inflows, particularly because much of the recent capital inflow was for short-term uses: for example, of the total estimated inflow of US $40 billion in 1991, foreign direct investment accounted only for about one quarter; medium- and long-term bank lending was less than 6 per cent of the total, the rest being raised through bond issues, commercial paper and other short-term money market instruments (UNCTAD 1992, p. 95). If a drop in inflow were to occur, a substantial devaluation will be necessary which would undermine macroeconomic stability through its effects on inflation and the fiscal deficit. The Mexican 'peso crisis' of December 1994 is proof to the fact that this scenario is not at all an unlikely one. Third, in many countries, a more sustainable trade balance may require cuts in domestic absorption in order to reduce imports. Finally, the recent increase in output was not sufficient to raise employment and, indeed, unemployment continued to rise in some countries, notably Brazil, but also in Argentina. It is for these reasons that the UN (1993, p. 5) cautioned that the 'new Latin-American take-off is still frail.'

For many countries of South Asia, the early 1990s were a difficult period owing to a widespread contraction of demand in both domestic and foreign markets, tight domestic policy, foreign exchange crises, and serious balance of payments deficits. In particular, growth slowed down in Bangladesh,

India, Myanmar, and Sri Lanka (UNCTAD 1992, p. 19). The domestic demand contraction resulted from stabilisation measures aimed at curbing import demand, credit expansion and persistent fiscal deficits. Depressed export demand, due largely to a slowdown in world trade and to the collapse of the Soviet Union, contributed to a widening of trade deficits. Various setbacks, ranging from the consequences of the Gulf war to domestic social and political unrest, a fall in private remittances from abroad as well as natural disasters, resulted in unprecedented shocks to some countries. In response to these problems, new strategies were put in place in many countries, including exchange rate and fiscal adjustment as well as structural reforms in the areas of trade, industry and finance. India is one of the countries where policy reforms have brought important changes (see Nayyar 1993). The major plank of the Indian reforms, as pointed out by Rakshit (1994), was a sharp reduction in the fiscal deficit, accomplished mainly through a cutback in public investment and subsidies (particularly on food and fertilisers), and partial disinvestment in shares of some public sector enterprises. Fiscal policy was supported by a restrictive monetary policy aimed at reducing aggregate demand. The industrial sectors were liberalised and deregulated to enhance efficiency and competitiveness of domestic firms, and to stimulate exports; financial reforms were pursued to encourage domestic saving and improve the investment climate for domestic and foreign investors; and the economy was opened up through the liberalisation of foreign trade, the introduction of exchange rate convertibility, and the easing of entry requirements for foreign capital. So far, the Indian reforms have met with only limited success: although the balance of payments has improved, the economy experienced persistent fiscal imbalances, industrial recession, increased unemployment, and continuously high inflation. Industrial growth appears to have picked up in 1994, but only at the cost of persistent high inflation and a failure to meet budgetary targets. Nayyar (1993) argues that underlying the poor performance is the poor quality of the fiscal adjustment, which by squeezing public investment, particularly in infrastructure, has resulted in a fall in private investment (due to reduced access to crucial non-tradable infrastructural inputs) and reduced growth.

The only group of developing countries to have grown consistently fast in the 1980s and 1990s are the East Asian economies, including the so-called newly industrialising economies (NIEs), whose growth performance has been held up – in Toye's (1993, p. 23) words – as 'a model for the development of countries still caught up in the toils of famine or debt'. Amongst the factors responsible for their superior growth performance the following ones are widely mentioned: the phenomenal economic growth of Japan during the post-World War II period (Chakravarty 1991); a relentless export drive, while the domestic market remained protected against foreign competition except in strategically selected industries (Amsden 1989; Wade 1990); stringent restrictions on international capital transactions (Amsden 1989); an ability nonetheless to draw in foreign capital on the strength of the export drive (Wade 1990); a steady and reliable access to concessional foreign resources (aid) also during critical phases of their development; remarkably high rates of investment (maintained on the basis of the capital inflows) together with high rates of domestic savings (Amsden 1989); the virtual non-existence of environmental regulations, which, for instance, enabled Korean industry to top the world in discharging pollutants (You 1993); land reforms carried out in the 1950s, which helped the accumulation process and released surplus labour for labour-intensive industrialisation (Bhaduri, this volume); their receptiveness to foreign technology (Amsden 1989); a paternalistic–authoritarian state that imposes discipline upon firms and workers and intervenes to promote growth, for instance by limiting risks to private investors, by lowering investment costs by fiscal and other means and by channelling investment into areas considered promising in the context of the international product cycle (Singh 1992); and finally a relatively weak level of organisation of the working class (Patnaik 1994), to the extent of permitting anti-worker repression (Lipietz, this volume). During the early 1990s, the growth rates of the NIEs accelerated slightly in spite of recessionary conditions. Importantly, while Japan had long been instrumental in fostering the NIEs' growth,[5] both as a supplier of capital and technology and as an export market, it was the interdependence of the NIEs and the other developing economies of the region[6] that has provided the impetus for their recent rapid development (UNCTAD 1993, p. 131). In fact, the successful export growth in the early 1990s was made possible by the rapid diversification of the NIEs – during the late 1980s – into the production of export items incorporating both high domestic value added and technological sophistication. This diversification into, for example, technology-intensive electronics production, was meant to compensate for the loss in international competitiveness of the older industries such as textiles, caused by domestic inflationary pressures, which in turn resulted from large current account surpluses and serious labour market pressures. It also led to – what Lipietz (this volume) calls – the 'primitive Taylorisation' of the region, that is, the resiting of the more labour-intensive and technologically less sophisticated production of the NIEs to lower-cost, more labour-abundant neighbours with very high rates of labour exploitation (in terms of wages, length and intensity of work *etc.*) – a trend which has accelerated rapidly in recent years with sharply increasing domestic production costs and currency appreciations in Singapore, South Korea and Taiwan (and also Japan).[7] The governments of the ASEAN countries welcomed the large inflow of foreign direct investment in order to speed up their own industrialisation and, in the process, the dependence of these countries on primary exports was much diminished (UNCTAD 1993, p. 131). Thus, the regional economic landscape was transformed by the fast expansion of export-oriented foreign direct investment and the complementary regional trade which followed. An additional and major contributory factor to East-Asian economic growth has been the growing participation of China in the world economy during 1978–90, the period of the 'open-door' policy. Underlying the rapid growth in Chinese exports (and production) was an increase in productivity, both in agriculture and industry, directly related to the economic reforms which began in 1978. Prior to 1978, substantial output expansion had been achieved by drawing in underemployed labour from traditional agriculture into land-improving activities and industrial production, but with hardly any improvement in productivity. Bhaduri (this volume) stresses that there is no obvious counterpart in capitalistic economic history to the Chinese way of tapping one of the major sources of economic growth (agricultural 'surplus labour') through a state-sponsored increase in employment and the participation ratio. While in other countries it proved difficult to shift from 'extensive growth' to a more 'intensive' higher productivity growth path (see Bhaduri, for the difficulties of sustaining extensive growth), the Chinese reforms, introducing 'flexibility' not only in factories but also in the countryside (Lipietz, this volume), turned out to be remarkably successful. The replacement of agricultural communes by family households in 1978 led to sustained agricultural output growth, and generated surplus rural savings and labour to further industrialisation, while the industrial reforms of 1984 and 1987, permitting the establishment of so-called non-state collective 'township and village enterprises', contributed to higher industrial growth and productivity (UNCTAD 1993, p. 139), based on 'primitive Taylorist' production relations (Lipietz, this volume).

The 'liberal–productivist' revolution[8]

As argued by some of the authors in this volume, the world economic conditions in the 1990s are very much the outcome of the 'liberal–productivist' policies adopted in the 1980s (see, for instance, Lipietz 1992; Toye 1993). The year 1979 is the major turning point, marking the introduction of these policies in the OECD countries. From Reagan's 'supply-side' revolution in the USA, to Thatcher's 'new monetarist' revolution in the UK and the policy of 'a strong franc' in France, the new policies involved greater reliance on market mechanisms and less on government, in the belief that this would yield both more stable prices and increased economic growth. Indeed, so strong was this belief that to reduce the presence of government in the economy became itself a goal of policy, not only in the OECD countries, but also worldwide; it is now also the centrepiece of the conditionality of the international financial institutions. The shift in policy was fuelled by governments' perceived failure to cure 'stagflation', that is, the simultaneous occurrence of high inflation, high unemployment and low economic growth (see Toye, 1993). Economic regulations, protection of certain industries as well as 'excessive' taxation were identified as depressants of the supply side of the economy. The remedy was a thoroughgoing liberalisation of the economy in conjunction with significant reductions in the burden of taxation and in subsidy expenditure. Logically implicit in many of these reforms is a reduction of the role of the state not just to some convenient point of choice, but – as is argued by Patnaik (1994) – necessarily to a point where the state has to perform only three main functions: (i) protecting and sustaining the functionings of markets; (ii) using whatever policy instruments are available to entice capital, both foreign and domestic, to come into or stay within the country; and (iii) undertaking certain minimum welfare expenditures to ameliorate the negative effects of the markets so as to make the system socially viable. Following Patnaik, we distinguish three strands of argumentation.

The first is the standard neoclassical–monetarist argument of the efficient use of resources, from which follows the principle that 'prices should be got right'. 'Right' is determined in terms of international prices, on the implicit assumption – as Patnaik points out – that world markets are characterised by all-round linearities, that is, no world-market imperfections, no export-demand inelasticities, no indivisibilities, no diminishing or increasing returns to scale *etc.*. State intervention distorts (relative) prices and causes inefficient resource use. From this it follows that the allocation of resources can be improved by getting markets to work properly, by 'liberalising' the economy (both internally and externally) and establishing the correct set of relative prices that will permit efficient long-run growth. In the OECD, particularly in Europe, this argument underlies much of the claim that the welfare state is an obstacle to economic growth and that a retrenchment in state spending on social security is necessary if growth is to be revived. For example, the Swedish Economics Commission (Lindbeck *et al.* 1994) has referred to 'the crisis of the Swedish model', arguing that it has resulted in institutions and structures that today hinder economic efficiency and economic growth because of their lack of flexibility and their one-sided concerns for income distribution, with limited concern for economic incentives. For Europe as a whole, Drèze and Malinvaud (1994) put forward a similar argument in a paper prepared for the European Commission. The solution to the crisis is, as is suggested by the IMF (1994, p. 36), more 'flexibility', particularly in the labour markets, which implies

less generous unemployment insurance provisions in terms of the level of benefit payments, duration of benefits, and qualification for benefits; wider earnings dispersions; lower levels of unionizations and less centralized wage bargaining; less government intervention in the wage bargaining process; fewer restrictions on hiring and firing of employees; and lower social insurance charges and other non-wage labor costs such as the amount of paid vacation.

The same argument underlies much of the reforms in the post- communist countries as well as the conditions attached to the IMF structural transformation facility, established in April 1993 to support the macroeconomic stabilisation and structural reforms in these countries. In the case of the developing countries, the neoclassical–monetarist argument has been used to justify the introduction of trade liberalisation and exchange rate reforms, the adoption of measures to attract foreign direct investment, the elimination of price controls and subsidies, and programmes of financial liberalisation and large-scale privatisation – reforms which started in the mid-1980s and continued into the 1990s. Often these reforms were accompanied by a 'structural adjustment loan' from the World Bank, the granting of which is conditional on the recipient country agreeing to privatise, deregulate, and liberalise. This is justified by World Bank economists Summers and Thomas (1993, p. 249) by arguing that '(g)overnments have done too much of the things they cannot do well'.

Instead, government policy should be 'market friendly', which means (World Bank 1991, p. 5): intervene reluctantly, apply checks and balances, and intervene openly.

The second strand emphasizes the intrinsic limitations of the state as an agency for economic intervention. Its basic point is that the state, far from being an exogenous force trying to do good is at least partially endogenous and the policies it institutes will reflect vested interests in society. Such a view of the state is not particularly new and goes back to Kalecki and Marx, if not earlier; also Glyn (this volume) and Braguinsky (this volume) treat the state as being non-neutral. What is important, however, in the present context is the inclusion of this argument in traditional neoclassical welfare economics through 'the application of standard tools of individual optimization to lobbies and interest groups' (Srinivasan 1985, p. 41). Traditionally, neoclassical welfare economics assumed that the Pareto-optimal quality of a market-based allocation of resources can be impaired by a number of well-defined 'market failures', but that a benevolent state, acting solely in the societal interest, and equipped with the needed information, knowledge and policy instruments, can intervene in an optimal way to correct any market failure and also provide public goods. The same assumption underlies Tinbergen's (1956) theory of economic policy. It is precisely this view which is rejected, with the argument that the state is pushed and pulled by lobbies and interest groups that are mostly interested in redistribution rather than growth. Two major strands of the literature on 'government failure' stand out. First, the collective choice analysis by Olson (1965) and associates argues that because of bargaining costs and the presence of 'free riders', 'distributional' coalitions will form within society to protect their own interests. Through lobbying for government regulation, these coalitions seek to redistribute income towards themselves, instead of increasing efficiency in the national interest. This retards the decision making process, leads to a highly distorted market structure, slows down a society's capacity to introduce technical change, and lowers economic growth. Second, Buchanan's (1980) public choice analysis elevates rent-seeking induced by government interventions – 'lobbying for state favours, paying a bribe to get an import quota or Pentagon contract' to use Taylor's (1993, p. 47) examples – to a deadly social ill. If public intervention is to be undertaken without giving rise to rent seeking, then it has to be done without creating differential advantages to some groups and, more importantly, a credible precommitment not to depart in future from the original intervention needs to be given. This, as observed by

Srinivasan (1985, p. 43), will be the more difficult the larger is the size of government and the extent and scope of its intervention. Thus, the public choice school arrives at the desirability of the minimal protective state supervising a competitive market – the latter condition to be guaranteed by international free trade.[9]

The third argument emphasises, in a neo-Schumpeterian fashion, the stifling of enterprise and innovativeness due to pervasive state intervention and ownership: the market, apart from being a purveyor of appropriate signals, and a disciplining device, is also a mechanism for unleashing enterprise, in the absence of which there is bound to be economic atrophy (see Patnaik 1994). This approach highlights the *creative* function of the market as distinguished from its *allocative* function. The neo-Schumpeterian argument is non-interventionist in spirit and relies on individual entrepreneurship to move the economy forward, while government intervention is held to destroy producers' incentives to produce, innovate and take risks in business. This argument is echoed in many recent EC policy documents including the EC White Paper (1993) on growth, competitiveness and employment.

To summarise, 'liberal–productivist' policies are based on the belief that, for all their faults, competitive markets are the most effective way yet found to get goods and services produced and distributed efficiently and that external and domestic competition provides the incentives that unleash entrepreneurship and technological progress. The market mechanism is superior to state intervention because the market, particularly the international market, is essentially a *disciplining* device (Patnaik 1994). The state, in contrast, is reduced to – what Fishlow (1991, p. 166) calls – a caricature, condemned to fail in its developmental efforts, and all state-promoted transfer of resources is relegated to unproductive distributionism.

Economic performance under 'liberal productivism'
After more than a decade, 'liberal–productivist' policy prescriptions are viewed in a more circumspect way for the following reasons.

First, the OECD experience during the 1980s did not turn out to favour the most significant experiments in labour market flexibilisation, based on 'neo-Taylorist' principles, notably in the USA, the UK, and France. 'Neo-Taylorism' is the elimination, as far as possible, of all subjective involvement by manual workers, by putting more emphasis on 'flexibility', by increased subcontracting, by encouraging casual work, and by locating production in other (developing) countries; accordingly, workers are even less consciously involved in the fight for higher productivity and quality than under 'Taylorism'. However, in a number of cases, 'neo-Taylorism' is being outperformed (in terms of raising productivity and quality) by the formidable competitive strength of 'non-Taylorist' organisations. According to Lipietz (this volume), recent economic experience in Japan, Germany and Sweden, where strong unions forced employers into making 'non-Taylorist' choices, shows that it is possible to have a labour process which is at the same time more intelligent, more efficient economically and potentially more attractive to workers. In particular, Japanese analysts (among other, Aoki 1990) have asserted authoritatively (because of Japan's extraordinary industrial performance in terms of productivity and quality) that their organisation of the labour process is superior: workers are grouped into teams and each team is given complete responsibility for its part of the production line, including checking for quality and tool repairs, periodic brainstorming sessions ('quality circles'), and the *kanban* method, in which the flow of components, parts, and raw materials is strictly rationalised. The superiority of 'more responsible autonomy' for workers is also shown by a recent comprehensive analysis of the determinants of firm-level productivity in the USA (Blinder 1990) where it was found that changes in the way workers are treated, involving particularly substantive participation in shopfloor decisions, raises productivity more than incentive pay schemes (for instance, profit sharing). In contrast, the separation of 'the scientific organisation of work' from its unskilled performance is found eventually to demotivate workers, reduce productivity growth and hinder quality improvement.

The second major problem found with 'liberal productivism' is macroeconomic – the recurrence of crises of overproduction, as happened in the early 1980s and again in the early 1990s. The main reason for this – as is documented by Glyn (this volume) for the OECD and by Nuti (this volume) for the post-communist countries - is a dramatic increase in uncertainty, faced by the entrepreneurs, in the 'liberal–productivist' order. Earlier, under centralised wage bargaining, growth in demand was in a sense programmed: entrepreneurs were guaranteed expanding markets, since all the employers gave their employees wage rises more or less in unison. Hence, it was in their interest to invest, which in itself raises demand for capital goods, increases employment and incomes, and so on. In the 'liberal–productivist' order, without coordination, entrepreneurs feel compelled (by international competition) to reduce the (real) wages of their employees, which limits the size of the domestic market, forcing them to rely more on exports. The growth in the demand for their products thus is no longer programmed. Entrepreneurs now invest if they think other entrepreneurs will also invest. This may lead to an economic upswing, until it is found that aggregate demand does not match recent investment, and the result is panic, stock-market crashes, and a drop in output (see Lipietz 1992). Increased producers' uncertainty combined with falling real wages is also a major factor underlying the poor investment performance of many developing countries under IMF-World Bank sponsored adjustment programmes (Taylor 1993; Nayyar 1993; UNCTAD 1993).

The third problem facing 'liberal productivism' is that, following the deregulation of commodity and, more importantly, financial markets during the 1980s, the scope for autonomous national economic policy has been attenuated (Banuri 1991; Banuri and Schor 1992). In response to the financial deregulation, international financial mobility has strongly increased: the US dollar value of transactions in the world foreign exchange markets now averages 30 times the dollar value of international trade in goods and services. In combination with deregulated world financial markets, liberalised trade was supposed to bring about both 'adjustment' of economies to each other, and the mutual encouragement of growth. However, virtually none of the anticipated benefits (see Friedman 1953) have materialised: flexible exchange rates and financial liberalisation have not improved allocative efficiency, reduced macroeconomic instability, or given individual countries a greater capacity to implement divergent national macroeconomic policies (Felix 1993, p. 49). Interest rate and exchange rate speculation have created inefficiencies in production and trade, because as Tobin (1978, p. 154) points out, goods and labour move, in response to international price signals, much more sluggishly than fluid funds, while prices in goods and labour markets move much more sluggishly than the prices of financial assets, including exchange rates. As a result, the global integration of national financial markets has far exceeded the global interlocking of national productive structures. This has greatly diminished the ability of national monetary and fiscal policies to achieve macroeconomic stability within a flexible exchange rate system even in dominant industrial economies such as the USA. Exchange rate instability has tended to disrupt commodity trade, and cross-border speculation in financial assets has intensified exchange rate volatility, which in turn has augmented speculative opportunities, and so has tended to be self-reinforcing, susceptible to 'bandwagon effects' and to inflate short- and medium-term financial bubbles.[10] Volatility in exchange rates and interest rates induced by speculation and capital flows can have real economic consequences devastating for particular sectors and whole economies. For example, as pointed out by Eichengreen *et al.* (1995), the appreciation of the US dollar against the Japanese yen in the early 1980s nearly destroyed the American automotive industry. The destabilising effects can be particularly harmful to the developing countries, which are less able, mainly because of their less diversified industrial structures, to adjust smoothly to external (financial) shocks – as is shown by data in Felix (1993, pp. 53–56). The Mexican 'peso crisis' of December 1994 is a clear case in point. National policy autonomy is further reduced as a result of 'imperfections' of world financial markets. International lenders typically secure their interests by creating a market which does not clear, as rationing ensures that only the safer borrowers get credit (see Banuri and Schor 1992). Heavily indebted countries in Africa, Eastern Europe, and Latin America often cannot borrow on world capital markets – at any price. This points to a fundamental asymmetry which is a persistent feature of world financial markets: capital outflows are highly responsive to interest rates, but capital inflows are unresponsive. The loss of policy autonomy for the indebted country clearly is severe. Finally, with high rates of interest being the norm, the major players in the international financial markets (such as institutional investors, banks, and large multinational corporations) find financial investments more profitable than producing goods, and stop investing in production. Hence, if countries are put together in a free-trade situation, without international policy coordination, the net result is a slow-down of output growth, but an expansion of the sphere of finance – the second of Sachs's 'decouplings'.

Fourthly, the emergence in the latter half of the 1980s of broad public concern over such environmental threats as global warming and ozone depletion has heightened public sensitivities to the idea that unchecked market forces may generate serious dangers that even the most powerful government acting alone is unable to contain. Thus the Brundtland Report, which initiated the process which led to the UN Conference on Environment and Development (UNCED) in Rio de Janeiro in 1992, argues that our present methods of using energy, managing forests, farming, managing urban growth and producing industrial goods are not environmentally sustainable, as is indicated by a slow but relentless deterioration of the earth's capacity to sustain life (see Sachs, this volume). Evidence of environmental sustainability is related to such processes as global warming, ozone depletion, acid deposition, toxic pollution, deforestation, land degradation, species extinction, water and fish depletion, non-renewable resources depletion, and congestion. The OECD production and consumption patterns are the driving force of many of these environmental stresses – a clear example of a negative feedback of economic growth on the environment in Taylor's matrix (this volume). Environmental problems in East and South have different causes requiring different solutions. Because their poor populations have no choice but to exploit the natural resource base, many developing countries suffer from serious environmental degradation – the 'low level equilibrium' situation portrayed by Taylor (this volume). On the other hand, in some of the fastest growing developing countries, industrialisation is accompanied by a rapid deterioration of environmental resources. For example, rapid industrialisation in South Korea was built on the comparative advantage in materials-, energy- and pollution-intensive industries created by the total disregard for the environment reflected in the virtual non-existence of environmental regulations (You 1993). Similarly, the environmental record of the post-communist countries is dismal (Nuti, this volume).

Finally, 'liberal productivism' has led to enhanced social polarisation. Under 'neo-Taylorism', individuals are integrated into firms in a variety of ways, from straightforward discipline to negotiated involvement, but all on the basis of the individual, not – as earlier – on the basis of collective individuality (class or job solidarity). This leads to a fragmentation of social existence (Lipietz 1992), with firms playing the role previously played by the nation ('we must stand together against competitors') and the world market becoming the operating environment. Sachs (this volume) describes the result as a 'two-tier' or a 'dual' society, with people above and people below, and the centre getting squeezed. Evidence of such 'dual' structures abounds for many developing countries, but also for the post-communist countries (see Nuti, this volume) and the OECD countries. For example, drawing on data for the USA, Reich (1992) and Hagan (1994) describe how residential segregation, racial inequality, and the concentration of unemployment and poverty structure the lives of millions of people in deprived neigbourhoods in a mutually reinforcing way. Glyn and Miliband (1994) provide ample evidence of Britain's 'dual society'.

What can we learn?

The economic legacy of 'liberal productivism' is summarised by the UNCTAD (1993) as: a substantial increase in cyclical and structural unemployment, a significant increase in economic inequality, a deteriorating environmental balance, persistent fiscal and trade imbalances, widespread financial fragility, and a weakening of international efforts to coordinate exchange rate and trade policy. Clearly, up to now, 'liberal–productivist' policy prescriptions have not yielded the desired results, but the question is whether traditional alternatives, whether Keynesian demand management, socialist planning, or social democratic welfarism, would have fared better. Each one of them takes the national economy as its framework of reference, which no longer seems adequate. What then can we learn from the economic history of the last two decades? Briefly, the following lessons emerge from the chapters in this book.

Labour–capital relations

In terms of productivity growth, quality improvements and innovations the performance of Japan, Germany and Scandinavia – all countries with an alternative, 'non-Taylorist' organisation of the labour process – is superior to that of countries with 'flexible labour markets'. The essence of these 'non-Taylorist' forms of organisation is that they reverse the logic of 'Taylorism': they reintegrate 'thinking' and 'doing' (Lipietz, this volume). This greatly increases the productivity of labour and capital; it also renders dysfunctional many types of skilled but highly specialised labour, and many layers of middle-management; and it requires much less unskilled labour. Productivity growth and quality improvement then depend crucially on the involvement of capable, multi-skilled workers and this in turn implies a significant investment in the training of workers (Hoogvelt and Yuasa 1994). Precisely because of this dependence, the 'non-Taylorist' model carries a considerable risk for the employers, for there is no guarantee that management can recoup its initial investment in training its workers. To secure cooperative attitudes and a strong commitment of the workers, employers are forced to negotiate a compromise with workers, offering them a voice in conceptual work and a responsibility in management. In Japan, this compromise ('Toyotism') consists of lifetime employment, heavily bonus-oriented remuneration, and the seniority wage scale system, which confers some security and benefit for individual workers, who will thus loyally stay with one company. However, as is stressed by Aoki (1990), firms where the practice is to negotiate involvement collectively have to be careful, because they operate in a liberal world. Their employees can be guaranteed something in return only to the extent that their commitment leads to increased sales, and this is not certain, since demand may fall or they may be outcompeted by a rival firm. Because of this, the collective compromise is limited to the smallest stable group of employees – the 'core workers' in large companies, forming only about one-fifth of all workers, who benefit from seniority and lifetime perks (see Hoogvelt and Yuasa 1994). For the other four-fifths of the labour force, working in small- and medium-sized enterprises, often subcontractors to large corporations, which act as a buffer or shock absorber in times of downturn, 'neo-Taylorism' is still virtually dominant.[11] In contrast, the Swedish or 'Kalmarian' compromise is negotiated collectively between unions and management in both public and private sectors (see Lipietz, this volume). It is based on (see Pekkarinen *et al.* 1992) the non-exclusion of any social group from the labour market and a high degree of equality in sharing both the benefits of increasing economic welfare and the burden of recession or adjustment. The state plays a critical role in sustaining this compromise, not so much through a reliance on *dirigiste* income policies (wage control has been the responsibility of the labour market organisations), but rather through its active labour market policies (for details, see Jayawardena 1992). However, the Swedish model has recently been discredited by a serious deterioration of economic performance leading to high unemployment and inflation. According to Glyn (this volume), in the late 1980s, the financial deregulation had generated a 'debt-led' boom with high demand for labour and strong inflationary pressures. Inevitably, there was a severe recession when the bubble burst, which was augmented by a 'harsh non-accommodative' policy stance of the then conservative government and by the collapse of its traditional export outlets in Eastern Europe and the former USSR. But there are two more fundamental problems, one internal and one external, facing the Swedish economy. Internally, as Glyn (this volume) points out, there is increasing opposition of employers to centralised bargaining. Externally, Sweden is faced with the structural competitive weakness of its 'Kalmarist' compromise in a context of liberalised (world) trade and capital flows, because – as Lipietz (this volume) argues – nationally negotiated compromises between capital and labour are dangerously generous to those industries with a low level of workers' involvement and low productivity gains. This generosity endangers the competitiveness of the more productive sectors and may lead to an increased outflow of direct investment and jobs from Sweden by its multinationals.

Complementarity between the public and the private sector

There is well-documented empirical evidence for many countries that there exists complementarity between public and private investment in many sectors. For example, findings from the 18 country studies of stabilisation and structural adjustment organised by WIDER, reviewed by Taylor (1988), indicate how in many countries, by undertaking lumpy and risky investment, the public sector complements private investment by way of creating necessary infrastructure in economic and social overheads, such as education and health services, and by providing critical inputs. Bhaduri (this volume) points out that this 'complementarity' between public and private investment is particularly important in developing country agriculture, both because of the nature of private property in land and because of the 'free rider' problem associated with large-scale land development, irrigation, drainage and rural communication networks.

A 'market guiding' industrial policy

There is also overwhelming empirical evidence that it pays – in terms of increased growth and employment – for a country to pursue a forceful and aggressive industrial policy. Taylor (1993) observes that collaboration and division of branches of industry among the state, foreign enterprise, and local private capital have for decades been standard practice in developing economies: production facilities in technically advanced branches may be publicly owned (as in Turkey, India, Brazil *etc.*) or just publicly supported (as were the *chaebol* in South Korea), but historically have not been the product of private initiative alone (see also Shapiro and Taylor 1990). Perhaps the post-war experience of Japan provides the most telling example of the effectiveness of industrial policy (see Singh 1992). At the end of World War II, the bulk of Japan's exports consisted of textiles and light manufactured goods. According to the Ministry of International Trade and Industry (MITI), although such an economic structure may have conformed to the theory of (static) comparative advantage, it was not viable in the long run. Hence, the government used a wide variety of instruments, including directed credit programmes, restrictions on entry and exit of firms in the domestic market, import controls and protection, control over foreign exchange and the importation of foreign technology, to bring about a structural transformation of the economy. The rationale of Japan's industrial policy was based on what Bhaduri (this volume) calls the failure of the temporal as well as intertemporal price mechanism to signal correctly towards the required direction of economic change. This rationale also provided the foundations of South Korea's and Taiwan's purposive and comprehensive industrial policies (see Amsden 1989; Wade 1990; and Singh 1992) which involved the use of long-term state-directed credit at negative real interest rates to foster certain industries; the subsidisation of exports and the 'coercion' to export, often at a loss, in compensation for being allowed to sell in the domestic market at inflated prices which was made possible by heavy protection; (sometimes) quantitative import restrictions; the strict control over multi-national investment and foreign equity ownership; a highly active state technology policy; fiscal investment incentives; and domestic content requirements. Importantly, particularly so in Taiwan, public enterprises have played a central role in creating new capacities in almost all industrial sectors – negating the 'liberal–productivist' assertion that public enterprises are invariably inefficient or in general performing badly.[12] The success of these policies is unequivocally an argument for adopting an industrial policy which 'guides the market'. This conclusion is particularly relevant to the post-communist countries trying to fill their 'systemic vacuum' (Nuti, this volume; see also Fry and Nuti 1992).

'Strategic' rather than 'close' integration[13]

The 'liberal–productivist' assertions with respect to the role of openness, external competition and closer integration with the world economy do not stand up to serious examination either at a theoretical level or empirically. The principal deficiency of the 'liberal–productivist' model is that its counterfactual world is one of harmonious market competition, 'as though the same special interests that present themselves in the political realm will meekly conform and market solutions will not concentrate power or impede efficiency' (Fishlow 1991, p. 166). This easy manipulable base for comparisons is greatly at variance with the real world of static and dynamic economies of scale, learning by doing, and imperfect competition. In such a world, even neoclassical analysis (e.g. Krugman 1987; Rodrik 1992) now accepts that the optimal degree of openness is not 'close' integration with the global economy through free trade. In that case, what is the optimal degree of openness for the economy? Keynes – in his famous *Yale Review* article of 1933 – had clear views on this matter:

> We do not wish ... to be at the mercy of world forces working out, or trying to work out, some uniform equilibrium according to the ideal principles, if they can be called such, of laissez-faire capitalism. ... The point is ... that we all need

to be as free as possible of interference from economic changes elsewhere, in order to make our own favourite experiments ... and that a deliberate movement towards greater national self-sufficiency and economic isolation will make our task easier ... (Keynes 1982, pp. 240–241).

Chakravarty and Singh (1988, p. 40) point out that it would be wrong to conclude from this that Keynes was a 'narrow economic nationalist', since, in the same essay, Keynes went on to express himself to be in favour of a free movement across national boundaries of people, culture, ideas, science and technology. The point is that he just did not believe that unfettered free trade was the best vehicle for international exchange, because it often led to underutilisation of resources, both nationally and internationally, and it also made an economy vulnerable to international economic fluctuations. In line with this, Chakravarty and Singh (1988) argue that 'openness' is a multidimensional concept: apart from trade, a country can be 'open' or not so open with respect to financial and capital markets, in relation to technology, science, culture, education, and inward and outward migration. A country can opt for 'strategic' but not 'close' integration with the global economy – that is, to be open in some directions (for example, trade), but not so open in others (such as foreign direct investment or financial markets) and thus integrate up to a point where it is useful to do so for promoting national economic growth. The most successful industrialisers in the second half of the 20th century – Japan, South Korea, and Taiwan – pursued such a 'strategic integration' path. The Japanese economy, as is shown by Singh (1992), operated under a regime of draconian import and exchange controls and a fixed nominal exchange rate during the 1960s and 1970s. Domestic capital markets were completely shut off from the world capital markets; only the government and its agencies were allowed to borrow from and lend abroad and foreign direct investment was strictly controlled. This protection provided Japanese firms with a captive home market, leading to high profits, which enabled them to increase investment, to learn by doing, and to improve the quality of their products. These profits, taken together with government-imposed restrictions on domestic competition, greatly aided exports. The same is true of South Korea and Taiwan (among others, Amsden 1989; Wade 1990), and also China, in spite of its 'open door' policy, is very far from being closely integrated with the world economy: it has aimed at 'strategic' rather than complete integration, maintaining a plethora of controls on imports and capital movements (Singh 1992). For large developing economies, Bhaduri (this volume) provides yet another reason for strategic integration: the external market cannot be relied upon for transmitting automatically the higher export demand to the domestic production structure. Hence, an important role for the state would be to integrate external demand impulses in the domestic production structure so that export promotion does not degenerate into islands of disjointed export enclaves. Finally, Lipietz (this volume) argues that strategic integration is crucial to sustaining 'non-Taylorist' compromises such as in Sweden.

Sustainable development
Addressing the gathering global environmental crisis requires a combination of fundamental structural economic change, substitution between factor inputs, and a more efficient use of the same input. This is a formidable challenge. Those who believe that environmentally sustainable GDP growth is possible are united with those who do not in arguing that it can only be approached by determined government policy. Hence, the environmental crisis has led to the awareness that markets do need to be governed. However, whether environmental policies will be able to promote GDP growth as well as environmental sustainability depends on – as is argued by Taylor (this volume) – the nature of ecology–economy interactions: whether we are facing a 'win–win' or 'trade-off' situation. One possible 'win–win' strategy is proposed by Sachs (this volume) who reasons that 'pro-active' policies fostering improved waste-management, more labour-intensive as well as ecologically more sound agriculture, biomass-based industrialisation (in which oil is replaced by biomass), and programmes of public works and social services, are required to raise employment globally in a sustainable manner.

Developmental state
The experience of many post-communist countries so far indicates that the discipline of the (international) market is not only compatible with, but often takes the form of, de-industrialising the economy, of introducing economic retrogression rather than growth. Hence, the disciplining device that is essential from the point of view of an economy is not necessarily introduced by market reforms. In contrast, the distinguishing feature of government intervention in Japan, South Korea and Taiwan is the ability of the state to use not only 'carrots' (tax concessions, preferential credit, subsidies *etc.*) but also 'sticks' (punishments) to influence firm behaviour. Indeed, the ability of the state to ensure discipline, not only of labour, but

also of capital is the *essence* of the successful East Asian 'developmental state' (see Amsden 1989; Wade 1990; Singh 1992). Why and how in certain contexts the state has been able to impose an overall discipline upon the economy, while in other contexts it has failed to do so, is a complex issue, analogous analytically perhaps to the question why particular firms succeed or fail. Nevertheless, it may be possible to pinpoint some elements of appropriate government intervention through empirical generalisations based on the foregoing discussion and the chapters in this volume. First, in successfully interventionist strategies, the government generally forcefully guides decentralised, market responsive decision making at the firm level. Guidance takes place through continual consultation among the state and employers and labour organisations. This consultation may be centralised as was the case with indicative planning in France and the Indian Bombay-Plan, and which still is true of Swedish corporatism and MITI in Japan, or it may be decentralised as in Brazil. The aim of consultation is to ensure feedback from producers and labour unions to the state, which centralises information and (selectively) shares it out among firms. Not only by feeding more market-related information into the formulation of policies than would have been the case in a top-down approach, but also by ensuring that it is the end result of a process in which representatives of employers and employees have participated, is the concerted effort meant to result in more coherent forecasting and policy decisions. Thus, MITI's functions were not simply those of completing the 'incomplete' markets in a neoclassical sense; rather, as is noted by Singh (1992), it was a much broader role to help create a social and business consensus in favour of MITI's specific restructuring and developmental goals. Second, to be successful, such bureaucratic transgressions of market rules need to be sanctioned by a national consensus on economic ends, different from the ones in South Korea and Taiwan which were maintained, if need be, with the help of an authoritarian framework based on 'primitive Taylorist' principles. By increasing the legitimacy of the policies pursued and the tolerance of the hardships involved and by 'resolving' the distributional crisis, the adoption of relatively egalitarian policies of 'shared growth' often are critical in supporting a national consensus – as is indicated by Glyn's (this volume) historical analysis of the OECD 'golden age' and is recognised by Nuti (who favours a 'social pact') and Sachs (who advocates a 'national project'). Third, state efforts should be targeted, with the state giving support only to 'thrust industries'. However, incentives must be given to business only in exchange for concrete performance criteria, such as export targets, training requirements, investments in technological capability and so forth, which are then monitored by a competent government bureaucracy. Sachs stresses the importance for the effectiveness of such consultation-based policies of 'meso-level' reforms, that is, the creation of intermediate forms of public, cooperative, market-oriented and private, individual and collective organisations, representing the various segments of society. Fourth, the question who bears the cost of such policies has to be addressed. A government that is fiscally constrained has few degrees of freedom – a point stressed by Bhaduri (this volume). Bhaduri reasons that it is crucial to the success of agriculture-demand-led industrialisation to devise ways of taxing private beneficiaries of public agricultural investment. Here, again, the issue of the disciplining power of the state arises. In that context, Braguinsky (this volume) underscores the importance of forging coalitions – necessary to support changes in policy – with those groups that are hurt by the prevailing *status quo*. Similarly, external circumstances may make intervention more feasible in some contexts than in others. Successful growth may be impossible in economies burdened by external debt without reduced payments, in which case foreign lenders would pay part of the adjustment cost. Finally, a major task for the state is to remove 'institutional obstructions' as well as provide an institutional framework supporting economic progress. For example, as is argued by Bhaduri, land reforms in South Korea and Taiwan were essential in raising agricultural productivity and thus providing them with an expanded home market for industrial goods, which has been used both as a testing ground for export promotion and as a complement to the export market to yield greater economies of scale.

Concerted international action

The large fiscal deficits and public debts and the sizeable trade imbalances facing many countries, including the major industrialised ones, have created a serious policy impasse, the negative effects of which are felt worldwide. The impasse can be resolved only by acting directly on the stock of outstanding debt. But, if all the major industrialised countries try to reduce debt by deficit reduction, the world economy as a whole will contract and unemployment will mount. Hence, adjustment through growth requires coordination of fiscal and monetary policies at the global level (see UNCTAD 1993, p. 87). Similarly, with respect to the prevailing trade imbalances, some regulation of international trade is required, which is unfortunately not offered by the World Trade Organisation (WTO) under the GATT. WTO will mainly serve to sustain protectionist practices and managed trade by the OECD, since many non-tariff means of protection, including 'voluntary export restraints', anti-dumping measures, and countervailing duty actions, which are increasingly being used by the OECD countries (following the downgrading of tariffs as an instrument of price policy), fall outside the GATT safeguard mechanism (UNCTAD 1993, p. 36). More fundamentally, however, any expectation that the world recovery from recession can be propelled by the worldwide liberalisation of markets without any modicum of regulation appears quite untenable, because one of the basic postulates underlying conventional trade theory, namely, that the transactors in international trade are in some basic sense symmetrically situated, is in practice violated, with the existence of transnational corporations (TNCs), strong oligopolies in certain world markets, and unequal access to technology, among other factors (Shapiro and Taylor 1990). The developing and post-communist countries, which are lacking in technical knowledge and the associated industrial structures, are at a considerable disadvantage *vis-à-vis* the OECD and, given the presence of significant external effects and/or increasing returns to scale, trade will be highly unequalising (see Chakravarty and Singh 1988). The same is true of the transfer of technical knowledge, which is the preserve of large TNCs located in the OECD, which are prepared to transfer knowledge only as part of a complete package. The developing countries will be placed at a further disadvantage by the GATT's rule on intellectual property rights favouring the TNCs which are likely to narrow access to industrial technology and information; under penalty of retaliatory measures against their exports, governments will now have to introduce laws protecting and enhancing patents and other intellectual property rights of the TNCs. For world trade to be more equalising, more stable and more growth-conducive, the developing and post-communist countries have to be included more fully as equal partners along the lines suggested by UNCTAD (1993) and Sachs (this volume).

To be effective, the 'international Keynesian order' must also include restrictions on international financial mobility – the dark side of which is evoking increasing concern. To discourage speculative behaviour that can impose significant costs on the real economy, some curbing of international capital mobility is required and new forms of regulation based on international cooperation have to be instituted. This is the direction many Keynesians advocate. For example, Tobin (1978) proposed to 'throw some sand in the well-greased wheels' of the world financial markets or, in Keynes's well-known phrase, 'to mitigate the predominance of speculation over enterprise', by putting a uniform transaction tax on trades involving foreign exchange. The tax would have to be administered by each government on all payments by residents within its jurisdiction that involve a spot currency exchange. This would create room for differences in domestic interest rates, allowing national monetary policies to respond to domestic macroeconomic needs – as was already stressed by Keynes in 1936. Proceeds from the tax would be paid to a central fund – controlled by the IMF or World Bank. Similar proposals have been advanced by Felix (1993), Harcourt (1994), Akyüz and Cornford (1994), and Eichengreen *et al.* (1995) and welcomed by Sachs (this volume). However, to be effective, the proposal would need to be implemented on a global basis, since if implemented in only a few markets, activity would quickly shift to other markets. This requires the collaboration of the major industrial powers. Is that at all likely? Mutual benefits are to be obtained by both industrial countries and developing countries from most of these proposals, but 'probably not enough to gain acceptance from the industrial countries, were they to respond according to the parochial self-interest that was ideologically acceptable in the Reagan–Thatcher era' (Felix 1993, p. 63). In fact, the IMF (1992, p. 26) already dismissed the global tax, apparently as too demanding of international coordination to be practical, whereas promoting global stability through the 'coordination of fiscal policy with respect to some structural aspects including tax reform' is apparently not impractical (Felix 1993, p. 53). In our world of fierce economic competition, cooperation is difficult to ensure and, without a hegemonic power to impose its will on weaker states, it may well prove impossible (see Banuri and Schor 1992), although the case for it is strong.[14]

Concluding remarks

This chapter has considered the origins, dimensions and implications of the recent economic crisis in the OECD area, the post-communist countries, and many of the developing countries. The historical evidence presented points to the limited effectiveness of 'liberal–productivist' policy responses to the current crisis, including privatisation, deregulation, liberalisation and 'close' integration in the world economy. We have argued that in a world of imperfect competition, economies of scale and learning by doing, there are sound analytical reasons for, as well as historical evidence of, the fact that vigorous 'market-guiding' policies, targeting strategic industries, carefully managing both market collusion and competition, promoting technical change, and managing foreign trade and investment, are successful in raising economic growth and reducing unemployment. What the papers in the present volume strongly suggest is the need to have a deeper understanding of the interface between 'market' and 'planning'. This may prove to be of strategic importance in solving the pressing economic problems of our time, rather than to seek salvation in the market system, whose self-regulating properties were questioned convincingly by Kalecki and Keynes more than half a century ago.

Notes

1. Alain Lipietz (1992, p. 163).
2. The 'home-grown' character of the current recession in the developed market economies is its most significant feature.
3. This is also the view of UNCTAD (1993, p. 74): ' ... the new policy experiments in the 1980s aimed at bringing about a shift in the distribution of income in favour of profits by disciplining the labour force through higher unemployment.'
4. Exports to other CMEA countries accounted for one quarter of total exports in Romania, about two fifths of Czechoslovakia, Hungary, and Poland, and three fifths of Bulgaria and the former Soviet Union. The collapse of intra-CMEA trade was as much a demand shock as a supply shock, because enterprises faced major changes in their input availability (UNCTAD 1993, p. 152). In particular, the Baltic states and other former CMEA members no longer had access to imports of raw materials, especially of energy from states of the former Soviet Union, at prices well below world levels.
5. For details of South Korea's dependence on Japan, see the inter-regional input–output analysis by Yamazawa *et al.* (1986).
6. These include the ASEAN countries (Brunei Darussalam, Indonesia, Malaysia, Philippines, Singapore and Thailand) and China.
7. The pattern of regional development in East Asia has been dubbed the 'flying geese' pattern. It is based on a vertical division of employment among countries at different stages of industrialisation, with competitiveness in previously established export sectors continuously shifting the advantage from countries at the higher stages to those at lower ones, and with those at the higher stages continuously acquiring competitiveness in new product lines.
8. This section draws heavily on Patnaik (1994).
9. There is a large literature on rent-seeking behaviour in developing economies, notably Krueger (1974) and Bhagwati (1982).
10. MacDonald and Taylor (1992) report two recent surveys of London foreign exchange dealers which show that, for time-frames of a month or less, over 90 per cent of the dealers relied on 'charting', that is, on identifying patterns of price movements that purport to capture the psychology of market players rather than on econometric models or news about 'fundamentals'.

11. Delbridge *et al.* (1992) plausibly argue that the Japanese compromise also includes 'sticks' which enforce cooperation and loyalty: strong peer pressure *via* 'teams' used to the point of nightmare surveillance; the personal assessment system in which the worker's immediate supervisor decides on matters of pay and promotion; the system of self-subordination by which workers discipline themselves by disciplining others when pointing out faults; and the use of corporate welfarism as a means to make workers accept continuous increases in work intensity. Also, Japanese enterprise unions and the dual economic structure continously weaken labour's position, thus making it cooperative (see Hoogvelt and Yuasa 1994, p. 299).

12. The results of the new developments in the theory of the firm and the theory of industrial organisation (agency theory, asymmetric information *etc.*) do not provide a theoretical basis for the argument that public enterprises perform necessarily less efficiently at the microeconomic level than similar large management-controlled private enterprises operating in oligopolistic markets and subject to the imperfect discipline of the stock markets. See Chang and Singh (1993)

13. This section draws on Chakravarty and Singh (1988).

14. However, political support for a global transactions tax is growing, witness the recent statements by Lionel Jospin, the socialist presidential candidate in France, and Jacques Santer, chair of the European Commission.

References

Akyüz, Yilmaz and Andrew Cornford (1994) Regimes for international capital movements and some proposals for reforms, *UNCTAD Discussion Paper No. 83.*

Amsden, A.H. (1989) *Asia's Next Giant: South Korea and Late Industrialization,* New York: Oxford University Press.

Aoki, Masahiko (1990) A new paradigm of work organization and co-ordination? Lessons from Japanese experience, in S.A. Marglin and J.B. Schor (eds).

Banuri, Tariq (ed.) (1991) *Economic Liberalization: No Panacea,* Oxford: Clarendon Press.

Banuri, Tariq and J.B. Schor (eds) (1992) *Financial Openness and National Autonomy,* Oxford: Clarendon Press.

Bhaduri, Amit (1993) The economics and politics of social democracy, in Pranab Bardhan, Mrinal Datta-Chaudhuri and T.N. Krishnan (eds), *Development and Change. Essays in honour of K.N. Raj,* Delhi: Oxford University Press.

Bhagwati, Jagdish (1982) Directly unproductive profit (DUP) activities, *Journal of Political Economy,* Vol. 90 (October), 988–1002.

Blinder, Alan (1990), *Paying for Productivity,* Washington: Brookings Institution.

Buchanan, James M. (1980) 'Rent seeking and profit seeking', in James M. Buchanan and Gordon Tullock (eds), *Toward a Theory of Rent-Seeking Society,* College Station: Texas A&M University Press.

Chakravarty, Sukhamoy (1991) Development planning: A reappraisal, *Cambridge Journal of Economics,* Vol. 15, No. 1, 5–20.

Chakravarty, Sukhamoy and Ajit Singh (1988) The desirable forms of economic openness in the South, Helsinki: WIDER, *mimeo.*

Chang, H.-J. and Ajit Singh (1993) Public enterprises in developing countries and economic efficiency: A critical examination of analytical, empirical and policy issues, *UNCTAD Review*, Vol. 4, 45–82.

Delbridge, Rick, Peter Turnbull and Barry Wilkinson (1992) Pushing back the frontiers: management control and work intensification under JIT/TQM factory regimes, *New Technology, Work and Employment*, 97–106.

Drèze, Jacques and Edmond Malinvaud (1994) Growth and employment: the scope for a European initiative, *European Economy*, No. 1, 77–106.

EC (1993) *Growth, Competitiveness, Employment. The Challenges and Ways Forward into the 21st Century*, White paper, Bruxelles/Luxembourg: Commission of the European Communities.

Eichengreen, Barry, James Tobin and Charles Wyplosz (1995) Two cases for sand in the wheels of international finance, *The Economic Journal*, Vol. 105 (January), 162–172.

Felix, David (1993) Suggestions for international collaboration to reduce destabilizing effects of international capital mobility on the developing countries, *International Monetary and Financial Issues for the 1990s*, New York: UNCTAD.

Fishlow, Albert (1991) Some reflections on comparative Latin American economic performance and policy, in Tariq Banuri (ed.).

Friedman, Milton (1953) The case for flexible exchange rates, in *Essays in Positive Economics*, Chicago: University of Chicago Press.

Fry, Maxwell J. and D. Mario Nuti (1992) Monetary and exchange rate policies during Eastern Europe's transition: some lessons from Further East, *Oxford Review of Economic Policy*, Vol. 8, No. 1, 27–43.

Glyn, Andrew (1992) The costs of stability: The advanced capitalist countries in the 1980s, *New Left Review*, 195, 71–95.

Glyn, Andrew and Paul Gregg (1994) Employment in the developed market economies, *paper prepared for the United Nations World Economic Report*, February.

Glyn, Andrew and David Miliband (eds) (1994) *Paying for Inequality. The Economic Cost of Social Injustice*, London: IPPR/Rivers Oram Press.

Gotz-Kozierkiewicz, D. and Gregorz W. Kolodko (1992) Fiscal adjustment and stabilization policies: The Polish experience, *Oxford Review of Economic Policy*, Vol. 8, No. 1, 14–26.

Hagan, John (1994) Crime, inequality and efficiency, in Andrew Glyn and David Miliband (eds).

Harcourt, Geoffrey C. (1994) Taming speculators and putting the world on course to prosperity: A 'modest proposal', *Economic and Political Weekly*, Vol. 29, September 17, 2490–2492.

Hoogvelt, A. and M. Yuasa (1994) Going lean or going native? The social regulation of 'lean' production systems, *Review of International Political Economy*, Vol. 1, No. 2, 281–304.

IMF (1992) Policy issues in the evolving international monetary system, *IMF Occasional Paper* No. 96 (June), Washington D.C.: IMF.

IMF (1993) *World Economic Outlook* (May), Washington D.C.: IMF.

IMF (1994) *World Economic Outlook* (May), Washington D.C.: IMF.

Jayawardena, Lal (1992) Foreword, in Jukka Pekkarinen, Matti Pohjola and Bob Rowthorn (eds.).

Kaser, Michael and Christopher Allsopp (1992) The assessment: Macroeconomic transition in Eastern Europe, 1989–91, *Oxford Review of Economic Policy*, Vol. 8, No. 1, 1–13.

Keynes, John Maynard (1933) National self-sufficiency, *Yale Review* (Summer), reprinted in Donald Moggridge (ed.) (1982), *The collected writings of John Maynard Keynes, Volume XXI, Activities 1931–1939*, 233–246, London: Macmillan and Cambridge University Press.

Kornai, Janos (1993) Transformational recession. A general phenomenon examined through the example of Hungary's development, *Economie Appliquée*, Tome XLVI, No. 2, 181–227.

Krueger, A.O. (1974) The political economy of the rent-seeking society, *American Economic Review*, Vol. 64, No. 3 (June), 291–303.

Krugman, Paul (1987) Is free trade passé?, *Journal of Economic Perspectives*, Vol. 1, No. 2.

Lindbeck, Assar, P. Molander, T. Persson, A. Sandmo, B. Swedenborg and N. Thygesen (1994) *Turning Sweden Around*, Cambridge: The MIT Press.

Lipietz, Alain (1992) *Towards a New Economic Order. Postfordism, Ecology and Democracy*, Cambridge: Polity Press.

MacDonald, Ronald and Mark P. Taylor (1992) Exchange rate economics: a survey, *IMF Staff Papers*, Vol. 39, No. 1, 1–57.

Marglin, Stephen A. and J.B. Schor (eds.) (1990) *The Golden Age of Capitalism. Reinterpreting the Postwar Experience*, Oxford: Clarendon Press.

Nayyar, Deepak (1993) Indian economy at the crossroads. Illusions and realities, *Economic and Political Weekly*, Vol. 28, 639–653.

OECD (1992) *Economic Outlook* (June), Paris: Organisation for Economic Co-operation and Development.

OECD (1994) *The OECD Jobs Study: Facts, Analysis, Strategies*, Paris: Organisation for Economic Co-operation and Development.

Olson, Mancur (1965) *The Logic of Collective Action*, Cambridge, Mass.: Harvard University Press.

Patnaik, Prabhat (1994) International capital and national economic policy. A critique of India's economic reforms, *Economic and Political Weekly*, Vol. 29, No. 13, 683–689.

Pekkarinen, Jukka, Matti Pohjola and Bob Rowthorn (eds) (1992) *Social Corporatism: A Superior Economic System*, Oxford: Clarendon Press.

Petras, James and Steve Vieux (1993), Russia: Transition to underdevelopment, *Economic and Political Weekly*, Vol. 28, December 11, 2717–2720.

Rakshit, Mihir (1994) Money and public finance under structural adjustment. The Indian experience, *Economic and Political Weekly*, Vol. 29, 923–935.

Reich, Robert (1992) *The Work of Nations. Preparing Ourselves for the 21st Century*, New York: Vintage Books.

Rodrik, Dani (1992) The limits of trade policy reform in developing countries, *Journal of Economic Perspectives*, Vol. 6, No. 1, 87–106.

Schor, J.B. (1991) *The Overworked American: The Unexpected Decline of Leisure*, New York: Basic Books.

Shapiro, H. and Lance Taylor (1990) The state and industrial strategy, *World Development*, Vol. 18, No. 6, 861–878.

Singh, Ajit (1992) 'Close' versus 'strategic' integration with the world economy and the 'market-friendly approach to development' versus an 'industrial policy'. A critique of the World Development Report 1991 and an alternative policy perspective, *mimeo*, Faculty of Economics and Politics, University of Cambridge.

Srinivasan, T.N. (1985) Neoclassical political economy, the state and economic development, *Asian Development Review*, Vol. 3, No. 2, 38–58.

Summers, Lawrence and Vinod Thomas (1993) Recent lessons of development, *The World Bank Research Observer*, Vol. 8, No. 2, 241–254.

Taylor, Lance (1988) *Varieties in Stabilization Experience. Towards Sensible Macroeconomics in the Third World*, Oxford: Clarendon Press.

Taylor, Lance (1993) *The Rocky Road to Reform*, Cambridge, MA: The MIT Press.

Tinbergen, Jan (1956) *Economic Policy: Principles and Design*, Amsterdam: North-Holland.

Tobin, James (1978) A proposal for international monetary reform, *Eastern Economic Journal*, Vol. 4, 153–159.

Toye, John (1993) *Dilemmas of Development*, Oxford: Blackwell.

UN (1993) *World Economic Survey 1993. Current Trends and Policies in the World Economy*, New York: United Nations, Department of Economic and Social Information and Policy Analysis.

UNCTAD (1992) *Trade and Development Report*, New York: United Nations publications.

UNCTAD (1993) *Trade and Development Report*, New York: United Nations publications.

Wade, Robert (1990) *Governing the Market*, Princeton: Princeton University Press.

World Bank (1991) *World Development Report*, New York: Oxford University Press.

Yamazawa, I., T. Nohara and H. Osada (1986) Economic interdependence in Pacific Asia: An international input–output analysis, *The Developing Economies*, Vol. 24, No. 2, 95–108.

You, Jong-il (1993) The Korean model of development and its environmental implications, *WIDER paper*, Helsinki.

PART ONE

The Developing Countries

2. Reflections on the Role of the State in Economic Development (with Special Reference to Large Predominantly Agrarian Economies)

Amit Bhaduri

Defining the problem

The state can be involved in economic development (or underdevelopment) in so many different and complex ways that it is necessary first to demarcate somewhat precisely the problem under discussion. Precision in this context means simplification, but hopefully not over-simplification to the point where it can become misleading.

It is useful to begin with a tangible and not too ambitious index of economic development. For that purpose, we shall assume that increase in per capita income is the main index of economic development. Despite the fact that the 'quality of life' is not determined entirely, or, at times even primarily by the level of income, the emphasis on per capita income with some attention to the pattern of income distribution is probably the best workable index that we have of economic development in the very poor countries. It bears emphasis that, when the overall labour productivity and per capita output are exceedingly low, neither significant redistribution nor environmental consideration alone can go very far in raising the quality of life. On the whole, therefore, it seems worthwhile to begin by focusing attention on per capita income or output as the strategic variable underlying economic development, with respect to which the role of the state may be discussed.

It is a matter of the simple arithmetic of weighted averages to decompose statistically per capita income into its three major components:

a. the participation ratio, i.e. the ratio of active to total population;
b. the occupational distribution, i.e. the distribution of the active population among (say) the three major sectors of the economy namely, primary (agriculture), secondary (industry) and tertiary (services); and finally
c. the sectoral productivity of labour, i.e. output of value added per worker in each of those sectors.

Together they yield the identity[1]

$$y = k \sum_j x_j w_j, \quad \sum_j w_j = 1 \tag{1}$$

where y = per capita output;
         k = participation ratio;
         x_j = labour productivity in sector j;
         w_j = proportion of labour employed in sector j
             (i.e. occupational distribution);
and j = a (agriculture), i (industry) or s (services).

This arithmetical truism decomposes the factors on the supply side influencing capita output as the index of economic development. Consequently, the role of the state in influencing the 'supply side' may be more conveniently discussed in terms of that decomposition. Note in this context that the state is also a fuzzy concept with the usual distinction – not operationally valid in some developing countries – between the legislative, the executive and the judiciary. In economic discussion, it is common to emphasise mostly the executive functions of the state, because it has a direct bearing on the formulation and execution of economic policies. We shall generally narrow down the problem by thinking of the role of the government, i.e. mostly the executive functions of the state in economic development. Nevertheless, its legislative functions, especially in terms of property rights in land in predominantly agrarian economies would also receive some attention in the course of our discussion.

Employment and the participation ratio
Particularly at times like the present, when the failure of central planning in earlier command economies has been only too apparent, it is worth reminding ourselves that the early years of central planning in most of these countries saw an almost dramatic increase in the participation ratio. By drawing in underemployed labour from traditional agriculture into land-

improving activities through various agricultural cooperative organisations, especially countries like China and Vietnam enjoyed a pattern of high extensive growth in the immediate post-revolution period, roughly for a decade or so.[2]

As far as can be judged from various historical experiences of capitalistic development, there is no obvious counterpart to tapping one of the main sources of economic growth through a state-sponsored rapid increase in employment and the participation ratio.[3]

The reason for the absence of any dominant pattern of extensive growth in the market economies is not far to seek. The rule of the market dictates labour to be used only up to the point where its use is profitable to the private employer at market prices, in other words, the marginal-value product of labour has to equal the wage rate. The short-term advantage of extensive growth arises from deliberately pushing the utilisation of labour beyond this point. So long as the marginal product of labour remains positive, something is gained by employing the hitherto unemployed labour, especially in rural construction works like irrigation, drainage, road-building *etc.*, which can be carried out in a labour-intensive manner. Nevertheless, it was a mistake of central planning to believe that such employment creation can sustain itself for long.

The pattern of extensive growth is beset with two different sets of difficulties. The first relates to the decline in labour productivity and the second relates to the problem of financing during the process of extensive growth. Since the logic of this strategy lies in more than recouping in terms of the volume of employment what may be lost in terms of labour productivity, there is a strong tendency for labour productivity to decline, at least in the early phases. The problem seems more manageable in the case of agriculture, because many of the simplest forms of capital formation in agriculture have a large component of construction work which can be carried out by almost bare-handed labour drawn from the large pool of open or disguised unemployment in the early stages of extensive growth. The consequent shift in the *composition* of output and employment in favour of immediate non-consumable (investment) goods with also a higher absolute level of employment implies that the quantity of consumption goods produced per *employed* person is lower, i.e. labour productivity measured in terms of immediate consumable goods must fall, although in the longer run this may be more than recouped through the higher capital formation in agriculture. The pattern of extensive growth in agriculture therefore implies a reduction in per capita consumption of the already employed population in the short period and a sacrifice of *their* present consumption for the future. For the society as a whole, it may mean no sacrifice as it implies redistribution of consumption from the already employed to the unemployed.

The 'financing' of the pattern of extensive growth hinges essentially on the question of how to effect the redistribution of consumption from the already employed to the formerly unemployed. Three broad options seem available: 1) direct transfer by the state through consumption rationing, 2) inflationary redistribution through the market mechanism, and 3) some forms of property tax.

Given a minimum socially acceptable real wage rate, any attempt to utilise labour beyond the point where the marginal product of labour falls below that wage would involve deliberate employment creation through redistribution of income by the state. If income from property is unimportant, this involves redistribution of income from the already employed to the unemployed, perhaps through some elaborate rationing system of consumption goods. However, this invariably creates a serious problem of incentives to work on the one hand and an elaborate bureaucracy on the other to handle the problems of rationing. Moreover, as the problem of incentives appear increasingly severe under this pattern of extensive growth, the government has an almost natural tendency to resolve them bureaucratically, e.g. by setting plan targets, trying to monitor work-in-progress *etc.*. Bureaucratisation of the planning process weakens the incentive structure even more. It is a vicious circle that we have observed as the common experience in so many centrally planned economies.

In the mixed, developing economy, attempts to raise the participation rate through extensive growth are likely to encounter a somewhat different type of problem. The real wage may still need to be reduced; but instead of direct rationing, it may come about through the mechanism of 'forced savings' associated with inflation. Essentially, the prices of consumer goods would have to rise faster in percentage terms than money wages to redistribute income in favour of property income. Since, by and large, the property owners would have a higher propensity to save than the wage- (and normal salary) earners, the reduction in the real wage rate entails higher savings to 'finance' the process of extensive growth.[4] However, two political implications of this process deserve special emphasis. First, inflation can be a very unjust and inefficient way of financing extensive growth in a mixed economy. Because it requires reducing the real wage to an extent where it not only finances the higher wage bill resulting from drawing in the unemployed workers into the extensive growth pattern, but also has to finance the higher consumption by the property owners, resulting from the redistribution of income in their favour. To put it dramatically, even an extremely regressive tax falling exclusively on wages could be less burdensome from this point of view than forced savings by the workers under inflation.[5]

Second, the financing of a higher level of investment through forced saving generated by inflation is not only grossly iniquitous, it can also become an ineffective instrument of policy. For instance, successful real wage resistance by the workers could lead to an unending process of inflation without generating the higher saving necessary to finance a higher level of investment. In that case, the economy would be exposed to all the social costs of unending inflation, without necessarily achieving a higher rate of (extensive) growth. Therefore, on grounds both of equity and of the danger of unending inflation, the price mechanism appears to be ill-suited to 'finance' the strategy of a high rate of extensive growth in a mixed economy.

The alternative to forced saving by the workers is to devise a scheme of taxation whose incidence falls mostly on property income. A particularly attractive solution that has been suggested from time to time in that context is the imposition of a sort of 'capital gains' tax on the various improvements in the value of private land which would be expected to accompany typically the process of extensive growth in a predominantly agrarian, mixed economy. However, such a scheme of taxation is likely to encounter severe problems posed by private ownership rights in land. It is not easy to design land improvement schemes on a large scale (e.g. major irrigation, road, drainage *etc.*) by respecting strictly private property rights in land; nor is it administratively or legally easy to ascertain and attribute the increases in land value to private holders of land, especially if such improvements are brought about without the prior consent of all the individual property holders in land who are likely to be affected by the scheme.[6]

This can be viewed as a classic case of 'external economies' generated by public investment while the benefits are internalised by private property owners in land. However, the market does not seem to offer any easily implementable solution as to how to finance the cost of creating these external economies in the first place. And yet, to create such external economies is precisely one of the central problems facing the development of backward agriculture.[7] It may be emphasised in that context that unless the state is empowered with legislative and executive rights to generate external economies through public investment whose cost it would recoup subsequently from taxing the private beneficiaries, the problem of recurring deficit in public finance (e.g. government budget) would arise. The sensible solution is not to preach the virtues of a balanced budget or financial austerity, but to devise ways to tax private beneficiaries of public investment.

Industrialisation and the occupational structure

The strategy for industrialisation of an underdeveloped, predominantly agrarian economy formed the core of traditional development economics in the post-war years. The question of industrialisation was closely linked with changing the structure of occupation. The empirically justified assumption underlying that discussion was the relatively high labour productivity in industry compared to agriculture which carries surplus labour. Consequently, industrialisation was seen as the route that allows overall productivity and per capita income to rise through intersectoral labour transfer from agriculture to industry. In discussing the role that the market might play in that context the main question was whether the price mechanism could be relied upon to induce industrialisation at a more or less acceptable pace.[8] Economic intervention by the state could be justified in terms of various forms of 'market failures', i.e. the failure of the temporal as well as intertemporal price mechanism to give correct signals towards the required direction of economic change. A remark in passing is that this paradigm assigns to the state primarily an executive role in economic development which is defined by the scope of conventional welfare economics, but overlooks largely the legislative role that it might also have to play regarding property rights, as mentioned earlier.[9] In more recent years, the 'market-failure' argument has been counterposed against the 'government failure' argument in various forms. Its gist is to point out that, if the market mechanism cannot be expected to function in a perfectly competitive manner, nor can the government be expected to act always more wisely than the market to satisfy the dictums of welfare theory.

The argument about government failure has two extreme versions. In the radical view, the government would seldom act in a wise, neutral manner, because it must attend particularly to the interests of the 'ruling class' that it represents. At the other end of the spectrum, we have the 'public choice' theory of the government, where the government acts more or less like a glorified, selfish individual to serve its own interest. For instance, it may regulate production to generate quasi-rents from the artificial restrictions on production in order to have a share in it. If, in the eyes of the radicals, the economic policies of the government are driven mostly by the interests of the ruling class, in those of the neo-liberal conservatives they are driven by a hopelessly self-seeking government which has only its own interest in mind. In either case 'government failure' looks no less (or more!) plausible than 'market failure' in guiding resource allocation for industrial development, because fundamentally the neutrality of the government as a social institution is questioned. And, even if neutrality could be assumed, one could argue that, while market prices may not contain adequate information, there is little reason to believe that the government would have better information. To put it in a nut-shell, lack of neutrality and lack of better information seem to be the two basic reasons for neo-liberal scepticism about government intervention in economic development.

Posed as a general problem of 'market failure' versus 'government failure', the issues must look indecisive. They can only be settled on the basis of political prejudices with little room for reason. However, this is subject to an important proviso. While political prejudices are extremely important we have also learnt from historical experiences. Government control in an extreme form resembling a command economic structure without any regard to the market forces has been known to encounter insurmountable difficulties in the longer run. This is despite the fact that it may raise the participation ratio in the short run and also provide essential public goods like higher literacy and better public health care. Experiences of many socialist countries point both to these short term gains, as well as insurmountable long term problems.

As a stylised fact, state-led industrialisation typically meant removing what are identified usually as the major macroeconomic constraints on development. Under central planning production of capital goods was rapidly increased by directing most of the public investment towards heavy industries, according to the orthodox Marxist postulate of 'the leading role of department I'.[10] In so far as industrial investments are concerned, this analytically meant putting the 'acceleration principle' in reverse. Thus, the positive feedback from increased demand (capacity utilisation) for consumer goods to higher investment for raising the capacity for consumer goods production ceased to operate. In its place, the volume and pattern of investments were guided by non-market and state-governed decisions, which through the multiplier and income elasticities of demand created a corresponding level and pattern of demand. Put more simply, under central planning, the increase in capital-goods production governed the production of consumption goods through time (acceleration principle in reverse), rather than the other way round. It meant that no strong feedback from the level and pattern of demand for consumption goods to the level and pattern of investments was accommodated in such an industrialisation strategy. Ignoring market forces in this way boiled down to getting the time sequence in the development of industries almost systematically wrong. It deserves emphasis here that, despite its ruthless bias against the poor, the market mechanism has been capable of fostering growth with interruptions of business fluctuations, by allowing the demand-generating multiplier effect of investment to interact with the acceleration effect, influencing the level and composition of investment.[11] In a fundamental sense, both the level and the pattern of investment in a market economy tend to be *demand-led*, i.e. the process of income generation reflected in the level and pattern of market demand determines what and how much should be produced. No doubt, it contains a strong bias against the poor, because their low purchasing power does not allow their needs to be reflected in the market. And yet, the alternative of a *supply-led* process of growth, where the level and composition of investment and output are largely state-governed and bureaucratically determined, encounters even more serious problems through time as the experiences of the centrally planned economies have shown. In this specific sense, the arguments about the failure of the government to govern the process of industrialisation have some validity in the light of the experiences gathered. It may often be true that the government is neither 'neutral' nor sufficiently 'informed' to sponsor a viable pattern of supply-led growth – as various critics of the role of the state in development have so frequently pointed out.

Nevertheless, the lesson to be learnt from this experience is not the ruling conventional wisdom that the state should have a 'minimalist' role, hardly going beyond investments in social infrastructure, like education and health. Experience and our theoretical understanding of it point to something quite different, namely that the economic role of the state must change according to the stage of economic development and the particular situation. Thus, with a lot of surplus labour in agriculture, the case is still overwhelmingly strong for the state in its executive as well as legislative capacity to be involved in a pattern of extensive growth. But at the same time, the fact must be recognized that extensive growth is a transitory, initial phase of capital formation in agriculture and the state has to withdraw subsequently rather than scuttling private incentives in agriculture over a long period.

On the other hand, the decision which industries to develop and in what sequence need not be a supply-led process even when the state has an active 'industrial policy' to pursue. The pattern of industrialisation, as already pointed out, must incorporate adequately the influence of the market. In essence, it must be a demand-led process. The state would still have an important economic role to play, but that must be directed more towards influencing the pattern of demand through time, than towards bureaucratic control of a process of supply-led growth.

In a developed market economy, demand management is identified almost exclusively with Keynesian expansionary fiscal and monetary policies. While these short-period policies are still important to overcome the short run deficiencies of effective demand, economic development also involves longer-term structural problems of demand management. And, even in a predominantly demand-led process of industrialisation, the role of the state in this respect deserves special emphasis. For instance, land reform, agricultural price support or an employment guarantee scheme are not only important on distributional or incentive considerations; they may be useful also for their influence on the structural aspects of demand management. The essential problem is easy to see. In a predominantly agrarian economy, demand management in the longer run would be highly problematic (and probably iniquitous), unless labour productivity rises rapidly in agriculture, because the volume of agricultural surplus plays a dual role. It provides essential wage goods and raw materials for industry on the supply side and it generates demand for industrial goods by agriculture on the demand side, at least in so far as the internal market is concerned. In that context, it is perhaps not altogether an accident that countries like Japan, Republic of Korea or Taiwan, which otherwise followed successfully a market-oriented, demand-led industrialisation strategy in the post-war period, had as their initial condition significant land reform aimed at productivity improvements in agriculture through various measures such as land redistribution, revision of tenurial conditions, agricultural credit, marketing reforms *etc.*. The improved agricultural productivity provided them with an expanded home market for industrial goods which in some cases could be a testing ground for export promotion and in others, it complemented the export market to yield greater scale advantages.

To avoid misunderstanding of the nature of demand-led industrialisation it should also be pointed out that the time sequencing of investment is not determined in this context simply by the backward and forward demand linkages of inter-industrial transactions, which featured prominently in the 'balanced versus unbalanced growth' debate in the 1960s. The time sequence of investment is determined instead by the level and pattern of *final* demand. In other words, it is the demand generated in the sphere of final rather than inter-industrial demand which has a critical role to play. Let two examples suffice to illustrate the point. First, if a developing country succeeds in promoting its exports rapidly, the external market plays a leading role. In that case, the investment sequence, operating through the 'acceleration principle', goes from developing those directly exported goods to the investment goods and services needed for exports. (Perhaps a small country like Singapore or Hong Kong concentrates more on services than on the manufacture of investment goods.)

On the other hand, if a country does not succeed in promoting its exports at a sufficiently rapid pace, the expansion of its internal market for consumption goods has to take the leading role. In that case, the 'acceleration principle' underlying demand-led growth, works largely by propagating the impulse of growth from the internal or home market for consumption goods to the 'derived' demand in the markets for services and investment goods. The role of the state could be market-friendly because it is demand-led, in both the former outward and the latter inward-oriented case. However, in the latter case, it has an even greater role in terms of demand management in the home market not only through monetary and fiscal policies, but also through structurally sustaining demand through measures such as agricultural productivity growth.

While demand-led industrialisation can proceed by relying primarily either on the internal or the external market, a special advantage of relying on export promotion is the international discipline it enforces in terms of quality and cost efficiency on domestic production. However, this needs also to be weighed against the greater difficulties encountered in transmitting the impulse of growth from higher exports to the domestic production structure of an underdeveloped economy. For instance, the capital goods and services needed to maintain the quality of export cannot usually be produced at home. When imported, they tend to weaken the demand impulse of the accelerator-type mechanism.[12] Thus, in contrast to the successful cases of export-led growth which integrate export promotion with domestic production structure, we also have frequent instances of 'export enclaves' that are mostly de-linked from the domestic production structure of the developing economy. The lesson seems to be that, even if the external rather than the internal market can play the leading role in a demand-led process of industrialisation, the external market cannot be relied on for transmitting automatically the impulses of growth to the domestic production structure. The state would have a role to play in integrating the external demand impulse in the domestic production structure so that export promotion does not degenerate into islands of disjointed 'export enclaves'.[13]

Sectorial labour productivity and the role of agriculture

An implicit assumption underlying the traditional strategy of industrialisation has been that a changing composition of GDP would also lead to a corresponding change in the occupational distribution. However, the assumption that industrialisation measured by a changing composition of GDP in favour of the manufacturing sector would also mean intersectoral labour transfer in favour of manufacturing has not been borne out by several recent experiences. For instance, almost all countries of South Asia in the post-World–War–II period have experienced a significant change in the composition of GDP in favour of industrial output, but with only a slight decline in the proportion of workforce in agriculture. This means arithmetically that labour productivity in agriculture has declined relative to the overall productivity level in the economy.[14] This declining agricultural productivity relative to other sectors needs to be viewed against the fact that the sectorial labour-productivity differentials between the developed and the developing countries tend to be highest in agriculture (about 15 times) compared to industry and organised services (three to five times).[15]

However, the relatively low labour productivity in agriculture is not purely, or even primarily, a technological phenomenon. It is not primarily a technological gap created by lack of technical knowledge; instead, very often its origin is in the socioeconomic structure of a developing country and in the nature of economic management. In other words, it is the consequence of economic policies and of production relations in agriculture. Better techniques improving productivity cannot be adopted on a large enough scale in agriculture because of the barriers created by the agrarian economic structure. Conventional market-oriented economics tends to be simplistic and to put the entire blame on wrong government price policies which do not encourage the peasants to produce more. There is some truth in this, especially in the case of sub-Saharan Africa until the mid 1980s.

However, like most half-truths, this can be a highly misleading over-simplification.

On the supply side, price response by the farmers requires a minimum of economic infrastructure such as control of water to grow alternative crops, credit and marketing reform to avoid distress sales and road links to the market. It is difficult to visualise how the price mechanism alone can create these pre-conditions for price response, especially by the small farmers, without involving the state. In a parallel vein, even long-term private investments in land improvement in the form of minor irrigation, feeder channels *etc.* are unlikely to occur on an adequate scale unless the state plays an active role in assuring ownership rights or long-term secured use–right of land to the tenants and consolidation of fragmented land-holding. These are pre-conditions which not the market, but the state can fulfil in its legislative and executive capacity, especially in a large, pre-dominantly agrarian economy.

It also needs to be emphasised in this context that the international gap in land productivity is considerably lower than in labour productivity. For instance, most of the poorest developing countries in Asia harvest between one to two metric tons of rice per hectare, while the new varieties of rice have raised average yields to over six tons per hectare in America, Australia, Japan and South Korea.[16] Thus, while land productivity differences are only about three to four times, the labour productivity difference is as high as 15 times between the developed and the developing countries. This points to the compulsion of intensive use of land with sharply diminishing return to labour in an overcrowded agriculture in many developing countries. In other words, the problem of agricultural productivity cannot be solved without creating greater opportunities for alternative gainful employment, especially of family labour in small-sized farms on the one hand and raising land productivity in agriculture on the other. The traditional answer of development economies to this question has been to rely on industrialisation to transfer labour out of agriculture. But all arithmetical projections in populous agrarian economies (e.g. in South Asia) suggest that the required pace of industrialisation would be almost certainly unfeasibly high to make any significant dent into the problem within a reasonable period of time.[17] In general, market forces cannot do the job of raising agricultural productivity without the pre-conditions being present and, for some of the reasons mentioned earlier, state-sponsored industrialisation has also failed to transfer labour from agriculture to industry in a gainful manner. The way out of this development impasse in large, populous and predominantly agrarian economies is far from clear. But two elements which reinforce each other in the process of development seem essential. First, the state needs to be actively involved in raising agricultural productivity, primarily through public investment in agriculture. Both the nature of private property rights in land as well as the 'free rider' problem, make public action essential for large-scale land development, irrigations, drainage and rural communication network. Fortunately, in the early stages extensive growth can provide some help in this respect. This has to be supplemented by adequate price incentives to the direct producers. But 'getting prices right' alone cannot be expected to do the job unless the state creates the pre-conditions, preferably through extensive growth. Second, higher labour productivity in agriculture would normally create also non-agricultural income earning opportunities in rural areas. And by raising the level of agricultural surplus available to be exchanged for manufacturing, it would also boost the demand for domestic industrial products and create the basis for demand-led, market-friendly industrialisation so long as the intersectoral terms of trade do not move drastically in favour of either sector.[18] The government needs to play a critical role, both in raising the level of agricultural productivity through public investment and in maintaining a steady expansion of the home market for manufactured goods through an intelligent intersectoral terms-of-trade policy as well as other demand management policies. Without such an active involvement of the government, there seems no escape route from poverty, with or without economic liberalisation, in large, populous and predominantly agrarian economies.

Summing up

1. Any attempt at raising the 'participation ratio' through extensive growth must be viewed as a transitory phase. While extensive growth requires large-scale government involvement, the danger of bureaucratisation of economic decisions is also exceptionally high in this phase. And unless this danger can be avoided, the extensive growth strategy may later turn out to be counter-productive (Section II).

2. The sterile controversy over 'market failure' versus 'government failure' needs to be avoided as far as possible. Instead, a fruitful focus of the enquiry could be the time sequence of investment decisions in the process of industrialisation. The main thrust of our argument has been that the sequence should be determined primarily by considerations of final demand in a process of demand-led growth but not by supply

linkages. In that respect, the analysis is Keynesian/post-Keynesian and differs from more conventional thinking in terms of only the supply side. However, demand management must also be 'structural', focusing on such factors as improvement of productivity in agriculture (Section III).

3. There seems no escape route from poverty in large, populous and predominantly agrarian economies without a rapid rise in labour productivity in agriculture. This would have the double potential of creating non-farm income opportunities in rural areas and expanding the internal market for manufactured goods. Public investment and involvement by the state to reorient property rights in land are essential for raising labour productivity in agriculture. Neither economic liberalisation nor the price mechanism can achieve this on its own.

Notes

1. Let X = income (GDP), N = population and L = labour force. Per capita income, y, is derived in the text as:

$$y = \frac{X}{N} = \frac{L}{N} * \frac{X}{L} = \left(\frac{L}{N}\right)\left(\frac{X_a}{L_a} * \frac{L_a}{L} + \frac{X_j}{L_j} * \frac{L_i}{L} + \frac{X_s}{L_s} * \frac{L_s}{L}\right) = k\sum_j x_j w_j , \ \sum_j w_j = 1$$

where $k = \frac{L}{N}$; $x_j = \frac{X_j}{L_j}$; and $x_j = \frac{L_j}{L}$

2. In analogy with the Ricardian idea of extending the margin of cultivation from the more to the less fertile soil, one could visualise the growth process as extending the margin of employment, rather than raising sectoral labour productivities through mechanisation. The latter would correspond to intensive growth.

3. Perhaps the closest analogy is the public works programme, especially followed by Hitler. However, in so far as public works programmes are undertaken in a market economy, their main purpose is to affect aggregate demand which may raise labour productivity also in the manufacturing sector through higher capacity utilisation.

4. This is also the essence of the so-called Cambridge (or post-Keynesian) theory of distribution, formulated by Kaldor (1955–6). See also Kahn (1972).

5. See Bhaduri (1986, pp. 189–190).

6. One needs to distinguish between the ownership and the use (tenurial) right of land, especially in the context of backward agriculture with extensive renting in and renting out of land on various terms.

7. Water management, consolidation of spatially fragmented land holdings, rural roads *etc.* belong to this category of creating 'external economies' in backward agriculture.

8. The 'dual-economy' literature initiated by Arthur Lewis' influential article (1954) has many variations on this theme. See especially Fei and Ranis (1961) and Lewis (1979).

9. See Chakravarty (1973) for an excellent analytical survey.

10. Formalised by the Feldman–Mahalanobis model. See Domar (1957) and Mahalanobis (1953).
11. Recalled that even the simplest multiplier accelerator interactions can produce either growth or fluctuations (but not both), depending on the structure of time-lags.
12. It may not even be feasible in terms of available foreign exchange.
13. However, this may be a more viable strategy in small economies, where the 'enclave' is the economy! The cases of Hong Kong and Singapore come readily to mind. But even in such cases, the export activities have to transmit the impulse to the domestic service sector for sustained growth.
14. For a survey of Indian experience, see Dandekar (1992).
15. Based upon computations made by the author, using 1980–81 data from the United Nations and World Bank sources.
16. For a scientist's view of some of these problems, see Perutz (1991).
17. Capitalist development in western Europe was greatly helped by migration to America. Such 'easy option' seems no longer available to today's developing economies. They have to rely on internal devices for bringing about changes in the occupational structure to reduce pressures on an overcrowded agriculture.
18. Both on the basis of analytical reasoning and an econometrically computable model (see Storm 1993) it has been pointed out in the case of India that 'too high' a price of agricultural (food) products reduces the real income of urban consumers and via Engel's law reduces the demand for manufacturing. On the other hand, 'too low' a price of agricultural products reduces the income of the agriculturists to depress the demand for manufacturing.

References

Bhaduri, A. (1986) *Macroeconomics: The Dynamics of Commodity Production*, London: Macmillan.

Chakravarty, S. (1973) Theory of development planning: An appraisal, in H.C. Bos, H. Linnemann and P. de Wolff (eds), *Economic Structure and Development*, Amsterdam: North-Holland.

Dandekar, V.M. (1992) Forty years after independence, in B. Jalan (ed.), *The Indian Economy*, New Delhi: Viking, 33–84.

Domar, E. (1957) A Soviet model of growth, *Essays in the Theory of Economic Growth*, New York: Oxford University Press, 223–261.

Fei, J.C.H. and G. Ranis (1961) A theory of economic development, *American Economic Review*, 533–565.

Kaldor, N. (1955–6) Alternative theories of distribution, *Review of Economic Studies*, 23, No. 2, 212–226.

Kahn, R.F. (1972) The pace of development, *Selected Essays in Employment and Growth*, Cambridge: Cambridge University Press.

Lewis, W.A. (1954) Economic development with unlimited supplies of labour, *The Manchester School*, May, 131–191.

Lewis, W.A. (1979) The dual economy revisited, *The Manchester School.*

Mahalanobis, P.C. (1953) Some observations on the process of growth of national income, *Sankhya,* 12, September, 307–312.

Perutz, M. (1991) Is science necessary, *Is Science Necessary,* Oxford: Oxford University Press, especially 7–35.

Storm, S. (1993) *Macroeconomic Considerations in the Choice of an Agricultural Policy,* London: Avebury.

Comment

Servaas Storm

Amit Bhaduri gives a clear analysis of the role of the state in steering large, predominantly agrarian economies onto alternative development paths. Decomposing per capita income into its major elements, *i.e.* the ratio of economically active to total population, the sectoral distribution of the labour force, and sectoral labour productivities, Bhaduri discusses the scope of and limits to a strategy of 'extensive growth', the rationale of an industrialisation-led growth strategy and its failure adequately to absorb rural surplus labour, and the critical importance for the economic development of some of these large developing countries of 'agricultural-demand-led' industrialisation. As a supplement to Bhaduri's analysis, I would like to give some empirical content to the 'arithmetical truism' decomposing per capita income into the already mentioned variables. Empirical estimates of these variables for the early 1960s and early 1990s are given in Table 2c.1 for a group of 14 large developing countries with a current population exceeding 50 million. Taken together, the populations of these 14 countries account for more than one half of the world's population in the early 1990s. In terms of agriculture's share in GDP and employment, most of these countries were predominantly agrarian in the early 1960s but are no longer so in the early 1990s. In all countries, agriculture's share in GDP has declined significantly, sometimes even dramatically (as in the case of Indonesia, Thailand and Turkey) in the relatively short period of 30 years. The share of the labour force employed in agriculture has also declined, though in general less than agriculture's share in GDP. Bangladesh, China, Ethiopia, India, Indonesia, and Thailand have remained predominantly agrarian when judged by the occupational structure of their labour forces. Table 2c.1 also includes estimates of the variable k (the ratio of the economically active population to the total population), defined by Bhaduri as the participation ratio. Under the conventional definition of the participation ratio – that is the economically

67

Table 2c.1 A decomposition of per capita income for selected large developing countries

		Year	Total Population (millions) (1)	Labour Force as % of (1) (2)	Proportion of Labour Force Employed in:		
					Agri-culture (3)	Indus-try (4)	Serv-ices (5)
1a.	Bangladesh	1961	50.8	34.3	86.0	4.8	9.2
1b.	Bangladesh	1985	101.6	30.4	56.5	12.3	30.2
2a.	Brazil	1960	70.1	32.3	51.6	24.8	23.6
2b.	Brazil	1988	141.4	43.2	23.3	22.4	50.4
3.	China	1982	1003.9	52.3	74.0	14.0	12.0
4a.	Egypt	1960	25.8	30.1	56.6	11.8	32.0
4b.	Egypt	1991	53.6	30.6	28.3	22.4	39.7
5.	Ethiopia	1991	55.1	40.5	88.0	2.0	10.0
6a.	India	1951	n.a.	n.a.	69.7	8.2	22.1
6b.	India	1961	438.8	43.3	72.4	11.3	16.3
6c.	India	1991	838.6	37.5	60.9	11.5	27.7
7a.	Indonesia	1961	96.3	35.9	68.0	7.5	19.1
7b.	Indonesia	1992	117.7	65.5	52.9	14.2	30.6
8a.	Iran	1956	19.0	32.0	54.8	19.6	23.0
8b.	Iran	1986	49.4	26.0	25.0	21.8	39.1
9a.	Nigeria	1963	55.7	32.9	72.0	10.0	18.0
9b.	Nigeria	1986	98.9	31.1	43.1	6.3	46.4
10a.	Mexico	1960	34.9	32.4	54.2	19.0	26.8
10b.	Mexico	1993	86.6	38.9	26.3	21.5	49.1
11a.	Pakistan	1961	39.4	32.4	59.9	15.8	24.3
11b.	Pakistan	1991	117.3	28.0	49.6	19.2	28.6
12a.	Philippines	1960	27.1	31.5	60.5	12.3	20.3
12b.	Philippines	1993	41.4	64.7	41.7	14.2	35.2
13a.	Thailand	1960	26.3	52.7	81.9	4.2	13.4
13b.	Thailand	1988	54.6	55.7	64.4	10.9	21.5
14a.	Turkey	1960	27.8	46.8	71.8	10.4	18.0
14b.	Turkey	1993	59.4	35.3	40.2	20.4	31.0

Sources: World Development Report 1984, 1988, World Bank; Human Development Report 1994, UNDP; Social Indicators 1991–92, World Bank; National Accounts Statistics 1991, 1993, UN; Yearbook of National Accounts Statistics 1964, 1966, UN; Yearbook of Labour Statistics, 1991, 1993, ILO.

Table 2c.1
(continued)

	Sectoral Shares in GDP: in percentages			Sectoral Labour Productivity: in US dollars			
	Agri-culture	Indus-try	Serv-ices	Agri-culture	Indus-try	Serv-ices	GNP per capita (US $)
	(6)	(7)	(8)	(9)	(10)	(11)	(12)
1a.	57.0	11.0	37.0	46	160	282	70
1b.	40.4	19.2	40.4	150	328	281	210
2a.	28.2	25.8	46.0	148	281	526	270
2b.	9.2	43.1	47.7	1056	5155	2538	2680
3.	40.5	50.7	8.9	202	1339	274	370
4a.	30.0	24.0	46.0	90	346	247	170
4b.	19.5	53.1	27.4	420	1447	421	610
5.	47.8	19.0	33.1	27	476	166	50
6a.	51.2	16.0	32.8	n.a.	n.a.	n.a.	n.a.
6b.	46.8	19.4	33.8	58	154	187	90
6c.	34.1	29.6	36.3	196	900	459	350
7a.	54.0	14.0	32.0	24	56	50	30
7b.	20.8	44.1	35.1	201	1583	585	510
8a.	33.7	28.0	38.3	154	357	416	250
8b.	27.5	25.0	47.5	2738	2857	3024	2490
9a.	18.8	33.1	48.0	120	1523	1228	460
9b.	8.2	31.8	60.0	471	12572	3222	2490
10a.	64.1	11.1	24.9	106	52	84	90
10b.	41.6	27.9	30.5	458	377	180	290
11a.	46.0	16.0	38.0	84	111	172	110
11b.	27.6	28.2	44.2	212	557	587	380
12a.	26.0	28.0	46.0	77	410	408	180
12b.	22.9	37.0	40.1	400	1903	832	730
13a.	40.0	19.0	41.0	68	633	428	140
13b.	16.8	35.9	47.3	370	4674	3126	1420
14a.	41.0	21.0	38.0	154	545	576	270
14b.	18.4	36.2	45.4	750	2909	2373	1640

active segment of the labour force as a percentage of the relevant population group, usually aged between 15 and 64 or so, itself consisting of all members of this age group willing to take up employment – raising the participation ratio implies either reducing unemployment and/or underemployment or inducing more people to join the labour force, or a combination of the two. Instead, Bhaduri's k, which is generally defined as the 'activity ratio', is much less amenable, at least in the short and medium run, to public policies, because it depends on demographic 'givens' such as the relative age structure of a given population and the rate of population growth. While observing that the activity rates in Table 2c.1 should be compared with caution (because of differences in labour force statistics among countries in the treatment of unpaid family workers, unemployed persons, part-time employees *etc.*), we may conclude that activity rates have declined through time in many countries, including Bangladesh, India, Iran, Pakistan, and Turkey. This reflects the relatively young populations (below the age of 15 or so) of these countries. The decline in k does not, however, imply a decline in the participation ratio.

Table 2c.1 further shows that the share of industrial employment in total employment has increased significantly in all countries, with the notable exception of Brazil, where industry's share in the labour force was already high in the early 1960s and marginally declined thereafter. This change in the occupational structure in favour of manufacturing, where labour productivity is substantially higher than in agriculture (see Table 2c.1), has contributed significantly to increased productivity growth. In countries where the change in occupational structure in favour of the industrial sector was quite large (for instance, Brazil, Egypt, and Turkey), but also in some of the other countries (notably India and Indonesia), the industrial-isation process was typically state-led, based on the idea of 'putting the accelerator principle in reverse'. It is precisely this idea which in Bhaduri's view, because of its neglect of final demand and market forces, has led to the creation of overcapacity in the capital goods sector and undercapacity in the consumer goods sector, poor export performance, and continued import dependence, all this eventually resulting in industrial stagnation and low productivity. Implicitly referring to the East Asian experience, he goes on to argue that despite its strong bias against the poor, the market mechanism has succeeded in fostering growth with fluctuations, by allowing the demand generating multiplier effect of investment to interact with the acceleration effect, influencing the level and composition of investment. I find the chapter's discussion of these points somewhat confusing. First, Bhaduri explicitly refers to centrally planned economies when making his argument against state-led growth, but does not link it to development planning in mixed economies, where planners were actually facing market constraints. The usual planning practice in mixed economies was to start from a GDP growth rate projection, next to derive its implications for final demand, and finally to determine the sectoral outputs ensuring intersectoral consistency. The crucial point is not that considerations of demand were not important, but that planners sometimes took the view that it is possible to separate the price system from the quantity system, that is, to assume that relative prices are fixed. Prices are accordingly ruled out as instruments of policy, thus leaving quantity-type instruments as the only option. As a result, policymakers chose to rely on 'planning by direction' rather than through the 'market', even when the latter was possible and probably also desirable. Hence, while Bhaduri's argument amounts to a case against certain types of planning, especially against the excessive central planning in some of the socialist countries, the more important issue in the context of the mixed economies is whether the 'plan' contains an appropriate mixture of incentives and disincentives for the different classes of economic agents, such as farmers, industrial workers, public sector managers, private capitalists *etc*. (see Chakravarty (1991) for a discussion of this matter).

Second, Bhaduri's argument distinguishes two (almost mutually exlusive) development alternatives: market-based and demand-led growth on the one hand, and state-supported and supply-led growth on the other hand. This distinction is overly sharp. Consider Japan's phenomenal post-war economic growth, for example, which is based on a state-led structural transformation of the industrial supply side, initiated by the state in consultation and cooperation with private industry in the mid-1950s in disregard of the postulates of comparative advantage (statically viewed), which fostered and developed certain 'strategic' industries, selected on the basis of such criteria as the income elasticity of demand for their products, prospects of rapid technological progress, and potential of sharp increases in labour productivity. This, as is stressed by Chakravarty (1991), is 'investment planning' in any operational sense of the term, but it is carried out through the market and it is based on longer-term demand considerations. Clearly, it is difficult, if not impossible, to do justice to Japan's development experience using Bhaduri's classificatory device. To avoid any misunderstanding regarding the nature of Bhaduri's argument in favour of 'demand-led' growth, it should be said that he is careful in emphasising the need for government intervention to tackle the longer-term supply-side constraints on demand-led growth, imposed by stagnating labour productivity in agriculture. While I agree with him on this matter, I would argue that it also makes the 'demand-led' development strategy a mixed strategy – a market-led, but at the same time state-supported growth strategy. It is market-led, because it must incorporate adequately the influence of the final demand; it is state-supported, because it includes public intervention, aimed at raising agricultural productivity and supply. Third, a very important point made by Bhaduri in this context is that, in many large developing countries, this 'market-based and state-guided' sequence of investment decisions can be achieved within both an inward-looking and an outward-looking development strategy. For these countries, because of the large size of their domestic markets, there is available an alternative to the export-led growth strategy propagated by the mainstream economics profession – namely domestic agricultural-demand-led industrialisation (see below). Bhaduri stresses that the very process of export-led industrialisation typically has to be initiated in the home market, which may even be protected for some time, and that it will be thwarted by any serious constriction of the home market, forcing these countries to rely prematurely on the world economy.

Bhaduri points out that the experience of most developing countries has shown that industrialisation is primarily a process of intensive growth, where some increase in average labour productivity is achieved through the intersectoral transfer of labour, but the industrial sector itself is unable to absorb the agricultural surplus labour at a sufficiently high rate. That conclusion seems to be supported by Table 2c.1, which shows that in most countries, although the share of industrial employment in total employment has increased significantly, there appears to exist an upper limit to labour absorption in manufacturing, constraining its share in total employment to a maximum of about one quarter. But there is more to the picture than meets the eye at first sight. On closer examination, it can be argued that the employment generating capacity of the manufacturing sector is often understated, because attention is paid only to the direct employment effects of industrialisation, while its indirect effects of expanding employment opportunities in the service sector through industry's demand for service inputs and income-induced demand for various types of services are neglected. Park and Chan (1989) show, on the basis of an interesting cross-country comparative analysis of input–output tables of 26 countries at different income levels, that industrialisation will generate substantial increases in employment in the service sector, owing to the strong backward linkage of manufacturing with distributive services (in the early stages of industrialisation) and producer services (in more advanced stages of industrialisation, when industrial activities become more skill-intensive and technologically sophisticated). An industrialisation strategy (whether market-led or state-led) thus contributes to a rise in per capita incomes through time provided it results in the transfer of (low-productivity) agricultural labour to (higher-productivity) employment in manufacturing and the service sector. However, even if indirect employment generation is taken into account, the ability of industry to absorb labour productively is limited. Therefore, an industrialisation-led development strategy no longer is a viable way out of the impasse. This is illustrated by countries like Bangladesh, India, Indonesia, Nigeria, and the Philippines, where (low-productivity) agriculture is still by far the largest sector of employment, while the proportion of the labour force employed in the (high-productivity) industrial sector is low (below 15 per cent) and the proportion of service sector employment rather high (above 30 per cent). Bhaduri is right in that, in these large and populous countries, the only way out is to raise agricultural labour productivity itself. He proposes a combination of extensive and intensive growth by raising the participation rate and labour productivity in agriculture in combination with 'agricultural-demand-led' industrialisation. This focus on agricultural growth stands in sharp contrast to the 'benign neglect' of agriculture characteristic of early development economists (Rosenstein-Rodan, Lewis, Hirschman, Jorgenson, and Fei and Ranis) who paid little attention to agriculture as a source of growth because of agriculture's weak backward and forward production linkages. Bhaduri observes that the early writers paid attention only to interindustry demands, neglecting the final demand out of the value added generated in agriculture. Once final demand – together with interindustry demands – is included in the analysis (as can be done in models based on a social accounting matrix or SAM), the contention that agriculture has weak backward and forward linkages can no longer be sustained. This is indicated by, among others, Vogel (1994), whose innovative decomposition of SAM multipliers for 27 countries shows that, at low levels of development, agriculture possesses strong backward linkages to non-agricultural production activities, which are mainly due to induced (final) rural household expenditure on nonagricultural commodities, while the agricultural backward input–output linkages increase during the development process. Vogel's results substantiate Bhaduri's conclusion that the time sequencing of investment needs to be determined not simply by backward and forward input–output linkages, but rather by the level and pattern of final demand.

A final point which I would like to raise concerns the assumption implicit in Bhaduri's argument in favour of an agricultural-demand-led development strategy that economic growth should be driven by the mass-consumption demand from the rural lower-income groups rather than by the demand for durable and other consumer goods from the upper-class segment of the population. It revives an old underconsumptionist argument, namely, that the size of the domestic market can be increased by redistributing income in favour of the poorer income classes, because these have a higher propensity to consume (particularly domestically produced goods), which will benefit the capitalists as well. A crucial question is whether the benefits of agricultural-demand-led industrialisation to private industrialists and big farmers will be large enough to induce them to support its implementation or whether they are likely to gain more from an alternative industrialisation strategy. For example, under export-led growth, if exports expand rapidly and if the rich get richer at a sufficiently rapid rate and spend and invest their increased incomes domestically, industrial growth may not be broad-based, but it can be fast as the recent history of countries such as South Korea and Brazil has shown. In mixed economies with a democratic political system based on private property, the support of the capitalist class is crucial to the success of any development strategy because of an inherent contradiction in the rules of the game of these systems – a point emphasised by Bhaduri (1993). While the rules of political democracy allow (social democratic) political parties, sharing or even controlling political power, to adopt a broad-based, redistributive, egalitarian development strategy, the rules of private property permit the private capitalists (including industrialists and landlords) to react against any economic measures which they find unacceptable by sharply reducing private investment, which in turn would reduce short-run demand and employment, and constrain economic growth in the longer run. While in the 1960s the governments of many large developing countries were restrained from pursuing egalitarian reforms by their fear for such an 'investment strike' by domestic capitalists, today, because of the increased degree of openness in trade and finance, the same governments are restrained by the threat of massive capital flight from their countries. Hence, to elicit capitalists' consent and avoid an 'investment strike', agricultural-demand-led industrialisation should offer them a sufficiently large part of the growing cake. However, as Bhaduri himself points out (Bhaduri 1993), in the final analysis, mass-consumption led expansion and active state intervention cannot go unchallenged for very long, as it will always tend to modify the social authority structure of capitalism in directions opposed by the capitalist class. The more open to trade and foreign capital a country is, the more likely its government will face the danger of an investment strike. This points to the crucial importance for national policy autonomy of 'strategic' rather than 'close' integration with the global economic system.

References

Bhaduri, Amit (1993) The economics and politics of social democracy, Pranab Bardhan, Mrinal Datta-Chaudhuri and T.N. Krishnan (eds), *Development and Change. Essays in honour of K.N. Raj*, Delhi: Oxford University Press.

Chakravarty, Sukhamoy (1991) Development planning: a reappraisal, *Cambridge Journal of Economics*, 15 (5), 5–20.

Park, Se-Hark and Kenneth S. Chan (1989) A cross-country input–output analysis of intersectoral relationships between manufacturing and services and their employment implications, *World Development*, 17 (2), 199–212.

Vogel, Stephen J. (1994) Structural changes in agriculture: production linkages and agricultural demand-led industrialization, *Oxford Economic Papers 46*, 136–156.

PART TWO

The OECD Countries

3. Growth and Equality since 1945: The Role of the State in OECD Economies

Andrew Glyn

It has become commonplace to divide the post-war history of the advanced capitalist countries (ACCs) into the 'golden age' of 1950s and 1960s (Marglin and Schor 1990; Maddison 1991) and the period of much slower growth after the first OPEC oil shock. In relation to the role of the state the fundamental questions raised by the post-war period are the following. Were state policies responsible for the golden age boom (for example demand management at a national or international level)? Were state policies responsible for the collapse of the golden age and the slower growth thereafter (welfare state, labour market rigidities for example)? Finally, can the appropriate package of state policies (be it interventionism in some form or more determined liberalisation) launch the ACCs, and in particular Europe, into a more satisfactory growth path (with due regard to environmental considerations)?

Government policy covers a huge and diverse range of interventions affecting demand (Keynesianism), the pattern of production (e.g. nationalisation), international relations (e.g. exchange rates, protection) and the regulation of social conflict (e.g. income distribution, trade union legislation). In an overview paper it is impossible to treat any, let alone all of the policies systematically; my focus, at the broadest level, will be on the impact of policy as a whole on the rate and pattern of growth and particularly on the distribution of that growth. A host of very important questions concerning the impact of the state on *relative* growth rates (role of Japanese industrial policy or French planning) will be ignored.

In order to approach our questions it is essential to start with a view of what drives the capitalist economies and where have been the problematic

79

elements in the key relationships of advanced capitalism. As argued elsewhere (Armstrong *et al.* 1991) the central driving force is taken to be the accumulation of capital which is both the most dynamic element of demand and a major determinant of the increase in productivity to meet that demand (see Scott 1992; De Long and Summers 1992; Englander and Mittelstadt 1988). Capital accumulation is dependent on an adequate rate of profit (Bhaskar and Glyn 1994; Glyn 1994), on steadily growing demand, and on reasonable stability in the international framework within which competition takes place. But most fundamentally it depends on an adequate degree of control by employers over the allocation of capital, the organisation of work and current and prospective rates of wages. It is, in my opinion, the balance of power between capital and labour which has been (and arguably still is) the key problematic element in the post-war history of advanced capitalism. If this is the case then it is the state's role in this sphere that is of central importance.

If attention is focused on the growth rate it is easy to visualise the golden age boom as emerging rather smoothly from the rapid expansion of the years of post-war reconstruction. But the history of the balance of power between capital and labour cannot concentrate just on 1973 as the single change in the trajectory of the ACCs. A more elaborate periodisation is suggested below, formed of successive stages of conflict (between capital and labour, open or suppressed), stabilisation (in the sense of restoration of a balance of power satisfactory for employers) and upswing (sustained rapid growth based on high investment).

Conflict	Stabilisation	Upswing
1941	1948–52/5	1952–68
1961	1979–199?	????

Tables 3.1 to 3.7, at the end of the text, give basic data for the USA, Japan, Europe and OECD as a whole for the following: GDP growth and unemployment (indicators of the pattern of growth of output and employment); inflation, the profit share, strikes and the budget deficit (indicators of class conflict over work issues and the distribution of income) and,

finally, the budgetary position and real interest rates (indicators of the overall macroeconomic policy stance).

Section I looks at the role of the state in the golden age, which necessitates a backward look at post-war reconstruction. Section II considers the responsibility of Keynesianism for the collapse of the boom and the problems encountered thereafter by expansionary policies. Section III analyses the general turn to stabilisation, with restrictive policies and deregulation, in the 1980s. Section IV outlines the successes and eventual crisis of the Swedish model. Section V notes the continued and current weakness of accumulation in the ACCs and speculates on the fundamental reasons for this and the space that remains for egalitarian policies.

The golden age of the state?

Keynesianism and the boom

It is not in dispute that the period from early 1950s to early 1970s was exceptional in terms of growth performance of the ACCs (see Table 3.1). The case that the state, and in particular the impact of fiscal and monetary policies on aggregate demand, played a pivotal role in securing the boom may be summarised as follows (see for example Boltho 1982; Matthews and Bowen 1984; Maddison 1991). There is a substantial list of permissive factors which contributed to the exceptional rate of growth in continental Europe and Japan. These would typically include: the possibilities of technological catch-up to the USA, ample labour supply which could keep wages in check, the possibilities for growth of trade after years of introversion. But these supply side factors, which could be seen as guaranteeing the potential profitability of even very high rates of very productive investment, were by no means unique to the post-war period. For example, whilst the US advantage in productivity levels had increased as a result of the war, it was not of a different order of magnitude from pre-war. The one unique factor after 1945 was the commitment of the state to high levels of demand and employment, and its ability to use Keynesian measures to deliver on that commitment. Hence, whilst the other ingredients (labour supply *etc.*) were necessary, priority has to be accorded to the one that made the decisive difference; that is the high level of demand which translated the supply side potential for very high investment rates into a sustained process of rapid and self-reinforcing growth.

Such an emphasis on the importance of Keynesianism has to deal with the following objections:

1. There was no tendency during the boom for governments to run deficits (thus pumping up demand in the text-book Keynesian fashion). On average between 1950 and 1973 governments were more or less in balance (Table 3.6). Deficit financing did not prevail, and the ratio of government debt to GDP tended to decline.
2. Attempts to examine whether government fiscal policy was actually stabilising (increasing demand when the economy sank below trend and vice versa) showed (Boltho 1989) that the effects were generally weak.
3. Governments of the most dynamic countries during the boom (Japan and Germany) were not committed to actively maintaining demand until the mid to late 1960s, long after the upswing began and indeed when it was beginning to run into difficulties. In the USA the first explicit use of Keynesian policies was in the early 1960s.

These are serious points against a simplistic Keynesian interpretation of the boom. A frequent response is that because business believed that the government would maintain high levels of demand, this bolstered confidence; the high level of investment spending which resulted then obviated the need for government deficits. This may have a good deal of force in the countries which were committed to government intervention to secure full employment (such as the UK), but is less persuasive for the important countries not so committed. Probably of greater significance for the system as a whole was the fact that the level of government expenditure was on average a much higher share of GDP even in 1950 than in 1929 (27 per cent on average as against 18 per cent according to Maddison 1991 Table 3.17). Moreover such figures exclude the investment by newly nationalised industries, which were important in some countries such as UK, France and Italy. The share of government spending also increased steadily throughout the golden age to reach 37 per cent of GDP in 1973. Even with balanced budgets, the growing weight of government spending acted to increase the average level of demand, and to contribute to steadily growing demand, since some part of the taxation raised would have been saved (the balanced budget multiplier). Moreover, by increasing the effect of automatic stabilisers (rising deficits in a recession for example) the growing weight of government expenditure contributed to the much smaller fluctuations of output in the post-war period (Boltho 1989). This in turn helped investment confidence. The fact that the most successful country in growth terms, Japan showed very little increase in the share of government spending before 1973 (when it was 23 per cent as compared to 19 per cent of GDP in 1929) does not disprove the beneficial effects of the spending on demand for the ACCs as a whole (in effect Japan was free-riding on high levels of government spending elsewhere, evident most clearly in the impact of the Korean war boom).

The motivation for the high level of expenditure was not the maintenance of demand but provision of welfare, reconstruction of infrastructure and defence. But this does not undermine the effect on demand which must have helped sustain the investment boom. However, continuation of the high level of government spending inherited from the war was not the only, or necessarily the most important, legacy of the period of post-war reconstruction. Nor was the role of the Marshall Plan in maintaining high levels of reconstruction expenditure, a kind of 'international Keynesianism', its most important contribution.

The state and post-war reconstruction

Attention will be focussed on continental Europe and Japan. It was there that the post-war boom was most powerful so that its evolution takes on a particular salience for understanding the period as a whole. The post-war phase of conflict was acute there, with a balance of power which was far from favourable to the employers. Thus the restoration of a adequate level of control for the employers, manifested in a period of economic stabilisation which followed, there was crucial for the golden age as a whole.

The characterisation of the middle 1940s as one of social tension and conflict is based on the following considerations (see Armstrong *et al.* 1991, for more detail):

1. Workers' organisations were much stronger than pre-war as a result of high employment and/or involvement in the resistance to fascism; they faced employers (in Japan and large parts of Europe) discredited by their association with the war. Employers' prerogatives, over dismissals in particular, were seriously curtailed; and this applied to a milder degree in the USA and UK where trade unionism was greatly strengthened by the years of labour shortage.
2. Inflation was very high in a number of European countries and Japan (see Table 3.2) where governments ran large deficits, caught between popular pressures to maintain high levels of spending (on subsidies for example) and difficulties in taxing sufficiently the already very low living standards.

3. Productivity was below pre-war levels (far below in Germany and Japan) reflecting in part employers inability to rationalise production.

The situation in 1945 and 1946 was far from being one of out and out open social conflict, however. The powerful labour movements were generally exercising discipline on their membership to co-operate in the process of post-war reconstruction, a process they helped to orchestrate via involvement in coalition governments. Thus strikes were at a low level, despite very low real wages. Investment was at quite high rates (save in Germany where the future shape of the country and economy was held in limbo), though much of it was financed by the state (including in the newly nationalised industries).

There was in effect a stalemate; labour was pushing for economic reconstruction rather than for a fundamental transformation of society, but was strong enough to circumscribe managerial prerogatives in a way which inhibited rationalisation. Moreover, labour had the potential for engaging in much more open conflict if the pressure from below built up or the line of the leadership was changed. The announcement of Marshall Aid signalled US support for a counter-offensive against labour (Communist parties were expelled from governments, trade unions splits secured, shop floor organisation weakened and dismissals carried through, budgets rebalanced with sharp cuts in welfare spending, unemployment rose and inflation squeezed out). Profits were already at high levels (save in Japan where they rose sharply) but were now much more secure. Not surprisingly after the turbulence of the previous years confidence was shaky, with share prices adjusted for inflation little more than one half of pre-war level in Europe and one fifth in Japan. It took several more years of sluggish growth before confidence was restored and private capital accumulation really took off, first in Europe and then in Japan.

Such an account places the importance of the Marshall Plan (and the comparable support to Japan) less in the fact that it helped sustain production through relaxing the acute dollar shortage and more as a registration of US support for the restoration of 'social and financial discipline'. Recent work (Eichengreen and Uzan 1992) estimates that the Plan had relatively small direct effects on investment, the balance of payments or public spending. It concludes that the main role for Marshall Aid was to provide a margin of resources which eased the 'distributional crisis' in Europe; whilst stressing that the subsequent rise in unemployment imposed disproportionate costs of stabilisation on the Left they ignore the decisive issue of recovery by employers of control in the factories, splits in the union movement and forth. The support of the state for this process, buttressed by US aid, played a central role. In this sense Marshall Aid was the first of the many 'stabilisation programmes' subsequently imposed on countries in the Third World, weaker OECD members and most recently the countries in what used to be the Eastern Bloc.

How does this account square with the picture of the golden age being based on a post-war 'settlement' involving capital's right to manage and invest being accepted by labour in return for full employment, rising living standards and extensions of the welfare state?

The position of the mass of workers the early 1950s, when stabilisation had been secured, was usually better than pre-war in that real wages were generally higher, unemployment much lower, welfare expenditure higher, and income distribution less unequal (the redistribution from the rich may have mainly benefitted the middle class: Kuznets 1966; Atkinson *et al.* 1989).

Yet, these gains do not demonstrate the existence of an explicit or implicit bargain between two parties of comparable strength recognising their dependence on the co-operation of the other. Sweden may be the best example of an explicit settlement with labour at least as an equal partner; Italy and France represent the other extreme of a settlement imposed in the wake of a period of defeats for the labour movement. Such defeats did not imply a radical deterioration in the living standards of most workers; the fundamental point was that their capacity to frustrate managerial prerogatives was much diminished and the danger that they would exert their bargaining power to the point where profitability was threatened was averted. In many countries (including Germany and Japan) the government commitment to full employment and the development of the welfare state arose as much out of the success of the boom, and the impact it had in reviving the bargaining position and political strength of labour, as from a prior bargain to secure labour's co-operation.

It would be one-sided therefore, to see the role of the state in setting the conditions for the boom as simply facilitating and underpinning a new social compromise which was then sustained by Keynesianism. In a number of key countries, the process of reconstruction had involved a decisive resolution of social conflict and tensions in the interests of employers. In the UK, by contrast, the trade unions pursued moderate wage claims but retained a good degree of shop-floor control, and avoiding a showdown in this period was to prove expensive for the employers.

The end of the boom

Keynesian and conflicting claims

The second question raised at the beginning of this paper concerned the responsibility of the state for the collapse of the boom into the period of slower growth. Perhaps the most influential version of such an argument was advanced (even before the event) by Milton Friedman's famous 1968 presidential address to the American Economic Association. This took the Keynesians to task for believing that they could trade-off lower unemployment for an acceptable one-off rise in the inflation rate, whereas in reality maintaining expansion beyond what the market 'naturally' delivers inevitably set off accelerating inflation. This can be extended into an explanation of post-73 stagnation with the addition of some 'hysteresis' elements. A long period of deflation was required to squeeze inflation out of the system, especially after the twist imparted by the OPEC oil price increases; this weakened capitalist confidence and pulled down investment rates and the growth rates, whilst a segment of the workforce became stranded in long-term unemployment as a result of state-imposed rigidities in the labour market (too high benefit levels, minimum wage regulations for example).

Rising inflation (Table 3.2) was indeed an important feature of the period before 1973. But to ascribe all the problems which culminated in stagnation to policy-induced excess demand would be a curiously thin account. Remaining at the economic level, accelerating inflation was accompanied by a severe decline in profitability (Table 3.4). In each of the major blocs the rate of profit fell by around one quarter to one third in the years before 1974, reflecting both a squeeze on profits (as product wages outran productivity) and a fall in the output–capital ratio. If the problem was simply temporary excess demand, as in Friedman's account, this would tend to raise profits. In our interpretation, declining profits reflected a situation of 'overaccumulation' when demand for labour had secularly, and not just temporarily, absorbed the excess supply of labour in open or disguised unemployment. This situation required an increase in product wages, a profit squeeze and a lower rate of accumulation to restore balance. A somewhat more subdued growth path was needed, not just the removal of temporary demand imbalance. In principle, as in a neoclassical growth model, there might be a smooth adjustment to such a new path. But the actual process of adjustment was so bumpy that the new growth path which emerged lay far below what was required.

The reason was that the mid-1960s brought not just economic strains but the expression of accumulated social and political tensions. This was reflected in strikes (Table 3.5), wage explosions, pressures for extension of workers rights and restraints on managerial prerogatives (most notably May 1968 in France and the Hot Autumn of 1969 in Italy and less dramatically elsewhere). This in turn reflected the legacy of the long period of high demand for labour which increased the bargaining position and organisational strength of labour. The effect of the commodity and oil price increases – directly inflationary, imposing cuts in living standards and cutting demand – exacerbated, rather than caused this turbulent situation. Profits fell very sharply, as cost pressures collided with heightened international competition as trade was liberalised and expanded rapidly.

Keynesian policies were not equipped to deal with intensely competing claims on the national output; a stronger labour movement pressed for wage gains and enlisted wider support for increases in state welfare provisions; third world producers were able to redress the earlier decline in the real value of primary commodities. Accommodation by the government would stoke up the inflation rate in the manner suggested by Friedman. Failure to accommodate, together with heightened international competition implied a further decrease in profits. Either way private investment was bound to suffer, exacerbated by challenges to managerial prerogatives in respect of work organisation and the allocation of capital (demands for participation in management, planning agreements between government and enterprises and even nationalisation).

Since a classic Keynesian expansion brings idle resources into use, it might seem an obvious solution to excessive claims for present output levels. The budgetary cost of unemployment makes the expansion doubly attractive as the cost of maintaining the unemployed is reduced (fiscal increasing returns). But even if there is significant spare capacity, expansion has to face further problems connected with foreign trade and the overseas sectors, with the private sector investment response and the impact on public sector borrowing and with inflation itself.

Given high marginal propensities to import (typically higher than the average propensities in Europe of some 25 per cent for the larger countries and up to 50 per cent or more for the smaller ones) then a significant part of Keynesian demand expansion leaks abroad. This is helpful in the very short-term, especially if capacity utilisation is quite high, in the sense that additional resources are provided to satisfy competing claims over and above what could be quickly generated at home. But unless the starting position is a very strong current account, an unusual situation when competing claims are intense, the deterioration in the balance of payments will be unsustainable. Real depreciation of the currency may in principle plug the balance of payments but at the cost of a deterioration in the terms of trade. This shaves off from domestic uses a part of the extra resources generated by the expansion. The extent of the terms of trade cost will be greater the larger the marginal propensity to import (and thus the proportion of GDP which has to be shifted into (net) exports to prevent current account deterioration) and the lower the trade elasticities (and thus the greater the real depreciation to secure a given shift into net exports). The trend towards higher trade shares (relatively slow during the 1980s) and perhaps towards lower trade elasticities (as a result of the growing internationalisation of production within multinational companies) has increased these terms of trade cost and made depreciation more costly.

The increased international mobility of capital has had contradictory effects. It has increased the ease with which balance of payments deficits may be financed if they are regarded by the markets as sustainable (without substantial future real depreciation); but it has also increased the possibility of exchange rates 'overshooting' downwards if policies are regarded as likely to lead to significantly higher inflation. Such overshooting · further increases the terms of trade cost. Import controls were frequently advocated on the left as an alternative to the costs of depreciation but they face overwhelming problems of retaliation from abroad. Exchange controls, whilst flying in the face of the furious tide of financial liberalisation, may offer some respite from speculation which anticipates, and thus contributes to, potential problems. They cannot, however, be expected to provide the finance which could support an 'unrealistic' real exchange rate which generated a large and rising current account deficit.

The extent to which a Keynesian expansion raises the government deficit depends on the response of the private sector. If the increased demand and profitability boosted private investment then the additional tax revenues raised from the expansion would substantially, or even wholly offset the initial budgetary deterioration. If on the contrary, because of the uncertainty connected with the outcome of the expansion, the private sector did not respond, or even cut its own investment, then the budgetary situation would worsen considerably. This could (given the starting point) give rise to fears of an unsustainable increase in public debt, destabilising the financial markets, forcing interest rates up and jeopardising the expansion. Direct measures to cajole the private sector to invest more, via planning agreements or other forms of 'interference', would be as likely to exacerbate as to improve the position.

Finally, there would be justifiable fears that an expansion would in fact worsen conflict over competing claims rather than ease them. The increased ability of groups with market power (strong unions and oligopolistic employers) to push their claims harder when demand was higher might outweigh the lubricating effect of the additional resources in moderating the conflict. Marshall Aid may have made a contribution to easing distributional conflict in the late 1940s, by allowing recovery to continue, but this was in the context of a reduced government deficits and an onslaught against the more militant unions. Expansion seems at best a temporary palliative for conflicting claims. It would only be by chance if claims were satisfied at the point where expansion reached its limits; more likely that higher demand and lower unemployment would leave a legacy of sharper conflict.

Problems such as those described above dogged attempts at expansion by radical governments from Whitlam in Australia in the early 1970s to Papandreou in Greece more than a decade later including en route, Wilson in the UK in the mid-1970s, Mitterrand in France (and examples also in countries outside the OECD such as Allende in Chile). They have afflicted the early years of such governments when the combination of unemployment and heightened expectations from supporters generated tremendous pressure to expand. Common to such experiences were deteriorating payments balances, increasing inflation, squeezed profits and very weak private investment; these were the costs of some gains in employment, real wages and welfare services. Typically the expansionary episodes were short-lived and were brought to a halt by one or more of the problems described above.

It is often said that the end of the boom and surrounding period of heightened tension and conflict involved a crisis of Keynesianism. If by this is meant that the boom collapsed because of inappropriate short-term demand management policies then it is quite unconvincing. If it is accepted that it was the long-boom and associated transformations of the ACCs (squeezing of the pre-capitalist sectors of the economy, strengthening of the labour movement) which led to a secular rise in the intensity of economic conflict (mainly distributional but also on the factory floor) then it is true that policies directed at maintaining full employment would not solve or contain this conflict. In this sense the period did indeed represent a crisis for Keynesianism and one which continues until the present.

Stabilisation and retreat from egalitarianism

The period of conflict which opened up in the middle to late 1960s lasted through the 1970s; the shift towards economic and social stabilisation occurred at different times in different countries and with varying degrees of open conflict – in Japan the decisive moment was the 1975 wage negotiations when Japanese workers accepted 11 per cent wage increases in the face of a going rate of inflation of 25 per cent; in France the Mitterrand government attempted some Keynesian style expansion (combined with redistributive policies and substantial nationalisations) as late as 1981–1983. But 1979 can be taken as the overall turning point with sharp deflation, especially through monetary policy (see Table 3.7 for the remarkable rise in real interest rates in the 1980s). This was combined with emphasis on free market policies of deregulation, especially of the labour market.

There was a marked decrease in social conflict and economic tensions. This was manifested most obviously in the decline of the inflation rate (by 1991–1994 at 3.2 per cent down from 10.3 per cent during 1973–1979 – see Table 3.2). There was also a strong reversal of the profit squeeze (by the end of the 1980s the manufacturing profit share had recovered very substantially in both Europe and the USA – see Table 3.4). This reflected a decline in real wage growth against a generally rather steady growth of productivity (Glyn 1994). There was also a dramatic fall in strikes. In the period 1990–1992 they were running at less than one tenth of the level of the period 1968–1973 in the USA, in Japan and in the average of the biggest four European countries. Exceptions to the pattern include Sweden (whose figures are dominated by a few major disputes) and Spain and Greece where there were extensive strike waves at the end of the 1980s.

The later 1980s saw a rather general reversal of the rising trend in budget deficits); by 1990 the average deficit was down to 1.6 per cent of GDP with spectacular reductions in a number of countries (Ireland, Sweden, Denmark, Japan, UK). Average ratios of public debt to GDP peaked in 1987 and were falling sharply in some countries (UK, Australia, Sweden, and Japan). But a number of others had stubbornly large deficits (Italy, Belgium, Netherlands, Greece) throughout the 1980s, with public debt in Italy reaching, and in Belgium easily exceeding GDP. The slow growth in the early 1990s (section V) pushed deficits up again (Table 3.6); raising taxation and/or restricting public expenditure has proved the most difficult aspect of stabilisation.

With due allowance for individual exceptions (especially the Southern European countries) the overall patterns are rather consistent. The conflict which had previously been manifested in high inflation, profit squeezes and strikes was widely moderated in the 1980s as inflation declined, profits recovered, the government's finances showed some improvement and strikes were at low levels. Moreover this stabilization was not simply a cyclical phenomenon; the faster growth at the end of the 1980s did not bring a rapid increase in inflation, more strikes or renewed profit squeezes. This suggests some considerable success for the change in policy regime in restoring domestic economic stability.

Partly as a by-product of restoring domestic stability, but also as a deliberate policy for the heightening of market incentives, the 1980s saw a pronounced shift away from egalitarianism. One of the most pronounced features of the golden age had been steady, if unspectacular, reductions in inequality. This was reflected in measures of household income inequality (Sawyer 1976) which fell quite strongly (USA, Japan, Sweden, France) or more modestly (UK, Germany, Netherlands). Whilst full employment itself played an important role in this (strengthening the organisation and bargaining position of unskilled workers for example) minimum wage legislation and above all social welfare also contributed (welfare expenditure rose from 12 per cent of GDP in 1960 to 22 per cent in 1975 (OECD 1986)).

In the USA the 'U-turn' to rising inequality occurred in the late 1960s as the average unemployment rate rose and earnings inequalities widened sharply. But in many European countries, by contrast, the period between the two OPEC oil crises saw a continuation and even sharpening of egalitarian trends as governments struggled to contain unemployment, welfare expenditure grew rapidly, wage dispersion was reduced (especially between men and women) and earned income grew much faster than the capital value of shares. It was not until the 1980s that the increase in economic equality was typically halted or reversed as:

- unemployment rose rapidly in Europe (Table 3.3); particularly for less qualified men the registered unemployment figures underestimated the loss of jobs as many disappeared from the measured labour force; only the 'social corporatist' countries of Northern Europe relatively immune (up to 1990) from the rise in unemployment;

- wage dispersion rose almost everywhere (Germany was an exception); the increase was probably strongest in the USA (Davis 1993); women's pay stagnated in relative terms;
- the financing of public spending became less progressive with cuts in the top rate of income tax (averaging 17 percentage points for OECD as a whole with a 40 point cut in UK);
- the growth of government expenditure as a share of GDP was much slower after 1979; between 1970 and 1979 the ratio of government expenditure excluding interest payments rose by 8.5 per cent of GDP in the OECD; in the next decade the rise was just 1.2 per cent; over the 1980s the share of welfare expenditure in GDP fell in a number of countries (including UK, Germany and the Netherlands);
- the distribution of household income became less egalitarian in a majority of countries in the 1980s, most strongly in the USA and UK but even where milder (e.g. France) increased inequality frequently represented substantial a reversal of the previous trend (Atkinson 1993; Green *et al.* 1992);
- capital gains, benefitting the best off, were very large, with share prices rising 8 per cent per year faster than wage earnings from 1979–1989 (having fallen by 13 per cent per year relative to earnings in the period 1973–1979);
- poverty (proportion of people in households with incomes less than 50 per cent of the average) increased in nine out twelve countries for the period 1979–1985 (O'Higgins).

Governments were responsible for halting or reversing the trends in welfare spending and for inegalitarian shifts in the tax burden. Macroeconomic policy, especially high interest rates, and market oriented policies, such as cuts in subsidies, contributed to rises in unemployment. Deregulation of the labour market (e.g. abolition of UK wages councils) contributed to increased earnings dispersion; pressure on benefit levels (indexation to prices rather than earnings in the UK for example) helped push up poverty. Macroeconomic and legal pressures on trade unions facilitated the rise in profits and consequent boom on the stock exchange. Whilst other factors were at work in the trend towards inequality (notably shifts in demand towards more qualified labour and company orientation towards performance related pay; Levy and Murnane 1992) government policy played a very important role overall. In some areas post-war gains were only eroded to a limited extent (for example expenditure on the welfare state by the end of the 1980s was typically in the range 1.5–2 times as high as a share of GDP as in the 1960s). But the change in *trend* towards inequality was very sharp, and in respect of the distribution of earnings, unemployment and poverty the deterioration in a number of countries was very large.

It should be emphasised that the turn to inequality was not based on strong evidence that it would improve economic performance. On the contrary, the macroeconomic evidence suggests that the more egalitarian countries have achieved better growth performance (Alesina and Rodrik 1992; Persson and Tabellini 1992); for the OECD countries in the 1980s this can readily be confirmed by noting that it has been the apparently more egalitarian countries (like Japan) which performed better than the highly unequal USA (Glyn 1992a). The reasons for this relationship are far from clear (less disruptive distributional conflict is one possibility). But there is one important proviso. Most measures of economic inequality focus on the personal income distribution and exclude retained corporate profits (or the large capital gains to which they give rise). Some countries with very low measured inequality (Japan, Korea) and rapid growth also had exceptionally high profitability. So the apparent positive relationship between growth and equality of *personal* income distribution does not contradict the positive relationship across countries between profitability and growth (especially in the Golden Age – see Glyn 1994).

A major attraction of increasing inequality in a period of slow growth is that the beneficiaries are thereby enabled to maintain their growth of living standards. A good example is the rationalisation of UK manufacturing industry in the 1980s when rapid increase in productivity (52 per cent) boosted dividends (73 per cent) and share prices (125 per cent), still allowed quite substantial increase in real wages for those who remained employed (28 per cent), at the expense of the one quarter of the labour force who lost their jobs (Glyn 1992c).

The Swedish model

The obvious inadequacies of reliance on demand management in the face of competing claims conflict does not mean that there is *no* solution other than relying on deflation and unemployment. Many Keynesians themselves recognized the problem in the form of the reconciliation of full employment and low inflation and proposed various forms of incomes policies in order to contain the conflict. Some of these policies, implemented by governments of the left in order to sustain expansionary and/or redistributi ve programmes, have been successful for a time. The Labour government's

94 *The state and the economic process*

incomes policy in the UK in the mid-1970s is an excellent example where the trade union movement accepted money wage increases way below the going inflation rate, and contributed to a remarkable disinflation by accepting a severe reduction in real wages. But the task of these policies has frequently been to try and hold the line after the early phase of social democratic expansion has opened up problems on the payments balance, government financing and inflation fronts. Thus the policies for involving the trade union movement in a planned distribution of resources have typically taken place when real wages have to be cut, public spending held in check and policies for extending one form or another of democratic control over enterprises have to be put in abeyance for fear of further undermining employer confidence. For workers to hold back from exerting their local bargaining power, in the name of restricting the rise in unemployment, puts great demands on their egalitarianism. Strains are particularly intense where union bargaining is traditionally relatively uncoordinated and geared towards extracting the maximum money wage increase from the particular group of employers.

All these difficulties help explain why the Swedish model, seen as a long-term strategy for full and rising employment, egalitarian wage bargaining and a major expansion of the public services has exerted such an attraction as a solution to conflicting claims conflict. The strength of the Swedish model became apparent when job opportunities were preserved and income inequalities further diminished even after growth slowed in 1974:

- Wage differentials which had roughly *halved* between 1965 and 1973 continued to fall (though more slowly) until the early 1980s (Calmfors 1993, Figure 3.8).
- In the period 1973–79 employment grew 0.9 per cent per year faster than the population of working age (compared to falls averaging 0.6 per cent per year in the main EC countries) as rising state employment in the welfare services and cuts in average hours worked (including more part-time work) more than made up for reduced total hours worked in the market sector. In the first half of the 1980s such 'spreading' of employment was less pronounced (Glyn 1992b) but Sweden maintained work opportunities through maintaining output and jobs in the market sector, with the help of industrial subsidies to slow the contraction of declining industries. By 1990 employment as a percentage of the population of working age was 81.9 per cent (nearly 10 percentage

points higher than USA and Japan and more than 20 percentage points higher than the EC); government employment was 31.7 per cent of the total (compared to 17.6 per cent in the EC).
- Transfers grew by 7 per cent of market output during 1973–1979 (to reach a share of GDP a little above the EC average – 19.7 per cent as against 17.5 per cent).

The productivity record in Sweden has been moderate; hourly productivity in the market sector has grown about two per cent per year since 1973 (one per cent per year slower than in the EC). This is extremely important in a context where average real wages have been squeezed far below the growth of hourly productivity by reduced average hours of work and especially by the tax increases, required to finance the rising employment in the welfare services and the higher transfers. Between 1973 and 1985 workers consumption (financed from their take-home pay) declined by some 1.7 per cent per year or about one fifth (it was rising at about 0.6 per cent per year in the EC).

The Swedish model was essentially a system for the egalitarian distribution of work, pay and social welfare amongst the mass of wage and salary earners. The squeezing of profits in the 1970s was not part of a strategy but, on the contrary, reflected the difficulties in maintaining the collective self-discipline required to implement the very strong redistribution. Egalitarian wages policy was supposed to force weaker firms to invest and modernise. The adverse effects of the profits squeeze on investment (and thus productivity growth in the 1980s) compounded the problems of that decade. For a long time the prerogatives of capital were never seriously threatened by nationalisation (always a much smaller proportion of the economy than in many parts of Western Europe), by intrusive industrial policy or plans for industrial democracy. When a major challenge was mounted in the mid-1970s, with the trade union proposal for wage-earner funds (incorporating strong elements of socialisation of ownership and control) this encountered violent opposition from the employers which watered down the scheme until it was little more than symbolic (Pontusson 1987).

In terms of redistribution as well the model seemed to have reached its limits in the later 1980s. In the second half of the 1980s the growth of state employment, reductions in hours worked and growth of transfers were much smaller and consumption per worker began to creep up. Earnings inequality also increased (though only reversing a tiny part of the previous reduction) and the (rather extreme) progressivity of the tax system was moderated. Finally, austerity policies in response to the inflation at the end of the 1980s has led to a precipitate rise in unemployment (currently some 14 per cent). This has swamped Sweden's famed 'active labour market policies' credited by many with having helped prevent the increases in long-term unemployment so prevalent in the EC.

The crucial question is whether the disastrous deterioration of Sweden's economic performance has finally put to rest hopes of sustaining, in the context of slow growth, the 'inclusionary' tendencies of the golden age – increased opportunities for work, decreasing inequalities of income and improvements in the welfare state. There seems to be widespread agreement that the situation in Sweden at present is partly to be blamed on disastrous macroeconomic policy since the later 1980s. Financial deregulation, espoused apparently with enthusiasm by the Social Democrats (as by Labour in Australia), generated a boom with extremely high demand for labour and inflationary pressures. Inevitably there was a severe recession when the bubble burst, consumers attempted to reduce their debts and speculative investments in new property collapsed. The incoming conservative government met this situation with very tight policies illustrating, according to a critic not of the left, 'how a "collision" between harsh non-accommodative policies and earlier inflation is bound to create a dramatic rise in unemployment' (Calmfors 1993 p. 58). Of the rise of the Swedish budget deficit some two per cent of GDP represented expenditures to bail out banking system.

Whilst these particular circumstances have dramatised the collapse of the Swedish model, there have been more fundamental forces at work. Indeed pressures on workers' consumption that had been accumulating from high taxation and wage restraint must have increased the attractions of financial liberalisation, with its promise that consumers could be released from their 'hard-budget constraints' by a kind of 'personal Keynesianism'. The list of fundamental underlying problems suggested by Rudolph Meidner (1993), one of the architects of the model, include the difficulties, both within and between the union confederations, of obtaining agreement as to appropriate wage differentials, the increasing opposition of employers to centralised bargaining and their wish to implement incentive-wage systems at the company, plant and individual level, and the outflow of direct investment (and jobs) from Sweden by its multinationals. A decade later than most, Sweden has joined the rush towards stabilisation and explicit anti-egalitarianism as the route to economic recovery.

A skewed recovery, stubborn recession, gloomy prospects

The recovery which followed the recession of 1979–1982 was rather long (lasting until 1990) but not very strong (except in the USA – see Table 3.1). The weakest link was Europe where growth was less than three per cent per year, hardly more in this prolonged upswing than during the whole cycle 1973–79. The specific characteristics of the recovery were:

1. Very rapid expansion of credit despite unprecedentedly high real interest rates which led to sharp falls in personal saving as households took on enormously increased debt burdens.

2. Real accumulation was twisted towards the services sectors particularly those most closely connected with the consumer boom (shopping centres and offices for financial institutions). Manufacturing investment was particularly sluggish and in a number of countries responded very feebly even to substantial recoveries in profitability (Glyn 1994). The UK was an extreme example of this phenomenon (the capital stock in manufacturing grew by an estimated 12 per cent over the period 1979–89 whilst the capital stock in the finance and business services sector – offices and computers *etc.* – grew by 105 per cent (Glyn 1992c). Japan was exceptional in the powerful recovery of manufacturing accumulation but not in escaping speculative excesses in property which left only Germany of the major economies relatively unscathed.

3. Productivity performance was very weak. Labour productivity growth (1.4 per cent per year) was no greater over the period 1973–1979, and if allowance was made for smaller cuts in working time, rather slower. Total factor productivity growth improved fractionally (from 0.5 per cent per year to 0.7 per cent per year) as the decline in the output capital ratio moderated. There were a few examples of a 'productivity miracle' in manufacturing, but the most spectacular example in the UK was based on the rationalisation of existing levels of production rather than investment in expansion.

The stagnation which succeeded the boom of the later 1980s left output growing by 1.1 per cent per year during 1990–1993 in the OECD. This was only a fraction higher than the previous OPEC II recession of 1979–1982 and only because of stronger growth in the USA. In Europe and especially Japan output growth was slower in the later period. The particular significance of the current recession is that it is entirely home-grown. Commodity and oil prices have been very weak and, apart from isolated cases such as Finland, the collapse of the USSR has not been a major factor. Government deficits have already increased by enough in the recession since 1990 to undo all the 'good work' of the 1980s in stabilising public finances undermining pressure for Keynesian expansion.

The fundamental reason for the stagnation is that there has been too low a rate of capital accumulation to propel the ACCs back into full employment and rapid growth. What is the underlying reason for the weakness of capital accumulation, that is the reluctance of the capitalists to invest? *Possible* hypotheses might be:

a. The fundamental problem caused by overaccumulation, the increased organised power of labour, has not been overcome despite the protracted period of high unemployment, despite the defeats suffered by the labour movement in key disputes (Fiat, UK miners, PATCO) and despite the organisational weakening of unions. The residual strength of organised labour underlies the fear that deliberate expansion will lead to accelerating inflation (if workers were not able to secure money wage increases to protect and increase real wages then any price increases induced by expansion would simply increase profits). On a microeconomic level the deregulation of the labour market has not gone far enough to reestablish the flexibility of the employment relationship which is necessary for high investment. Capitalism needs mass unemployment to discipline workers and, as Kalecki predicted fifty years ago, full employment policies would be abandoned. This approach would see the persistence of very high real interest rates as confirmation that the authorities fear that an expansion could soon become inflationary and that political difficulties with reducing government deficits force reliance on monetary tightness.

b. The post-war boom was based on a certain technological paradigm (Fordism) which has exhausted itself and is reflected in the slowdown of labour productivity growth and falling output capital ratio. The post-Fordist solution, just in-time production of much more sophisticated consumer goods, may have only offered an apparent solution during the yuppie boom of the mid to late 1980s where consumer credit and growing inequality led to unprecedented growth in luxury consumption (Nissan has recently announced a programme of reduced model ranges and increased standardisation of parts in order to slash costs). Falling output capital ratios in particular would mean that maintaining growth of the capital stock requires ever increasing investment shares (an environmentalist, or Ricardian, twist to this could offer decreasing accessibility to, and thus increased capital costs of extracting, natural resources and increased costs of installing anti-pollution equipment as contributory factors to falling output capital ratios).

c. Increased international competition, together with see-sawing real exchange rates has undermined confidence in the predictability of market growth in the crucial traded-goods sector (above all manufacturing). Financial liberalisation has vastly increased exchange rate instability. Interpenetration by foreign investment, which increased rapidly in the 1980s may be more of a defensive response to heightened uncertainty than the route to a higher overall investment rate. The problem, it must be emphasised, is not a (relatively) diminishing market for manufactured goods. Although the market for manufacturing is growing as fast as GDP (between 1979–90 manufacturing production grew at 2.6 per cent per year in the OECD, whilst GDP grew at 2.7 per cent and with net exports of manufactures declining absorption of manufacturers grew faster). But import shares of manufactures rose both due to increasing intra-OECD trade and, more threateningly, as a result of higher imports from outside the OECD (now constituting 12 per cent of OECD imports of machinery and transport equipment and 23 per cent of other manufactures).

None of the three explanations for the underlying sluggishness of the ACCs is individually wholly convincing. Declining unionisation and increased fragmentation of wage bargaining have served to substantially weaken the power of organised labour. Outside Germany in particular (which is very important of course for the rest of Europe) it may be difficult to see fear of organised labour as the break on expansion (however satisfying for the symmetry of this paper's argument). Limits to profitable investment stemming from loss of technological possibilities is hard to square with the developments in electronics (and it is important that the 1980s saw a halting of downward trend in the output–capital ratio, when measured at current prices, with the relative price of investment goods falling substantially). Limits-to-growth explanations, which had a certain plausibility in the mid-1970s when productivity was declining in the extractive industries of the ACCs and when relative prices of commodities rose so sharply, carry less convictions now that most resource prices are, in real terms, below those of the 1960s (energy is an important exception, but even there the increase in the relative price has been strongly eroded). International competition, may seem more convincing as an explanation of the form the stagnation is taking (elimination of labour intensive industries in the ACCs) rather than its underlying cause. It cannot explain why governments in Japan even now and until recently Germany, both with very strong payments balances, refused to expand further.

Nevertheless in combination these hypotheses may provide some insights. In the early 1950s, after the previous phase of stabilisation, each of these factors were more favourable:

a. Whilst the mid-1940s saw intense class conflict it was relatively short-lived and could be written off to the exceptional circumstances at the end of World War II, the impact of which was snuffed out by the Cold War. The more extended period of turmoil set off in the late 1960s, however, even if less fundamentally threatening, flowed from the very success of the boom and thus constitutes, potentially, a recurring threat.
b. For Europe and Japan there was a very obvious route to follow at the end of the war, in terms of the patterns of production and consumption already mapped out by the USA and spread throughout the world by popular culture. This is in contrast to current uncertainties reflected in speculations about 'the information society', 'post-industrialism' and the succession of managerial vogues for 'synergies', 'core businesses', 're-engineering', 'flexibility', 'lean manufacturing' and so forth.
c. The golden age, as emphasised by the French Regulation School (Boyer 1986) was founded on relatively insulated home markets; exchange rates were predictable and the international system had a commanding leader. The contrast with the present situation is obvious.

None of these factors making for stagnation seem likely to be rapidly reversed. Perhaps a further decade of weakening collective bargaining and employment legislation might banish the spectre of wage pressure as a barrier to expansion. Possibly a move to greater economic coordination within regional blocs, based on the USA, EC and Japan respectively (between which at present trade flows are a modest 1–2 per cent of GDP), might reduce the sense of disorder in the world economy. But just as we have concluded that Keynesianism was responsible for neither the boom nor subsequent stagnation so there is no obvious policy package to restore growth rates to anything approaching the golden age either for one country or for the group of ACCs as a whole. Whilst desirable from the point of view of pressure on the environment, the prospect of continued slow growth of GDP may seem to imply the inevitability of further rises in unemployment and inequality.

But even if the prospect within the ACCs is for slow growth this still leaves open the question of how that slow growth will be distributed. Whilst there are some underlying economic forces making for increased inequality (such as technical progress being biased away from unskilled work) these can be offset by active retraining, tax and benefit and regulatory policies. The fact that inequality of earnings in particular has been rising at very different rates, and apparently falling in a few countries like Germany, shows that there is no overriding economic imperative whatsoever which demands that inequality must rise. Within a given growth of GDP there are a range of possibilities for the growth of total employment (and thus how many are excluded from work), for the pattern of distribution of the additional earned income (whether the new jobs are well paid or adding to the bottom end of the earnings distribution), for changes in the distribution of taxation, for the overall growth and structure of public expenditure, and for the balance between earned and unearned income (dividends, interest payments, capital gains).

It would be tempting, but misleading, to argue that it is only the employers who gain from casualisation of the labour market and the inegalitarian trends in employment and social welfare. But large numbers of well-paid and secure employees in the large and competitive companies also gain directly from many service jobs being poorly paid (reducing the cost of the services) and from public provision of many services (such as health and education) kept at safety-net levels (reducing tax rates). Contrary to Mrs Thatcher, however, there *is* such a thing as society. The systematic economic exclusion of large sections of a society from the high living standards and reasonable job prospects, which are continually presented as the main index of personal worth and self-esteem, will inevitably bring huge costs to the rest of society as a result of the 'anti-social' response of the excluded. Well managed economic policy will not allow these problems of distribution to be ducked. The fundamental task is the political one of convincing the relatively secure that their interests lie in accepting the immediate costs of combatting this exclusion, rather than in concentrating what will otherwise become a diminishing amount of total social welfare (if not GDP) on themselves.

Table 3.1 Output growth 1945–94

GDP average annual % changes	USA	Europe	Japan	OECD
1945–51	0.4	7.8	10.1	2.9
1951–68	3.4	4.7	9.2	4.4
1968–73	3.2	4.9	8.7	4.6
1973–79	2.4	2.9	3.6	2.7
1979–90	2.6	2.0	4.3	2.8
1990–94	2.3	1.0	1.6	1.6

Note: Prior to 1960 data for Europe and OECD is weighted average of 12 and 16 countries (Maddison).
Sources: Maddison (1991), OECD *Historical Statistics, Economic Outlook*.

Table 3.2 Inflation 1947–94

Consumer prices 8average annual % changes	USA	Europe	Japan	OECD
1947	15.5	26.3	115.0	19.4
1950	0.9	3.0	-6.9	2.0
1951–68	1.7	3.3	4.1	2.6
1968–73	5.0	6.1	7.1	5.8
1973–79	8.5	11.7	9.9	10.3
1979–90	5.5	7.1	2.6	6.4
1990–94	3.1	3.9	1.7	3.2

Note: Prior to 1960 data for Europe and OECD is weighted average of 12 and 16 countries (Maddison); after 1960 OECD excludes Turkey and Iceland.
Sources: Maddison (1991), OECD *Historical Statistics, Economic Outlook*.

Table 3.3 Unemployment 1950–94

Average % rates	USA	Europe	Japan	OECD
1950–51	6.2	4.5	1.8	
1960–67	5.0	2.8	1.3	3.1
1968–73	4.6	3.4	1.2	3.4
1974–79	6.7	5.1	1.9	5.1
1980–90	7.0	9.0	2.5	7.3
1991–94	6.8	10.2	2.4	7.9

Note: Prior to 1960 data for Europe and OECD is weighted average of 12 and 16 countries (Maddison).

Sources: Maddison (1991), OECD *Historical Statistics*.

Table 3.4 Profitability 1952–90

Manufacturing net profit share % of value added	USA	Europe	Japan	G7
1955–66	20.7	26.0	34.2	23.6
1967–73	19.3	21.8	39.4	20.0
1974–79	17.4	16.6	22.8	18.1
1980–87	14.8	17.6	20.1	17.1
1989–90	21.5	23.1	22.7	22.3

Note: Europe is weighted average of largest four countries.

Source: Armstrong *et al.* (1991) updated from OECD *National Accounts, Capital Stocks and Flows*.

Table 3.5 Strikes 1953–90

Average days per year per 100 workers in industry and transport	USA	Europe	Japan	G6
1953–66	101	40	38	50
1967–73	141	130	20	114
1974–79	47	52	11	44
1980–90	13	28	1	21
1990–92	14	9	0	8

Note: G6, Europe are unweighted averages of largest six, four countries.
Source: Armstrong *et al.* (1991) updated from *Employment Gazette*, ILO *Labour Statistics*.

Table 3.6 Budget deficits 1951–94

General government balance, % of GDP	USA	Europe	Japan	OECD
1952–67	−0.9	0.6	1.4	−0.2
1968–73	−0.6	−0.3	0.9	−0.2
1974–79	−1.4	−3.3	−3.4	−2.5
1980–90	−3.5	−4.1	−1.1	−3.3
1991–94	−3.5	−5.5	0.8	−3.0

Sources: OECD *National Accounts, Historical Statistics, Economic Outlook*.

Table 3.7 Real interest rates 1956–93

Long-term bonds less GDP deflator average %	USA	Europe	Japan	OECD
1956–67	1.4	2.1	(2.2)	1.8
1968–73	0.6	0.8	0.2	0.6
1974–80	−0.3	−1.2	0.5	−0.3
1981–93	5.6	4.7	4.3	5.0

Sources: Rowthorn (1993) (from OECD *National Accounts, Historical Statistics, Main Economic Indicators*).

Notes

1. My thanks to Carla Naastepad and Servaas Storm for their most helpful suggestions. For more detailed presentation of the arguments and data see Armstrong *et al.* (1991) and Glyn *et al.* (1990) in respect of sections I and II, Glyn (1992a) for section III and Glyn (1992b) for section IV.

References

Alesina, A. and D. Rodrik (1992) Distribution, political conflict and economic growth, in A. Cuckierman, Z. Hercowitz and L. Leiderman (eds), *Political Economy, Growth and Business Cycles*, Cambridge, Mass.: MIT Press.

Armstrong, P., A. Glyn and J. Harrison (1991) *Capitalism Since 1945*, Oxford: Blackwell.

Atkinson, A. (1993) What is happening to the distribution of income in the UK, *STICERD Discussion Paper No. 87*.

Atkinson, A., A. Harrison and J.P.F. Gordon (1989) Trends in the shares of top wealth owners in Britain 1923-1981, *Oxford Bulletin of Economics and Statistics*, 51, No. 3, 315-332.

Bhaskar, V. and A. Glyn (1994) Profitability and investment: Evidence from advanced capitalist countries, in J. Epstein and H. Gintis (eds), *Economic Policy in the Conservative Era*, Cambridge: Cambridge University Press.

Boltho, A. (ed.) (1982) *The European Economy: Growth and Crisis*, Oxford: Oxford University Press.

Boltho, A. (1989) Did policy activism work, *European Economic Review*, 33, 1709-1726.

Boltho, A. (1991) A century of Japanese business cycles, *Journal of the Japanese and International Economies*, 5, 282–297.

Boyer, R. (1986) *Theorie de la regulation*, Paris: La Decouverte.

Calmfors, L. (1993) Lessons from the macroeconomic experience of Sweden, *European Journal of Political Economy*, March.

Davis, S. (1993) Cross-country patterns of changes in relative wages, *NBER Macroeconomics Annual 1993*.

De Long, B. and L. Summers (1992) Equipment investment and economic growth: How strong is the nexus, *Brookings Papers on Economic Activity*, 2.

Eichengreen, B. and M. Uzan (1992) The Marshall Plan, *Economic Policy*, No. 14, April.

Englander, S. and A. Mittelstadt (1988) Total factor productivity: Macroeconomic and structural aspects of the slowdown, *OECD Economic Studies*, No. 10.

Glyn, A. (1992a) The costs of stability: The advanced capitalist countries in the 1980s, *New Left Review*, September/October.

Glyn, A. (1992b) Corporatism, patterns of employment and access to consumption, in Pekkarinen *et al.* (1992).

Glyn, A. (1992c) The productivity miracle, profits and investment, in J. Michie (ed.), *The Economic Legacy 1979–1992*, London.

Glyn, A. (1994) Does profitability *really* matter, *mimeo*.

Glyn, A., A. Hughes, A. Lipietz and A. Singh (1990) The rise and fall of the golden age, in S. Marglin and J. Schor (eds), *The Golden Age of Capitalism*, Oxford: Oxford University Press.

Green, F., A. Henley and E. Tsakalotos (1992) Income inequality in corporatist and liberal economies: A comparison of trends within OECD economies, *University of Kent Studies in Economics*, 92/13.

Kuznets, S. (1966) *Modern Economic Growth*, New Haven: Yale University Press.

Levy, F. and R. Murnane (1992) US earnings levels and earnings inequality, *Journal of Economic Literature*, 30, 1331–81.

Maddison, A. (1991) *Dynamic Forces in Capitalist Development*, Oxford.

Marglin S. and J. Schor (eds.) (1990) *The Golden Age of Capitalism*, Oxford.

Matthews, R. and W. Bowen (1984) Keynesian and other explanations of post-war macro trends, in W. Eltis and P. Sinclair (eds), *Keynes and Economic Policy*, Oxford: Oxford University Press.

Meidner, R. (1993) Why did the Swedish model fail, *Socialist Register*, London: Merlin.

OECD *Historical Statistics*, annual.

OECD (1986) *The Future of Social Protection*.

OECD (1989) *Economies in Transition*.

O'Higgins, M. (1990) Poverty in the EEC, in R. Teekens, V. von Praag and S. Jenkins (eds), *Analysing Poverty in the European Community*, Brussels.

Pekkarinen, J., M. Pohjola and R. Rowthorn (eds.) *Social Corporatism*, Oxford: Oxford University Press.

Persson, T. and G. Tabellini (1992) Growth, distribution and politics, in Cuckierman *et al.*, op. cit.

Pontusson, J. (1987) Radicalisation and retreat in Swedish social democracy, *New Left Review*, No. 165.

Rowthorn, R. and J. Wells (1987) *Deindustrialisation and Foreign Trade*, Cambridge: Cambridge University Press.

Sawyer, M. (1976) Income distribution in OECD countries, *OECD Economic Studies*.

Scott, M. (1992) A new theory of economic growth, *Oxford Review of Economic Policy*, Winter.

Comment

Dirk J. Wolfson

Andrew Glyn's chapter convincingly argues that the Rise and Fall of Keynesianism cannot explain what has happened to growth and equality in the Western world since 1945. Clearly, a high level of post-war demand has helped to translate the supply-side potential for high investment rates into rapid and self-reinforcing growth, but the combined effects of reconstruction and continued defence spending, European integration, a more equal distribution of income and relatively low commodity prices provide a stronger explaination for the sterling performance of the 1950s and 1960s than demand management as such. I even doubt that there actually *was* such a thing as a balanced budget multiplier of a rising share of public spending in GDP, as the propensity to invest out of private resources was high anyway. Conversely, I cannot believe that any intellectual argument could link the economics of Keynes to the poor performance of the 1970s and 1980s. It may be so that Keynesian policies were not equipped to deal with intensely competing claims on the national output, as Glyn points out, but that should not surprise us, as Keynes deliberately addressed himself to situations of insufficient effective demand. In doing so, however, he explicitly recognized the bottlenecks developing 'where the supply of particular commodities ceases to be elastic and their prices have to rise to whatever level is necessary to divert demand into other directions' (Keynes 1936, p. 300). I have always held the view that it is too easy a way out to blame 'Keynesianism' for the collapse of structural adjustment in the Western world. It was not Keynesian *economics* that did us in, but *politics in the name of* Keynes, together with the combined failure of government and public administration to replace the market mechanism as the change agent in a dynamic society.

As I can find little to disagree within Glyn's treatment, I will extend his argument by dealing more explicitly with the crucial micro- and meso-levels of shop-floor and wholesale policymaking. Macroeconomic balance sets the stage all right, but it takes more to have a good performance. As a starting point, I would like to support Glyn's view that the balance of power between capital and labour is the key dramatic element in the post-war history of advanced capitalism. Schouten (1980; 1983) taught us to perceive this relationship as shifting endogenously from monopoly capitalism to monopoly labourism, and back again, as a buyers' market for labour forces adjustments that create a sellers' market, and *vice versa*. So the system may be self-adjusting, after all, but only through time, and at considerable social cost. At all levels of policymaking – macro, meso and micro – the question therefore seems to be what ways we have to reduce adjustment time and hysteresis, with the concomitant social cost to both labour and capital.

The answer depends, first and foremost, on the paradigmatic views we hold on the ways in which wealth is accumulated and distributed. As there seem to be more paradigms than economists, nowadays, the Central Planning Bureau (1992) has done us a service by condensing our various beliefs into three basic visions: the Equilibrium, the Coordination, and the Free-Market perspective, as held by the stereotypes of *rational, cooperative* and *competitive* Man.

The Equilibrium perspective is grounded on neoclassical and new classical theory. As such, it reflects a vision in its own right, but I will use it here as the counterfactual against which the other perspectives are developed. In this counterfactual, on the assumption of a well-functioning price mechanism, prices are seen as reliable, adjustable and reliably adjusting information carriers, leading to a balance between supply and demand at all levels in all markets. The economic subjects are *rational*; they even have *rational expectations*. The government is rational as well (remember, we are dealing with a counterfactual!); it confines itself to pure public goods, which cannot develop by means of the price mechanism because of non-excludability and non-rivalry (indivisibility) characteristics.

For those of us who do *not* believe that the system is – readily – self-adjusting, there is the Coordination perspective, grounded on Keynes and the tradition of disequilibrium economics, from Malthus to Marx and beyond (to Morgenstern, Modigliani and Malinvaud, as my favourite big-Ms). They recognise the paradigm of rational expectations as the neurosis of mathematical economists afraid of behavioural science, and see the economy as driven by animal spirits or, at best, by satisficing behaviour. And, in a game-theoretical mood, they recognise that the extent of market failure and the prisoner's dilemmas involved are underestimated in the neo-classical perspective, and should be overcome by coordination and cooperation. Hence their christening as *cooperative men*.

The Free-Market perspective brings together the neo-Austrians, supply-siders and monetarists[1] who feel we should not cry over losers. In that view, the will to win and the fear to lose should be allowed to drive the dynamics of an economy in the perennial gale of creative destruction. Hail to the *competitive man*!

As a child of the neo-classical/neo-Keynesian synthesis, I do not particularly care for neo-Austrians, supply-siders and related ideologists. Admittedly, their self-serving articulation of no nonsense as a value system draws considerable support among the elite in charge of present-day policy making. Perhaps that is a blessing in disguise, forcing those who prefer to see the survival of the fittest as a positivist rather than a normative proposition to come up with better answers.

I submit that there is a missing link in the approach of both Glyn and the Central Planning Bureau: the socio-institutionalist perspective of what I would call the *social man*. The economics profession typically concentrates on interpretations of rational self-interest and on market coordination as *pars pro toto* of what makes society tick; but there is more between heaven and earth: there is a broader motivation of altruism and aiming to please, which goes a long way in explaining Schultze's do-no-direct-harm theorem of targeting social services and public goal-setting in general (1977), and explains a lot about the difference between the market place and other mechanisms of coordination.

In a socio-institutionalist perspective, attitudes towards growth and equality in the OECD countries change endogenously in a Schouten-type cycle around a more structural trend towards individualism at the micro level, more diversified allegiances at the meso level, and a more international outlook at the macro level. *Cyclically*, periods of prosperity breed contempt for the capitalist ethic, as evidenced by the end of the 1960s and the early 1970s. The subsequent decline in economic performance makes way for the free marketeers again, as evidenced by the 1980s. Meanwhile, the scale of consumption and production seems to be driven in different directions by more *structural* developments. The scale of things crumbles into individualism at the micro-level, proliferates into a variety of competing lifestyles at the meso level, and challenges our achievements through an increasing international mobility of capital, good, services, and even labour, at the global level.

So much for the socio part. The institutional scene has difficulty in keeping up with all this, as it is ignored by the neo-classicists, idolised by the coordinators, and just hated by the free-marketeers. The neo-classical tradition just *assumes* that governments behave rationally and properly, just as markets are supposed to do. It holds a Weberian and static view of bureaucracy, in benign neglect of what zealots or shirkers may do to the public good, once the bottom line is removed that would hold them accountable in a market mode. One would hope that the coordination perspective, with an eye for the dynamics of disequilibria, would have recognized the potential of the market as a referee on the efficiency and effectiveness of the public performance, and as an agent of change through time; but it has not. Cooperative men fear the market as they fear the free-marketeers, in a misconception that perceives the market mode as a *goal* rather than an *instrument*. As a result, public policy is caught between future shock and organisational slack. Meanwhile, the free-marketeers tell the government to go 'back to core business' – whatever that may be. It is beyond them to recognise that the quality and sustainability of wealth and welfare might be better off if the public mode and the market mode were made more compatible. And yet, that is precisely what the 1980s have taught us about the need to reconcile the role of the state with that of the market.

Notes

1. The Central Planning Bureau also includes Hayek and Schumpeter among the role models of this perspective. I could not. Both are honourable men. Hayek is just a neo-classical economist, in my view, and so is Schumpeter, who put neo-classical economics in a dynamic frame without becoming a free-marketeer.

References

Central Planning Bureau (1992) *Scanning the Future, A Long-Term Scenario Study of the World Economy 1990–2015*, Den Haag: Sdu Publishers.

Keynes, J.M. (1936) *The General Theory of Employment, Interest and Money*, London: MacMillan.

Schouten, D.B.J. (1980) *Macht en Wanorde*, Leiden: Stenfert Kroese.

Schouten, D.B.J. (1983) On the general and concrete structure of an economic/political system, *The Netherlands Journal of Sociology*, 19, 47–64.

Schultze, Ch.L. (1977) *The Public Use of Private Interest*, Washington: Brookings.

4. The New Core-Periphery Relations: the Contrasting Examples of Europe and America[1]

Alain Lipietz

Since the beginning of the 1980s, 'Fordism', the dominant model of development in the post war period, has clearly broken down. The developed countries have looked at various ways to construct an alternative. Some have prefered 'flexibility', others 'mobilisation of human resources'. At the same time, the newly industrialised countries have increased their competitiveness and have become more differentiated. This has resulted in a vast reordering in the world economic hierarchy.

Another tendency which has been revealed with growing force is the concentration of international economic relations into continental blocs (Europe, America, Asia). Asia is certainly the most varied, most dynamic and most fascinating bloc, nevertheless at the present moment the two blocs bordering the Atlantic remain the most important. Further, their economic relations are more codified. Europe (with the European Union and the European Free Trade Association) has a thirty five year lead and its institutional apparatus is already highly elaborated. The Americas and in particular North America (with the North American Free Trade Agreement) are moving in the same direction.

The two blocs have in common the heterogeneity of the economies which they unify. It is precisely the *coexistence of countries with different wage regimes within an integrated continental bloc* which is the subject of this article. The emphasis will of necessity be on Europe, and North America will be used as point of comparison.

In the first section the different ways the dominant countries have attempted to escape from the crisis of Fordism is considered. Next the analysis is enlarged to include the other countries of the South and the East. Then in a third section the hypothesis of a new international division of labour (the third!) is outlined. Finally the fourth and fifth sections return to the contrasting examples of Europe and North America.

The central crisis of Fordism and the way out of it
Throughout the post World War II period, two models of development were proposed to the developing countries: the western model and the 'socialist' model. This latter has now recognised its complete failure, and the various countries which claimed allegiance to it have abruptly rallied to some kind of capitalist model. At the same time capitalism in the North West of the world was experiencing its Golden Age. The development model of the Golden Age (which is here called 'Fordism') has been in a state of crisis during the 1970s and 1980s, but no one thinks of it as being 'the final crisis of capitalism'. On the contrary many reforms have been proposed for this model, and at the end of the 1980s these reforms seem to have come together to give more or less promising results. We can conclude that the future of Fordism and the ways out of its crisis will once again determine the future of capital labour relations throughout the world. Hence the decision to start with Fordism, its crisis and the ways out of it, and to then extend these considerations to the South and the East.

The rise and fall of the Golden Age[2]
First a brief reminder of what Fordism is. As with any model of economic development it can be analysed on three levels:

- As the general principle for the organisation of labour (or 'industrial paradigm'), Fordism is Taylorism plus mechanisation. Taylorism implies a strict separation between on the one hand the conception of the production process, which is the task of the Organisation and Methods Office, and on the other hand the execution on the shopfloor of standardised and formerly defined tasks. Mechanisation is the way that the collective knowledge of the methods office is incorporated into the material apparatus (both the hardware and the software). According to this principle, the involvement of the workers is considered to be unnecessary in carrying out the Methods Office's orders.

- In so far as it is a macroeconomic structure (or regime of accumulation, or social structure of accumulation), Fordism implied that the productivity gains resulting from these organisational principles were matched by on the one hand a growth of investment financed out of profits and on the other hand a growth in the purchasing power of workers wages. The result was that the share of wages and salaries in value added and the capital coefficient (in value terms) remained more or less constant. Hence the rate of profit was also roughly stable, and the demand for consumer goods and investment goods grew in line with productivity.
- In so far as it is a system of rules of the game (or as a mode of regulation), Fordism implied long term contractual wage relations, with strict limits on redundancies, and a programming of the growth of wages indexed on prices and the general growth of productivity. What is more, a vast socialisation of incomes through the Welfare State assured a guaranteed income for wage earners. The other side of the coin was the accceptance by the unions of management prerogatives. In this way both the principles of the labour process organisation as well as the macroeconomic structure were respected.

The success of the Golden Age model was thus wage-led in the internal market of each advanced capitalist country. There were only limited external constraints because of the limited importance of the growth of international trade relative to the growth of the internal markets, and because of the hegemony of the United States. Nevertheless, at the end of the 1960s, the stability of the Golden Age growth path was beginning to be questioned. The first and the most obvious reason appeared on the 'demand side'. There was little competitive difference between the United States, Europe and Japan. The search for economies of scale resulted in an internationalisation of production and of markets. The growth in the price of raw materials imported from the South (in particular oil) stirred up competition in export markets at the beginning of the 1970s. The regulation of the growth of the internal market through the wage policy was compromised by the need to balance external trade. Faced with this 'demand side' crisis, the first reaction of the international elites was clearly Keynesian. The main plan was to coordinate the maintenance of world demand, via the OECD, the International Monetary Fund, the Trilateral Commission, the Summits of the Big Seven, *etc.*. This was very clearly the line taken by the first Summit at Rambouillet in 1975. It has since been noted that the policies actually carried out were sub-optimal from the point of view of demand.[3] But at least it was understood by everyone that it was necessary to be concerned with effective demand. In fact the growth of real wages slowed spectacularly, more and more firms moved their enterprises to non-unionised zones, or subcontracted in third world countries, but the basic structures of the existing mode of regulation were maintained in the advanced capitalist countries.

However, at the end of the 1970s, there was a change in the state of mind of the international elites of the capitalist world. The management of the crisis by demand side policies had certainly avoided a depression. But a major limitation appeared: the fall in profitability. This was due to a number of 'supply side' reasons: the slowdown in productivity growth, the growth in the total price of labour (including the indirect wages of the Welfare State), growth in the capital–output ratio and growth in the relative price of raw materials. In these conditions the Keynesian recipes, such as the growth in real wages (however limited it might have been) and lax monetary policy, could only lead to inflation and the erosion of the value of monetary reserves, in particular the international money – the dollar (Lipietz 1983). Hence the turn to 'supply side policies', that is to say towards 'labour relations', a sphere which has certain aspects in common with the industrial paradigm and the mode of regulation.

Even within the theoretical framework used here, the supply side problems encountered by Fordism can be interpreted in two different ways. In the first, following the tradition going back to Kalecki, the growth in the relative price of labour and raw materials is considered to be the result of the long boom of the Golden Age. The profit squeeze was the result of the preceeding expansion and of full employment. Furthermore, the Welfare State had spectacularly reduced the cost of job loss (Bowles 1985), which could also explain the slowdown in the growth of productivity.

We will return to a complementary explanation, but the fact is, that at the end of the 1970s, the profit squeeze analysis had become the official explanation. Profits were too low because workers (and raw materials exporters) were too powerful. This in turn was because the rules of the game were too 'rigid', which led to difficulties in the restructuring of the productive apparatus and the risk of failing to take advantage of the opportunities offered by the technological revolution. Such was the analysis of the 1980 Big Seven Summit in Venice, after the second oil shock. This proclaimed that the 'first priority' was to combat inflation (rather than unemployment). This was to be done by increasing productivity and redistributing capital from the declining sectors to the growth sectors, from the public sector to the private sector, and from consumption to investment. They undertook to *'avoid measures protecting particular interests from the severity of the adjustment'*. In other words, the *'rigid'* social compromises were to be repudiated.

This policy of 'liberal flexibility' was carried out by the British and then the US governments, and was finally followed by most of the OECD countries including the French Socialist–Communist government. The renunciation of the social compromise was carried out to different extents and conducted on different fronts – from the rules concerning wage increases (inflation plus productivity) to the extent and depth of social provision, from the liberalisation of redundancy procedures to the proliferation of precarious employment. This process was carried out in an authoritarian manner (governments and management grasped the opportunities provided by the defeats of the trade unions and the political successes of conservative parties) or as a result of negotiations between capital and labour in a context of a rising cost of job loss (for the workers). After a first period of recession at the beginning of the 1980s, there was a recovery starting in 1983. However this upturn was largely the result of a return to Keynesian budgetary policies (Lipietz 1985a, 1992) and it is difficult to affirm that it was solely the result of the liberal policies of flexibility. Moreover the experience of the 1980s did not favour the most serious attempts at flexibility – the United States, United Kingdom and France. On the contrary these countries have experienced both deindustrialisation and a worsening of the balance of trade in manufactured goods. At the end of the 1980s, the winners in the competitive struggle (Japan, West Germany, the European Free Trade Association) appeared to be characterised by other solutions to the supply crisis.

Returning to 'the supply side' explanation of the crisis of Fordism, an alternative to 'the full employment profit squeeze' theory, or rather a complementary explanation insists on a reduction in the efficiency of Taylorist principles. Full employment can explain the fall in the rate of profit at the end of the 1960s, but not the continuation of this tendency, with a growing capital coefficient, in the following years. More importantly, the elimination of all involvement of shopfloor workers in the tuning of the production process now seems to be of limited value. It is a good method for ensuring that management has control over the intensity of labour. But greater 'responsible autonomy' of shopfloor workers can lead to a superior organisational principle, especially when it is a case of setting in motion new technologies, or 'just-in-time' management of production flows, which requires the involvement of the intelligence of shopfloor workers and their willing cooperation with management and engineers.[4] This was precisely the alternative way chosen by numerous large companies in Japan, Germany and Scandinavia. There, pressure from the unions and organisational traditions led to the choice of the *solution by negotiated involvement* to the crisis of Fordism (Mahon 1987).

At the end of the 1980s the superiority of this choice is being more and more recognised, not only among this second group of countries, but also in books on management and in the press. Certainly, the international competitive success of this second group has played an important role in this evolution of ideas, but the difficulties encountered in the setting up of the new technologies in the context of liberal flexibility have also encouraged a change in management style. However it seems possible that liberal flexibility and negotiated involvement are policies that could be combined *à la carte*. This idea is the basis of a conception of 'post Fordism' as 'flexible specialisation' as found in Piore and Sabel (1984). The mutual coherence of these ideas will now be looked at.

After Fordism, what?[5]

The overview of recent economic history which has just been carried out can be summarised as follows:

- Initially great importance was attached to the demand side. Then this problem was forgotten, as if it had become without interest because internationalisation had made demand impossible to control, or because the boom of the second half of the 1980s had made it unnecessary to support demand.
- The development of two doctrines concerning the supply side: *liberal flexibility* and *negotiated involvement*.

The first question will be returned to when the macroeconomic coherence of labour relations at the level of continental blocs is considered, for the moment we will just consider the supply side.

In fact, the two doctrines for getting out of the supply crisis can be considered as two escape routes related to the two characteristics of Fordist labour relations. On the one hand the rigidity of the wage contract; on the other Taylorism as a form of direct management control over the activity of workers (see Figure 4.1). The first doctrine proposes an evolution from 'rigidity' towards 'flexibility' in the employment contract, and the second an evolution from 'direct control' towards 'responsible autonomy'. Using a different vocabulary, the first axis refers to the 'external labour market', to the link between the firms and the labour looking for work and wages. The second axis refers to the 'internal market', to the form of organisation of cooperation/hierarchy within firms.[6] On this axis as opposed to Taylorism we could speak of *Ohnism*, in recognition of the role played by the theoretician of the Japanese methods of production developed in particular by Toyota (Coriat 1992). On the first 'external' axis both rigidity and flexibility have many dimensions, as has already been remarked. The rules of the game may include the rules about the way direct wages are formed, the rules on hiring and firing, the rules on the allocation of the indirect wage – the external market is a more or less organised one. The axis is thus a synthetic axis. Moreover, the rules can be established at various levels – the individual, the firm, the sector, or society as a whole.

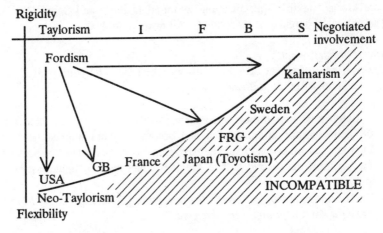

Figure 4.1 Evolution of post-Fordism: the advanced capitalist countries

On the second 'internal' axis, there are also many dimensions: 'involvement' may signify qualification, cooperation between workers, participation in the definition and monitoring of tasks *etc.*.[7] Here again it is a case of a synthetic axis. But this time, for reasons which will become apparent, it is necessary to take into account the level of the negotiation about the involvement of the workers:

- The involvement can be negotiated *individually* and satisfied by, for example, bonuses or promotion systems. This option is limited though by the *collective* nature of the involvement required in most of the processes of cooperative production. Also the individually negotiated involvement (I in Figure 4.1) can be extended to a team or a workshop. This remains compatible with a flexible work contract.
- The involvement can be negotiated *firm by firm*, between management and unions (F in Figure 4.1). Here the firm and its labour force share the rewards of specific skills accumulated over the course of a collective learning process. This implies an external rigidity of the wage contract, that is limits on the right to fire workers already in the firm, but this compromise clearly does not include workers outside the firm.
- The involvement can be negotiated *at the industry level* (B in Figure 4.1), this limits the risk to firms of competition through 'social dumping', and encourages them to set up communal institutions for training *etc.*. As a consequence the external labour market is likely to be more organised, and in general more rigid and with a greater socialisation of labour income.
- The involvement can be negotiated *at the level of society as a whole* (S in Figure 4.1), with the unions and the employers organisations negotiating the social orientation and the sharing of production at the regional or national[8] level, it being understood that the unions will ensure that 'their people' will do their best on the shopfloor or in the office. Here the external labour market is likely to be at least as well organised as in the more corporatist or social-democratic forms of Fordism.

On the other hand, the collective involvement of workers can only occur if firms and the workforce share common aims, in a context of external flexibility at whatever level (individual firms, industry or territory). Thus the limit of the consistency between flexibility and involvement appears as a curve joining the two axes; outside the curve is an excluded triangular region of inconsistency, where flexibility and negotiated collective involvement coexist.[9] The two axes themselves constitute the privileged lines of evolution, that is to say two real paradigms (see Figure 4.1):

- External flexibility associated with direct hierarchical control. This leads to some kind of Taylorist form of organisation of the labour process, without the social counterparts of Golden Age Fordism. We call this paradigm 'neo-Taylorism'.
- External rigidity of the work contract associated with the negotiated involvement of the producers. We call this paradigm 'Kalmarist', in honour of the first car factory (Volvo) reorganised following these principles in a social-democratic country – Sweden. This factory is closed today; we will see why later.

The recent experience of the OECD countries can be analysed as follows. They appear to lie on a curve, with the USA and Great Britain preferring flexibility and ignoring involvement, some countries such as France introducing individually negotiated involvement, Japan practising negotiated involvement at the level of the (large) firm, Germany carrying it out at the industry level, and Sweden finding itself closest to the Kalmarian axis. What then is the attractive power of these axes? The experience of the United States shows that it is difficult to negotiate involvement at the level of the firm in a flexible liberal context, however individually negotiated involvement can be carried out there. Towards the other extreme West Germany appears to have a less socially advanced form of the Kalmarian paradigm. Japan appears to occupy an intermediate position which could be called '*Toyotism*', with a strong duality (rigid–flexible) in its external labour market.[10] This point will be returned to when the global coherence of the paradigms is considered. But first let us glance at the non-OECD countries.

The South and the East: towards which post-Fordism?
While the East had developed completely original forms of labour relations (self designated as being 'socialist', though not all would agree with this), the South could be described as the group of countries who had not succeeded in imitating either the Western or the Eastern model.

In the 1960s it was widely thought that the most rapid route of development for the South was the Eastern one. This followed from two kinds of consideration:

- The East was already an example of accelerated growth, at the time more rapid even than in the Fordist countries. The Stalinist Soviet

Union could then be considered as an ex-underdeveloped country which had succeeded thanks to its superior mode of regulation.
- The West itself seemed to be opposed to the industrialisation of the South. Not only had the colonial system been explicitly based on an 'international division of labour', with the South being allocated the production of primary products, but also the automatic dynamics of free trade reproduced the same division of labour in the neo-colonial relations existing after independence. This fact had been theorised in a positive form in Ricardo's theory of comparative advantage, it was now theorised in a negative way under the title of 'dependency theory'.

Since then heterodox models (that is to say including certain features of the Eastern model) have appeared to be the way for the South to catch up with the West, even among the non-socialist countries. In fact counter examples already existed such as Finland which was a part of the old Russian Empire which had become a Fordist social democracy. But it was the success of the Newly Developing Countries, which contrasted with the lack of success of the peripheral (or even central socialist countries), which led to the change in the general appreciation, rather than Rostovian rhetoric. It is thus appropriate to start the analysis with Eastern Europe.

The rise and fall of the Iron Age
The Stalinist Soviet Union adopted its own model of development which could be called the 'Iron Age' model, contrasting it with the Fordist Golden Age model:

- The Taylorist industrial paradigm was explicitly imported into revolutionary Russia by Lenin.
- The accumulation regime was based on an extensive accumulation of the productive forces, through import substitution, and without any major growth in mass consumption.
- The rules of coordination (or mode of regulation) were based on centralised planning, and that was the 'socialist' aspect. The idea (among stalinist economists) was that it was 'the anarchy of the market' which was the bad aspect of capitalism. With more 'organisation' and 'hierarchy' Taylorist rationality spread throughout society.

Certainly it was a very efficient model in a Lewis-type situation (that is to say with an immense peasant reserve army). They thought that

Taylorism was well adapted to putting to work new unskilled workers. Extensive accumulation has no great need for flexibility, and it increases average productivity in the economy as industrialised and mechanised production replaces pre-industrial forms. With slowly growing real wages an enormous surplus could be accumulated. The centralised organisation of demand eliminated the demand constraint, but with the risk of the appearance of a 'supply side constraint' (Kornai 1979). As for the labour relations, their initial harshness was progressively stabilised into an acceptable compromise (according to the standards of the 1950s). In exchange for its Taylorist subordination, the industrial and tertiary labour force had virtual security of employment. This combination (Taylorism plus tenure) was the 'cousin' of the Fordist one, hence their similarity and their competition in the 1950s.

However new problems came to the surface when the Lewisian reserve army of labour was used up, or had never existed (as in Czechoslovakia and the German Democratic Republic). As Köllö (1990) has shown, the impossibility of organising inter-firm relations to the same extent as the relations within firms resulted in bottlenecks and waste. In return, the anarchy in social planning was reflected in the disorganisation of the firms. The involvement of the workers was discouraged by the erosion of revolutionary ideals, by the anarchy of industrial relations, and by the lack of any kind of incentive, be it negative (cost of job loss) or positive (access to higher levels of consumption). The compromise of 'job security (or tenure) plus low wages' was thus completely stagnationist.

However different it might be from Fordism, the 'socialist' paradigm of the Iron Age also finally resulted in a 'supply side' crisis. The main differences were the following:

- there was no demand side crisis;
- socialist 'tenure' was far more rigid than Fordism;
- the rigidity also included all other aspects of industrial organisation;
- the non-involvement of the workers seemed to be more the result of management incompetence than excesses of Taylorist 'scientific management'.

It became obvious that the Eastern mode of regulation needed more flexibility in its economic organisation. Hence the common choice of East European reformers in favour of autonomy in the management of firms. But the first bit of freedom claimed by the firms is the freedom to adjust their labour force to match their needs, given the potential productivity of existing installations and social demand. Very quickly liberal flexibility in the labour relations – that is external flexibility and the end of socialist tenure – seemed to be a panacea. Ten years after the West, all the ex-socialist countries (except, in 1994, Cuba and North Korea) rushed to embrace this new panacea, forgetting the other side of the problem: the internal organisation of the labour process.

How can this situation be depicted in the figure? On the vertical axis 'tenure' can be represented as 'excess rigidity'. But on the internal axis (organisation) the situation is less clear. The trade-off is less between 'direct control' and 'responsible autonomy' than between 'inefficient control' and 'irresponsible autonomy'. In the East the shopfloor worker has a degree of autonomy, due either to a revolutionary tradition or an industrial tradition (East Germany and Czechoslovakia), and in any case as a result of the inability of management to scientifically organise any direct control. On the synthetic axis this position could be placed between 'negotiated involvement at the firm level' and 'negotiated involvement at the industry level', since as Köllö has shown, the negotiation of a compromise requires participation of the Ministry for the sector, the directors of the firm and the workers. From this point of departure (shown in Figure 4.2) the movement will certainly be downwards, that is to say towards greater flexibility in the wage contract. But after abandoning the tenure compromise will the workers be able to negotiate some kind of social-democratic type Fordism, or will they be obliged or persuaded to accept the panacea of 'liberal flexibility'? This remains an open question at this level of our analysis and at this stage of the historical process.

The situation on the horizontal axis is also an open one. The main tendency of the new 'autonomous' direction of firms will certainly be to implement a full system based on Taylorist principles, especially in the less developed countries (Poland, Hungary, Romania, and most of the Soviet Union). But they will encounter strong resistance from skilled workers, especially in the areas influenced by the West German and Scandinavian examples of the Kalmarist paradigm (the ex-German Democratic Republic and the Czech Republic).

To summarise this first discussion, in response to the challenge of the crisis in their supply side industrial paradigm, the countries of the East will attempt to eliminate the most obvious problem, that of rigidity. This will mean the end of the tenure system in their labour relations. Since Taylorist principles have not yet reached their limits, because they were never fully implemented, the main attraction will be the 'Taylorism plus liberal flexibility' menu, that is to say the neo-Taylorist paradigms which seem (to these countries) to be the basis of the West's success.

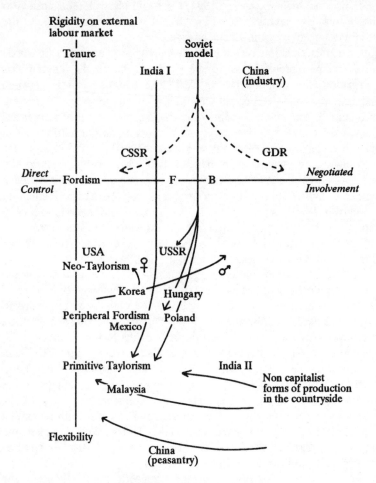

Figure 4.2 Around Fordism

The rural giants with islands of industrialisation
China and India are two immense countries of the South which have most closely adopted the development model of the Soviet Union. The big difference between these countries and those of Eastern Europe is the size of their peasantry, about a third of the world's population. The big difference between China and India is the spectacular agricultural revolution in China.

China has benefited from its agricultural reform, and its strict organisation of rural life, with the result that up to the end of the 1980s it had not witnessed a massive exodus towards the towns. This was a form of 'hidden Lewisism', with an artificial shortage of urban workers dedicated to a quasi Soviet strategy of extensive accumulation oriented towards import substitution. This strategy was pushed by Maoism to quasi self-sufficiency. Further the Great Leap Forward and the Grand Proletarian Cultural Revolution can be understood as the first attempt to make a critique of 'capitalism' (in fact of Taylorism) from the supply side, as a system of direct hierarchical control. After a first attempt to return to strict Stalinist principles, the Deng Xiaoping regime was the first one in the socialist world (with Hungary) to recognise the organisational dead-end, and to reintroduce flexibility not only in the factories but also in the countryside. The Maoist attempt to involve the workers in the running of firms and local communities was destroyed, and all that remained was a tradition of local involvement in management. The liberal reforms revealed the Lewisian situation in the countryside. The entrepreneurs (both within and outside state property) found themselves with a labour force which was very flexible, extremely badly paid and yet with a considerable 'cost of job loss', and with a very authoritarian regime. These are the conditions which later on we call 'primitive Taylorisation', a model which the newly industrialised countries of East Asia experimented with in the 1960s and 1970s. In Figure 4.2, the Chinese trajectory can be shown in the following way. Starting from the Soviet model, and after a sharp turn towards involvement on the 'internal' axis, industrial China is moving rapidly to the bottom of the graph in the direction of primitive Taylorisation. This is shown below neo-Taylorism (because the conditions of the workers is worse than in the dreams of even the most extreme supply-siders). Further, the peasants are immediately set to work under the primitive Taylorisation paradigm.

In India there has not really been any land reform, the country was never 'state socialist', it has never had real centralised planning. Yet there are many traces of the Soviet model visible in its history since independence. The State's policy of import substitution encouraged the development of a large tertiary and industrial sector oriented towards the internal market, where the workers benefited from the tenure principle (sector I following Mohan Rao 1990). These workers were less involved than in the socialist countries, and yet they were not exactly Taylorised. The big difference with China is a permanent flux of primitive Taylorisation of workers excluded from pre-capitalist relations or integrated into capitalist relations through some kind of putting-out system – sector II following Mohan Rao (1990). So a second archipelago of industrial wage relations appeared in rural India. For historical and cultural reasons, Taylorisation has not attained the absolute level of direct control of a Methods Office (which hardly exists). In Figure 4.2, this process is represented by an arrow entering the capital–labour diagram at the bottom right. The liberal economic trend of the 1980s will probably push the labour relations in India towards the classic form of primitive Taylorisation. With the opening of the market to international competition, sector II will be led to adopt deeper forms of direct control without any noticeable increase in real wages or improvements in social legislation. The tenure principal will have to be abandoned in sector I, however it is possible that the priviliged fraction of the labour force will be able to negotiate a limited liberal flexibility and social benefits of the Fordist type in exchange for the rationalisation of the labour process.

This Indian model is extremely interesting, because it is a caricature of a certain evolution in the Latin American countries of the 'Economic Commission for Latin America (ECLA)' type, that is to say the evolution which reflects the theoretical ideas of the ECLA which combine:

– the construction, based on import substitution, of a modern industrial sector, often under the guidance of a populist state;
– the existence of an agricultural sector with more or less antiquated social relations which leads to a continuous flow of labour from the countryside; this is found in different forms, from Mexico to Argentina;
– a 'sector I' where a relatively 'rigid' labour aristocracy had a brutal flexibilisation imposed upon it and a 'rationalisation' (in fact a Taylorisation) of the organisation of work;
– a 'sector II' of peasant origin which has become urbanised and joined the industrial and tertiary workforce, either as a result of the chaotic

process of the formation of an informal sector or by direct entry into Taylorised firms with flexible wage contracts.

This new type of peripheral industrialisation (relative to the Indian, Chinese or ECLA models of import substitution) will now be looked at in its own right.

The Newly Industrialised Countries: where are they going?

The 1970s witnessed the appearance of the Newly Industrialised Countries (NICs). Brazil and South Korea are the most important examples. Certain aspects of their development models have been examined elsewhere under the rubric of 'primitive Taylorisation' and 'peripheral Fordism' (Lipietz, 1985a):

– *Primitive (or bloodthirsty) Taylorisation.* This concept is concerned with the relocation of limited sections of industries to the social formations with very high rates of exploitation (as concerns both wages and the length and intensity of work *etc.*), the output being in general exported to the more advanced countries. In the 1960s the free zones and the workshop-states of Asia were the best illustration of this strategy, which is expanding today. Two characteristics of this regime should be noted. First the work in general follows Taylorist principles, but there is relatively little mechanisation. The technical composition of capital in these firms is particularly low. This strategy thus avoids having to import investment goods, which is one of the inconveniences of the import substitution strategy. Another aspect is that since it mobilises a largely female workforce, it incorporates all the knowledge gained from domestic patriarchal exploitation. Secondly this strategy is 'bloodthirsty' in the sense that Marx talked of the 'bloodthirsty legislation' on the eve of English capitalism. To the ancestral oppression of women, it adds all the modern arms of anti-worker repression (official unions, a lack of social rights, imprisonment and torture of opponents).

– *Peripheral Fordism.* Like Fordism it is based on the combination of intensive accumulation and the growth of final markets. But it remains peripheral in the sense that in the world wide circuit of the industries, skilled labour (especially in engineering) remains to a large extent external to these countries. Further, the outlets follow a particular combination of local consumption by the middle classes, a growing consumption of durable goods by the workers and low priced exports to the core capitalisms.

Take the two examples of Brasil and South Korea. Brazil started its industrialisation earlier and with greater success than India. Agricultural reform was just as limited as it was in India, the supply of the reserve army of labour was Lewisian and, since the Vargas period (during the Second World War), a policy of import substitution led by the state was put in place in the urban sector by the national capital. This was combined with corporatist social legislation (not that different from Fordist principles). However there were two major developments which made a difference. First the developmentist state while protecting its internal market from imports did not hesitate, under Jocelino Kubitschek, to open the doors to capital, and its technology, from the 'North West of the World'. Next the 1964 military takeover suppressed the social advantages of the Vargas legislation (precisely out of fear of union power under the presidence of Goulart). As a result the 'scientific organisation of work' developed without any limit other than technological dependence, and the bloody repression of the unions offered capital a 'flexible' labour force. At the end of the 1960s and the beginning of the 1970s Brazil developed a very competitive industry, completed its import substitution and developed its industrial exports.

This led to primitive Taylorisation. However Brazil did not clearly follow a simple strategy of import substitution. The investment goods were mainly paid for by the export of primary products and by borrowing. The benefits of primitive Taylorisation were reinvested in the development of a dualist peripheral Fordism. A fraction of the population – the new middle class – set themselves up with a quasi Fordist life style. The workers benefited in the second half of the 1970s from the productivity growth resulting from the mechanisation and rationalisation. This fraction comprised the major part of the 'formal sector' (Amadeo and Camargo, 1990), not *all* of it, but still the major part of the working class, which at the end of the 1970s had regained some of the advantages guaranteed by the Vargas legislation. But on the other hand there was a large section of workers who remained excluded from the benefits of the Brazilian miracle – the 'Lewisian' ex-peasants, the informal workers and the badly paid formal workers in small firms.

In the 1980s the debt crisis blew up, followed by a movement towards democracy. The resulting evolution is fairly complex. On one side the democratisation increased the negotiating power of the workers and their legal guarantees, but on the other side high inflation reduced their ability to control the evolution of their real wages. Distributional conflicts were at the forefront of industrial conflicts. Labour relations could not stabilise in this permanent storm involving the marginalised Lewisian reserve army, the informal sector and the different levels of the formal sector. In this chaotic situation there are three possibilities for the future of Brazil. A return to primitive Taylorisation, a consolidation of peripheral Fordism, and even an evolution towards Fordism with local Kalmarist aspects.

In comparison the 1985–87 revolution in South Korea inherited a much better situation. At the base of everything is the agrarian reform of the 1950s followed by income support for peasants. Primitive Taylorisation in Korea was not under the pressure of a Lewisian reserve army. All the labour force was hired with a flexible work contract, but was formally hired. Moreover the state was careful to painstakingly plan export capacity to ensure that debt could be repaid. Women were terribly over exploited, especially in the export sector, but workers family incomes grew throughout the 1970s and accelerated in the 1980s, with the result that Korea saw a transition from primitive Taylorisation to peripheral Fordism. Moreover among the male working class enterprise consciousness developed in such a way that it could lead to the copying of certain aspects of the Japanese form of negotiated involvement at the enterprise level (You 1990).

The democratisation process will probably encourage these tendencies, since there is no longer any debt constraint, though there is still a competitivity constraint. Korea could evolve towards a form less and less peripheral to the centres of Toyotism.

Towards a third international division of labour

We are not going to continue the discussion of the stability (macroeconomic, sociopolitical or ecological) of the different national models of the evolution of the capital labour relations.[11] We are going rather to discuss the possibility of the coexistence of nations with different models in a world which is more and more internationalised (that is to say where geographic, legal, tarrif or cultural barriers are becoming less of a hindrance to the free circulation of technical knowledge, capital and goods).

This is a question which concerns the theory (or rather theories) of international trade. But the theory of international trade is particularly handicapped today by its assumptions which correspond more to a past reality. It is either assumed (with Adam Smith and the Marxist-dependency tradition) that there exists *one* best way to produce each commodity, and that this best way must in the end dominate, to the benefit of the country which has the knowledge – the theory of absolute advantage. Or it is assumed that there is a curve of production possibilities which combines the factors of production within a unique technological paradigm. In this case there is a division of labour based on the inital endowment of the different factors – the Ricardian theory of comparative advantage. This international division of labour must gradually dissappear as the barriers to the international mobility of the factors fall.

Today we have precisely the situation where the 'factors' capital and labour are completely mobile,[12] but where the *way* they are combined (technological paradigm, labour relations) is different from one country to another. This situation is significantly different from previous periods when the hegenomic model dominated.

The two first international divisions of labour
The 'first international division of labour' which existed practically up to the 1960s shows the pertinence of Adam Smith's intuition. As soon as certain goods become the objects of international trade, their production tends to be concentrated in places where the conditions of production are favourable or are mastered (natural conditions such as climate or cultural conditions such as social organisation or knowledge). This concentration becomes in its turn relatively stable because economies of scale protect the old centres of production against new ones. New centres can only appear under the protection of a 'natural' monopoly such as distance or an artificial one such as the protection of 'infant industries'.

From the time that manufacturing, and more importantly heavy industry, started up in England, the major part of world manufacturing production was concentrated in that country, and in a few others who, with varying amounts of protectionism, were able to adopt the same industrial paradigm. Other countries could only enter world trade by doing 'something else', that is making *other products* and specialising in industries where they also had an *absolute* advantage (most often geographic) over England. The first international division of labour (manufacuring exports/primary goods, agricultural or mining exports) is thus an *inter-industry* one.[13]

Ricardo's explanation of the trade of English textiles and Portuguese wine, which he claimed was based on comparative advantage, is more apologetic than accurate. In fact Portuguese wine outclassed absolutely English wine (and there was no great merit in this), and English industrial textiles equally absolutely outclassed Portuguese artisanal textiles. Even the relative failure of import substitution models in the 1960s, be they Soviet or ECLA models, can be explained by the theory of absolute advantage. Neither the Soviet Union nor Argentina have become major exporters of manufactured goods, because the Fordist model has turned out to be more competitive even with wage levels which over time have become much higher.

In the NICs primitive Taylorisation and above all peripheral Fordism appeared nevertheless in a new international configuration. Now a technological paradigm appeared to be partially transferable, and at little cost, from one country to another, so that the least skilled and the least mechanised sections of the Fordist labour process can be localised much more competitively in low cost regions or countries. Is this the revenge of the Ricardian theory of comparative advantage? Far from it.

a) Firstly it is not a question of comparative advantages between endowments peculiar to each industry, but differences in the cost of factors of production for different segments of the production process within a single industry, or at the very least between the successive stages of production of a single product, organised within a single technological paradigm. The Fordist division of labour can in effect be schematised into three kinds of task:

- conception, engineering and organisation of work;
- skilled fabrication (in particular of machines); and
- unskilled fabrication or assembly (or more generally routine tasks including services).

To put it in another way, the standardised procedures typical of Fordist mass production allow there to be a geographical disconnection between these three kinds of task, from which it is 'natural' to localise these tasks where the corresponding labour exists at the best quality–cost relation. Research centres are not set up in places where there are no engineers; it is worth while setting up routine production where qualified labour is cheapest. It is a question therefore of *absolute advantage in the division of labour within an industry*. Primitive Taylorisation therefore corresponds to the localisation of sections of type 3 in very low wage countries; peripheral Fordism to the localisation of sections 3 and 2 in countries with low wages but already having a supply of skilled workers and more developed technical capabilities. This is the 'economistic' schema of the second international division of labour.

b) The reality of the dynamism of the NICs cannot be reduced to this economistic schema of relative labour costs however. Firstly, industrial organisation, transport costs and the localisation of markets *is important*. Activities of type 3 and 2 cannot be localised anywhere. There must be a certain local balance between the skills on the labour market, the industrial fabric and the structure of local demand. The schema of the Free Zones of Asia, or of the 'maquiladoras' of the northern Mexico border, where some links of a productive process are relocated to 'the South' (where wages are very low) to serve the final markets of 'the North' (where the demand is more affluent) in fact corresponds to only a very small part of world manufacturing production. Above all, and still keeping to the supply side, the discriminating factor (in this case labour) is a social construction. If it was simply sufficient for labour to be abundant ('Lewisian'), then all the countries of the Third World would have become NICs. Labour also needs to be free from other constraints (rural, family, religious), to be unorganised as a result of repression or tradition (female labour) and moreover to be used to industrial work discipline. In short, the 'endowment of labour' looked for is its suitability for the flexible Taylorist paradigm which has been identified in the first part of this paper,[14] a socially constructed characteristic of local society.

The coexistence of post-Fordisms

When at the beginning of the 1980s the Fordist compromise was openly criticised and judged obsolete, the spontaneous tendency was, once again and following the lessons of history, to look for 'the' new form of hegemony in the capita–labour relation. The first part of the decade, marked by the success of Reaganism, saw the triumph of the idea that 'the' way out of the crisis of Fordism would be the (external) flexibilisation of the wage contract. 'Euro-sclerosis' was criticised and blamed on the rigidity of the wage relationships. Then after the crash of 1987, the decline of the United States and the impasse it had been led into by Reagan's 'deregulation' became obvious, and the technological and financial superiority of Japan and Germany became clear. It was recognised that models for escaping from the crisis based on the 'mobilisation of human resources' outperformed those based on flexibility. Today (in 1994), the difficulties faced by Germany and Japan show that things are not so obvious, and competition from the NICs of Asia and even Latin America seems capable of imposing on the whole world a single standard of ever lower wages and ever more flexible wage contracts. In any case, is it reasonable to think that one of the two paradigms distinguished in the first two sections of this chapter will have an absolute advantage over the other and will end up by eliminating it?

The fact that it is not yet possible to say *which* must however give cause for thought. First it is clear that the two paradigms are not sufficient to define a coherent model of development for the whole world. There is a lack, at the very least, of a mode of regulation of international effective demand. Competition in the world market has become global and hence cyclical, as it was before 1950. There is no reason why the cycles should spare the dominant model (be it the USA, Germany or Japan). Next, exceptional events such as the dissolution of the 'socialist' bloc and its conversion into market capitalism, for the moment successfully in China and unsuccessfully in Europe, cannot but influence the economic situation and even the structure of neighbouring countries (especially the unification of the two Germanies).

But even taking into account these conjunctural considerations, we are prepared to risk the following strucural hypothesis. *The world will organise itself into three continental blocs, and within each there will be a division of labour between the centre and the periphery based on different combinations of the two basic paradigms of post-Fordism.*

The first point – the tendency for the world economy to break up into continents (Asia and the Pacific around Japan, the Americas around the United States, and Europe around Germany) – is not essential to the argument. This integration within continents results in the first place from a 'revenge of geography' – with the 'just in time' method of organisation, distance and transaction times take on greater significance. It is also the result of the attempts to control the international economy, which on a world scale is too difficult to achieve, but which has got some chance of success between neighbours.

Within each of these blocs there are clearly countries at quite different levels of development with core-periphery type relations between them, be they within the first or the second type of division of labour. These hierarchies are changing, there is progress in the peripheral countries, the dominant countries get out of the crisis with varying degrees of success, and above all they use different ways to do so, emphazising one or the other of the paradigms shown on the axes defined earlier.

The second hypothesis put forward here is thus the possibility of the coexistence of the two paradigms within the same area of continental integration, with an international division of labour of the third type between countries where one or the other of the two paradigms dominates. Note that it is not a question of producing in different ways quite different products as in the first international division of labour, nor to specialise, as in the second international division of labour, in different kinds of task within the same paradigm and within the same industry, but rather to produce similar products in a *different way*.

This is only possible if neither of the two paradigms completely outperforms the other, and which one dominates depends on the industry or sub-industry. At this point the Ricardian formalism finds its heuristic value if the notion of 'initial endowment of factors' is replaced by that of '*social construction of the adoption of a paradigm*'. This social construction is a complex fact about society that is not elaborated here (but see Leborgne and Lipietz 1988). Here it is simply noted that the adoption of the 'flexible' and 'negotiated involvement' paradigms correspond, respectively, to 'defensive' and 'offensive' strategies, on the part of the elites of the nation or region considered, for getting out of the crisis.

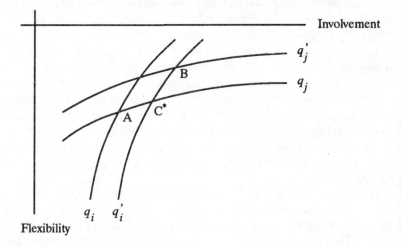

Figure 4.3 Comparative advantages

Suppose that in industry i it is possible to produce, at the same cost, in either of the two ways – firstly by 'mobilising human resources' with contractual guarantees and with relatively high wages corresponding to a high level of skill, or alternatively with Taylorist methods and in this case with less skilled labour and with wages sufficiently low. Assume also that this choice between involvement and flexibility allows for intermediate positions on a continuous curve which can be represented as a fixed price curve for a quantity q_i, very much like the classical production function which combines capital and labour. This is shown in Figure 4.3 where the axes are labelled (somewhat confusingly) Flexibility–rigidity and Taylorist–involvement following Figures 4.1 and 4.2. In this picture neither paradigm is completely dominated by the other. It is possible for sufficiently low wages to be equally competitive with a 'Taylorist' work organisation as it is with a 'Ohnist' organisation which requires higher wages.

In order to be more competitive, and produce a quantity q_i' greater than q_i for the same cost, it is necessary for a given level of involvement and skill, to find more flexible and less well paid workers, or for a given wage find workers with a greater level of involvement and skill. The constant price curves with growing competition move away from the origin. But industries are not all equally sensitive to changes in flexibility and involvement. In industry i with a high level of skill, it is necessary to have a considerable reduction in wages to compensate for the advantages of a small change in the mobilisation of human resources. For industry j the opposite is true, here it is a standard industry where involvement does not matter very much.

Consider two countries A and B, or two segments of the labour market in the same country but well insulated from each other (by gender or ethnics for example). In the figure the point A is superior to the point B for industry j (because $q_j' < q_j$), but it is the other way round for industry i. Note however that the point C is superior to A for both industries. This can be put as follows (adapting Ricardo's theorem): *the industries most sensitive to skill will tend to look for the relatively more skilled and less flexible segments of the labour market, the industries most sensitive to the low cost of labour will tend to look for the more flexible segments of the labour market.*

This helps to understand the success of the 'Toyotist' model, because if within a given society the two types of labour market can be found, then the ability to negotiate wages at the level of the firm would enable there to be an optimal adaptation for all industries. The more 'Kalmarist' national models would be handicapped by the rigidity and excessive cost of labour in the more standard industries. The more flexible national models (neo-Taylorist) would be handicaped in industries requiring a high level of skill. On the other hand countries where there is a classical Fordist relation (rigidity plus Taylorism) will be gradually outperformed 'from above and from below'.

If differences within countries are abstracted from, and only their relative position in Figure 4.2 is considered, then it can be seen that within a given continental bloc all the different possibilities may coexist. Industries with the most skilled labour will tend to be found at the top and the right, where there will be high salaries, high skill levels, the highest internal flexibility and hence the greatest ability to introduce new processes and to invent and test new products. In a word they are found in 'core' countries. As industries become more standard, they are found in countries more and more to the bottom and left of the figure, who can remain competitive only by a more and more savage flexibility and with ever lower wages, and with the risk of being accused of 'social dumping'. Figure 4.4 shows how as you move down the steps toward the periphery you – first – find the old Fordist countries become more and more neo-Taylorist, then the peripheral Fordist and finally the primitive Taylorisation countries.

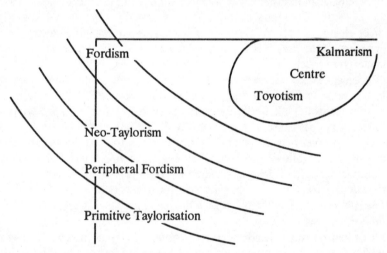

Figure 4.4 The new hierarchy

This hierarchy is fine on paper, but in the field things are not ordered quite so neatly as will be seen when Europe and America are compared.

Europe - a well ordered hierarchy

Europe - a hierarchical continental bloc[15]
The most important market in the world both in population and in wealth, Western Europe is also the centre of world stagnation since the beginning of the crisis. It is the only advanced capitalist centre where unemployment has remained high despite the demographic stagnation. This paradox is in no way linked to a lack of technological or social innovation, as can be seen in the Scandinavian countries and in the 'alpine arc' of Southern Germany, Austria, Northern Italy and Switzerland. A glance at the figures (see Table 4.1) clearly shows the fundamental problem. In the 1980s the only countries to avoid stagnation and unemployment were Norway, Sweden, Austria and Switzerland, that is countries who were not members of the European Community. This stagnation specific to the EC is the disquieting phenomenom which will have to be explained. But first consider the changes in the way that Western Europe as a whole (the EC plus EFTA) is inserted into the world economy.

The first characteristic of Europe is that it is composed of ferocious exporters - seven out of the world top ten - but who are struggling mainly between themselves. Between 1967 and 1986 intra-European trade (EC and EFTA) grew from 37.6 per cent to 40.5 per cent of total world exports. But when inter-zone exports are excluded, then the west European export share fell from 15.3 per cent to 13.8 per cent and the import share from 17 per cent to 11.8 per cent over the same period. Thus Europe as a whole is in surplus while seeming to slowly loose importance in world trade. To this should be added the fact that Europe is the only zone in the world with a positive balance on the services account excluding payments to factors. Inveterate competitors with each other, the European countries taken as a whole do not offer any outlets for other countries to balance their accounts.

This general European 'self centredness' takes on a more dramatic form at the sector level. What stands out in an analysis by industry (CEPII, 1989) is the reduction in imports, especially in the agro-food sector but also energy and non-ferrous metals. The only sectors with growing imports were textiles (where Europe is in balance), motor vehicles (where Europe has a surplus) and electronics (where it has moved into deficit). It is the same with exports where the only growth sectors are energy, electronics (where Europe is in deficit) and the chemicals 'bastion'. The time when Europe was the workshop inundating the world with its manufactured goods and importing its industrial raw materials and food from the less developed world is clearly over. Europe is *de facto* moving to a kind of self sufficiency. The springboard of this evolution is the powerful constraint of internal competition. Each country in Europe is attempting to balance its account at any price. This self-centredness is also made possible by the internal diversity of Europe, with its countries with a strong manufacturing tradition, its newly industrialised mediterranean countries, its great temperate plains strongly encouraged to guarantee (and more) self sufficiency in food thanks to a productionist common agricultural policy, and even its reserves of fossil fuels. Europe (EC plus EFTA) forms an 'integrated continental bloc' illustrating well the hypothesis of this paper.

The productive weight of western Europe will be looked at next. Gross domestic product can be aggregated and compared in two ways – in volume (evaluated at purchasing power parities) or in value (at current exchange rates). Since the end of the 1960s Western Europe has become less important in volume terms, but much less so in value terms. The decline in both value and volume terms is particularly clear *vis-à-vis* Japan, in Latin America however the volume share grew like Japan's did, and even more so, while the value share fell even more rapidly than Europe's. This brings out the two ways that a zone can be inserted into the world market. At one extreme the value of the production grows as a result of a kind of quality improvement, and at the other extreme there is a growing volume of exports but at a lower and lower price on world markets. From this point of view Western Europe finds itself between the Japanese path and the Latin American one.

This diversity is also found within Western Europe. In volume terms every country lost shares in world trade with the exception of the 1960s newly industrialising countries of Southern Europe – Spain, Greece and Portugal.[16] But these latter countries, like Latin America, saw their values stagnate. The British Isles (Great Britain plus Ireland) lost as much in volume as in value, the Federal Republic of Germany, France and Italy lost in volume, but Germany and Italy grew in value. So in broad terms the picture is one of a more or less stagnant Northern Europe, and a Southern Europe which is growing, but which – with the exception of Italy – is only able to realise the output of its workers at low prices. This new indication of a European sickness will become more clear when account is taken of the complexity of the reciprocal adjustments within Western Europe.

Some countries, in particular those of Southern Europe, play the 'defensive' low wages card. Others, especially Scandinavia, on the contrary play the 'offensive' card of the negotiated social mastery of new technologies. Almost every point on the curve of outlets to the crisis is represented in Europe, and there is both a 'core' which grows in international values, and a periphery which can only grow in volume terms. This is not sufficient to counter, in motor vehicles and electronics, the organisational superiority of the Japanese, or in textiles the competition from third world countries with a very high level of exploitation of labour. This is why Europe also plays the protectionist card against Japanese cars, Asian textiles, beef from Argentina *etc.*. But it would be a big mistake to reduce European selfcentredness to protectionism, its anti-dumping passion underlines the importance it attaches to the maintenance of its internal social compromises. Now this varies both between regions and nations, and the greatest threat to it comes from the internal structure of Europe. This will be analysed next.

The macroeconomics of the single market
The fundamental problem of any 'economy of work in the Single Market' is that onto any interregional differences in the strategy adopted to escape from the crisis of Fordism are superimposed the internal European national frontiers. Every country, whatever strategy is adopted at its own level, must balance its external account. A stylised view of this is presented next, followed by a consideration of possible outcomes given the present state of the Single Market Act and the Maastricht Treaty.

A stylised model of the situation of the EC[17] up to 1993 (that is, before the breakdown of the European Monetary System) can be characterised as follows:

1. The EC is potentially self sufficient.
2. There is a free market in goods and capital, and real exchange rates are fixed.
3. Each country has to adjust to the external constraint without any explicit coordination with the others (non cooperative game).
4. Each EC nation can be thought of as being composed of some regions adopting a neo-Taylorist strategy as a way out of the crisis, and of other regions with a negotiated involvement strategy.
5. The offensive strategy (negotiated involvement) is superior (in competitiveness) to the defensive (flexible) strategy, but the superiority is less in the labour intensive industries where a sufficiently large wage difference can give the advantage to the defensive strategy.

From the first three hypotheses the normal Keynesian considerations (beggar-my-neighbour policies: Glyn *et al.* 1988; Lipietz 1985a) result in a tendency to stagnation – each country being obliged in the short term to react to the pressure from the others by reducing incomes and attempting to increase exports by reducing unit labour costs. A tendency which, as has been seen, was confirmed by the experience of the 1970s and 1980s. It is also to be expected that in the medium term countries with weak social protection and low wages would develop a competitive advantage over the others, which would in turn lead to a general erosion in social protection (social dumping). This would certainly be the case if the forms of work organisation were everywhere the same, and competition only functioned at the level of wages and 'defensive flexibility'.

This analysis must be modified, though, when hypotheses 4 and 5 are introduced. The application of the 'transposition of Ricardo's theorem' of the previous section means that each region will tend to specialise in the industries which use most intensively the 'factor' with which the region is best endowed, that is to say either flexible and Taylorised labour, or skilled labour and negotiated involvement. Since there is free movement of capital and the market really is a single one, the division of labour within the EC tends to get divided between regions by industry (or sub-industry) according to this special kind of 'comparative advantage'. This allows Denmark, for example, to exist side by side with Portugal where wages are five times as low.

The totality of the single market is thus determined by the relatively high wages in the countries where involvement dominates, and the relatively low wages of the countries with flexibility. The weaker are the redistributional options in the first group of countries, the more is the second group constrained to low wages (and to flexibility and unemployment). In the absence of a concerted policy to expand the economy (point 3) the macroeconomic choices of the first group impose themselves on all the others and in this way define a kind of equilibrium with underemployment at the European level.

It must be emphazised that in the regions of the core, gains in productivity are redistributed in the name of collectively negotiated involvement within the strict limits defined by the competitive quasi-rent which is conferred on them by the productive advantage of the involvement of their workers. This quasi-rent itself is constrained by the difference in competitiveness between the two groups of regions, its preservation implies a structural 'excessive redistributional prudence' in the first kind of region, because it is at permanent risk of being reversed by a growth in wage costs relative to the second type. In other words, while Fordist macroeconomics was based on a general and foreseeable national redistribution, the regional social compromises based on involvement, within a Europe without common social legislation, can only be maintained if account is taken of productivity differences between regions, and if they tend to be affected (pulled by demand) by growth in other regions.

However the result is less catastrophic than the one based only on the first three hypotheses. Instead of a reciprocal erosion of the national social compromises by intra-EC competition, there is a two speed Europe, a geographical 'leopard skin'. Moreover the regional 'marks' of a network of firms with an 'offensive' social compromise will often include subcontracting and business services sectors, and homeworkers where the social security cover is weak and highly 'flexible'; these intra-regional differences can be based on gender and ethnic differences.

In any case this Europe with two social speeds is, by the mechanism we have just analysed, a Europe with but a single economic speed – and that is a slow one.

Where are we?

The considerations above shed some light on the facts evoked at the beginning of this section – the relative stagnation of Europe and high unemployment rates, even in countries with balance of payments surpluses, and this despite a surplus for the European zone as a whole. They also shed light on the contrast between countries (the Federal Republic of Germany, but also Italy thanks to its Northern and Central regions) which are growing by increasing the value of their labour on the international market, and those who are growing by devaluing their labour (mainly the Iberian Peninsular, and partially the British Isles), as a result of their choice between neo-Taylorist and negotiated involvement labour relations.

Up to 1993, the EC institutions are becoming more and more like the stylised hypotheses above, especially with the ratification of the Single Act: a free exchange zone without a common social policy (except in agriculture). The European Common Market had hardly impeded the Golden Age growth of Fordism because all the countries used to simultaneously follow a policy of growth of their internal market. The balance of payments disequilibria were periodically purged by devaluations, or by short term cooling down policies, and even by 'failsafe clauses' permitting the establishment of some customs tariffs. In the 1960s these margins for manoeuvre were little by little abandoned, even though the growing internationalisation of the economy increased the commercial war between member countries. Deprived of the possibility of changing its exchange rate by the rules of the European Monetary System (EMS), the only way for each country to achieve balance of payments equilibrium is by growing less rapidly than its neighbour, a policy of 'competitive austerity'.

In reality growth in Europe is strictly limited by the growth of the most competitive, and thus surplus, economy, that of the Federal Republic of Germany which has chosen the strategy of negotiated involvement. But since the second phase of the crisis, German governments of the left or right have preferred monetary and budgetary orthodoxy despite a high rate of unemployment in the Northern and Central regions. As a result of the EMS and the Single Act, the hegemonic weight of the Federal Republic of Germany has allowed it to act as the Economics Minister for the whole of Europe. In particular it controlled the size of the 'monetary adjustments' within the EMS, and its restrictive domestic monetary policy forced excessive interest rates on all its partners until 1993. In refusing either to stimulate its own economy or to allow its partners a competitive devaluation, it condemned them to oscillate between stagnation and deficits *vis-à-vis* itself. The commercial power of the EC is in some ways reduced to the commercial power of Germany, and that relative to the rest of Europe. The Federal Republic of Germany obtains the main part of balance of payments surplus from the rest of Europe, thus forcing these countries to have a positive balance with the rest of the world in order to pay for their imports from Germany.

Nevertheless, at the end of the 1980s, Europe (EC plus EFTA) seemed to be a 'tranquil force' progressing in a more stable and certain way than the Americas, less rapidly certainly than Asia but with an incomparably higher standard of living. It appears to be organised exactly as in the core–periphery schema of Figure 4.4. At the top the Kalmarist countries of Scandinavia. In the middle Germany and the 'alpine arc'. A bit below lies France which is evolving from Fordism to a fairly defensive flexibility, but with a few more offensive islands. Then neo-Taylorist Great Britain, and Spain which remains peripheral Fordist, finally Portugal still more peripheral and flexible. Further on lies Morocco and all the countries of the Agreement of Preferential Interest (basically: Southern Bank mediterranean countries). Further still lie the African, Caribbean and Pacific (ACP) countries of the Lomé Agreement which remain in the first international division of labour and are trying hard to be part of the second, in the position of primitive Taylorisation.

But the fall of the Berlin Wall will change all this. On a macroeconomic level the reconstruction of Eastern Europe could have played a dynamic role in Western Europe if there had been a 'Marshall Plan' policy with associated low interest rate. The opposite happened, and after a two year Keynesian stimulus, the restrictive German monetary policy progressively smothered not only the reconversion in the East, but also any internal dynamism in West Europe. But on top of this error of economic policy, the erruption of an ultra-flexible but yet skilled labour force has arrived to upset the pre-1989 equilibrium, in particular in the top right hand corner of Figure 4.4. In a way the opportunties of flexibilisation prevail over the advantages of involvement (Lipietz 1992).

It is first of all the Scandinavian model which is put into a state of crisis. Suddenly deprived of its traditional outlets in the East (while they could have hoped for a 'hanseatic virtuous circle'), Finland and Sweden are faced with the structural competitive weakness of their 'Kalmarist' compromise in a context of liberalism, since nationally negotiated compromises between capital and labour are dangerously generous to those industries with a low level of involvement and low productivity gains. This generosity ends up by also endangering the competitiveness of the more productive sectors – significantly the eponymous Kalmar factory is now closed. There is thus a tendency to slip down the curve towards the bottom and the left, that is to say towards negotiation by industry and abandoning the 'solidarity wage' (Mahon 1993).

But Germany itself is being pulled along by the same forces. Chancellor Kohl's 'initial lie' concerning the financing of reunification is leading to a general destabilisation of labour relations in West Germany despite the fact that the Ohnist industrial paradigm remained less perfected there than in Japan. The industry aggreements have been repudiated. The employers of the small and medium-sized enterprises are attempting to disengage themselves from the industry negotiations which align their wage contracts to those obtaining in the large firms, who themselves are not hesitating to threaten to move production to more flexible countries such as Portugal or Malaysia (Duval 1993). So to summarise there is a generalised movement towards Toyotist rules of the game.

This 'flooding' of the core by the ocean of peripheral flexibility remains for the moment contained, and could be reversed by social and environmental legislation at the continental level. Unfortunately the

Maastricht Agreements ignore these two essential points and on the contrary, through exchange rates and interest rates, reinforce the rigidity of the macroeconomic links between countries. However the difficulties encountered in applying the Agreement, as a result of the two crises of the EMS in September 1992 and July 1993, increase the margins of manoeuvre of national macroeconomic control and mutual adjustment between countries, but it is not a good sign for the future fundamental treatment of this issue which requires more Europe rather than less. Paradoxically the difficulties of the NAFTA will demonstrate the same thing.

North America - a paradoxical bloc

A glance at Figure 4.4 shows the two differences between North America and Europe:

- the dominant force in the continent, the United States, is not engaged in the dominant world industrial paradigm;
- since the core and the periphery of the continent are engaged in the *same industrial paradigm*, they can only compete with each other through the degree of flexibility.

So the first paradox is that the core which dominates the American continent, the United States, is no longer dominant, either technologically or financially, on a world scale. And the only purpose served by its military power is to allow it to manage the enormous public order problem brought about in the whole hemisphere by the decadence of its own social compromises – the war against drugs. As for organising the economic network of its sphere of co-prosperity – the word is not well chosen! – that is another matter. The United States only controls one market, Mexico, its feudal border country. The whole of South America, with countries which previously seemed so promising – Brasil and Argentina – is now caught in a historical backwater. It is too endebted, too far from the United States which has become too weak, and waiting for Japan or Europe to become interested in it again, which already seems to be the case in Chile.

In September 1991 I was able to visit several factories on Mexico's northern border.[18] This was only a very small sample of five factories, but the fact that my Mexican colleagues had been able to arrange for me to visit them indicates that the managers were particularly proud of what they had to show me. Of the five factories four escaped from the technological or financial domination (or both) of the United States. The four were:

- the Sony factory at Tijuana: obviously escaped from both dominations;
- the Rockwell factory at Nogales: American equipment, but it has just been bought by Alcatel of France!;
- the cement factory at Yaqui (a magnificent ultra modern cathedral to productivism): all the machines were Swiss;
- the equally modern Ford factory at Hermosillo: most amusingly, everything, except the Mexican labour force and a few spare parts from the Mid West, was Japanese – the robots, the presses, the steel, even the GTI engines, and of course the discourse were imported from Japan.

All the same I did visit a genuine *maquiladora* (subcontractor) of a gringo firm, a sawing machine tool factory in Hermosillo. But this was only to discover that the parent company, where the parts were made, was also going to move to Mexico. And that is the worst part of the drama of American industry; having chosen for itself the strategy of low wages and and a low level of skill, it no longer has any reason to keep the heart of its productive apparatus on its own soil as Germany and Japan have done. All United States manufacturing is tempted to slip towards the use of Mexican labour, with machines more and more often of European or Japanese origin.

In this way the serious consequences of the second characteristic of the North American block become apparent. Instead of the constituent countries being aligned from the core to the periphery along the diagonal line from Kalmarism to Neo-Taylorism, here Canada, the United States and Mexico are aligned on the vertical axis of growing flexibility, but with a uniformly Taylorist industrial paradigm, so that most industries can only compete with the assistance of low wages and a reduction in workers job security. The implication is that a general movement of firms (or at least their type 3 Taylorist jobs) towards Mexico is inevitable and can only be slowed down by the requirements of just-in-time management for the close proximity of supplies.

This law first became obvious at the time of the first Canada–United States free trade agreement in 1990. Canada, with 'permeable Fordism' (Jenson 1989), had to a large extent escaped the 1980s social deregulation of Reaganism, but without being able to endow itself with a qualification globally superior to that of the United States, with the result that it rapidly lost employment to its neighbour.[19] But it is with the arrival of NAFTA that the problem became really important. Mexico is in effect evolving in the Indian direction (as discussed earlier) with the following characteristics:

- A general increase in flexibility of the wage relation for the old 'labour aristocracy' in State enterprises. This flexibilisation is accompanied by a rationalisation in the organisation of labour.
- A very rapid exodus from the countryside, further accelerated by the freeing of the market in the common lands (*ejidos*). This resulted in an explosion in the urban informal economy and an overabundant supply of labour for primitive Taylorisation.

During the 1980s these two movements converged, the import substitution sector changed to an export-led one, and the primitive Taylorisation sector of the Northern border became stronger, increased its mechanisation and was more and more allowed to work for the internal market. So a true peripheral Fordism is emerging in Mexico. This transformation is perceived by some Mexican researchers as a process of Japanisation, or is presented as such by the elites, in the sense that it combines flexibility and the mobilisation of the responsibility of shopfloor workers. In fact Japanese firms do not have, *at the same time*, an Ohnist organisation of production and a flexible regulation of the wage relation. Moreover the organisation of work, even at Ford Hermosillo has nothing in common with Ohnism. There is no question of negotiating the involvement of workers in the perfectioning of the productive process, but rather to incite them individually, by persuasion or by bonuses, to keep strictly to the prescriptions of the methods office, in the pure style of Frederick Taylor or Henry Ford I!

The Japanisation of Mexico is thus in fact nothing more than showy *Japanisation*. But it has succeeded in putting the country's industry in such a competitive position relative to the United States that, in 1992, the negotiations on the Free Trade Agreement, brought out to a fanfare of trumpets by the liberal administration of George Bush, is being questioned by the US side itself. Large sections of opinion are recognising that in the new rules of the game it is Mexico which will have an absolute advantage over the United States for the semi-skilled labour in most industries.

The less dogmatically liberal Clinton administration is reconsidering the whole issue, and without denying the United States interest in extending the NAFTA to Mexico, is demanding and obtaining in July 1993 the signature to two additional protocols against social and environmental dumping. This has not succeeded in disarming the opposition of the unions and the ecologists of the three countries.

A few words of conclusion

In North America as in Europe, competition between divergent models to escape from the crisis always results in a powerful pressure to align social conditions on those of the least favoured part of the working class. The strength of Scandinavian and German unions has however succeeded in imposing on northern continental Europe solutions based on negotiated mobilisation of human resources. These solutions have succeeded in winning on a global scale, in the sense of permitting the regions where they exist to consolidate their central positions in the framework of post-Fordism. They have even allowed them to coexist, on the basis of a socially constructed comparative advantage, with countries in the same continental bloc with much lower wages and much more flexible wage contacts.

However, the eruption on the doors of western Europe of an abundant, flexible and relatively skilled labour force increases the temptation of the employers in the core to play the card of moving to the zones of flexible labour. This scenario is already occurring – with even greater force since the whole of North America is essentially following the same Taylorist industrial paradigm – between the United States and Mexico.

It is an irony of history that NAFTA which was launched on a more liberal basis than the EC has been forced to adopt the rudiments of a 'social and ecological continental space' more constraining than that of Maastricht.

Notes

1. Original title *Les nouvelles relations centre-peripherie: Les exemples contrastes Europe-Amerique*. This paper was presented at the *Intervention au Colloque: A periferia europea ante o novo seculo*, Saint-Jacques de Compostel, 29 September – 2 October 1993.
2. The sub-section which follows is a résumé of Glyn *et al.* (1988), Lipietz (1985a, 1990 and 1992).
3. This is the well known position of Ajit Singh – see Glyn *et al.* (1988). The position of Lipietz (1985a) puts more emphasis on the success of the credit economy of the 1970s.
4. See Aoki (1987, 1988). A long time ago Andrew Friedman (1987) had already opposed 'responsible autonomy' and 'direct control' as being two tendencies which were in *permanent* conflict within the capitalist organisation of work. In Aoki's writings the opposition between 'semi-horizontal' and 'vertical' structures of coordination in work is related to more general considerations of industrial organisation. Significantly he starts by showing the superiority of the first over the

second in the case of just-in-time management (Kanban) of on-stream productive processes (car assembly lines). Next he admits the superiority of responsible autonomy in most kinds of productive processes.

Note the relative independence of labour relations, not only *vis-à-vis* technology, but also *vis-à-vis* other aspects of internal management of the firm and industrial organisation. This independence remains relative and the view taken here is that the new technologies *underline* the superiority of responsible autonomy (without however determining it as suggested by Piore and Sabel 1984). Further, responsible autonomy is perfectly consistent with sophisticated forms of industrial organisation such as just-in-time and 'networks of firms'. But this is going beyond the field of the current paper. See Leborgne and Lipietz (1987, 1988).

5. The final part of this section and the following one is the result of collective work organised at an international level by the World Institute for Development Economics Research (cited in the bibliography as the WIDER project), now published in Schor and You (forthcoming).

6. See Doeringer and Piore (1971). The term 'market' can be confusing, even the external labour market is not a true market, and the internal market is certainly not one at all.

7. As is shown, the negotiation of the involvement (and the involvement itself) can involve aspects external to the firm, such as skill formation and the participation of the unions in directing committees at the interprofessional level or at the industry level (as in the 'corporatist' states such as Austria and Sweden).

8. Or even at the international level! The problem of which geographic field is suitable to the social paradigms is one of the most difficult and least explored (see however Lipietz 1985b). This point will be considered again later.

9. This combination is still however possible, if it concerns different segments of the labour market within the same society. What is *in general* not possible is the negotiated involvement of a group of flexible workers. That is to say the Piore and Sabel model.

10. Take care! Toyotism is not Ohnism! It combines Ohnism as an industrial paradigm with a certain mode of labour relations.

11. See, however, Lipietz (1988).

12. The limits to the mobility of capital (and with it of technology) have practically become non-existent. As for the limits on the mobility of labour, they are largely the result of countries judging that they have an excess supply of labour.

13. In reality, it is *also* a division of labour between different modes of production or different forms of organisation of labour, because certain forms of production outperform absolutely the waged workforce in those industries. See Lipietz (1977).

14. It is also necessary that this Taylorisable and flexible labour is faced with an elite of employers and civil servants who are capable of setting in motion such a model, which is in general far from the case. On all these conditions, see Lipietz (1985a).

15. The following is based on a first approach in Leborgne and Lipietz (1990).

16. See CEPII (1989) and Lipietz (1985a). Freire de Souza (1983) has shown that this same contrast exists between Portugal (growth in volume) and Spain (growth in international value).

17. Here only the EC is considered. EFTA is more homogenous in its choice of negotiated involvement as the way to get out of the crisis, and above all it has retained its monetary sovereignty.
18. I would like to thank Lilia Orantes (University of Sonora) and Jorge Carillo (Colegio de la Frontera Norte) for the organisation of these visits.
19. Mahon (1992) shows nevertheless the possibilities for an 'upwards' adaptation in Canada. Lapointe (1992) gives the example of the aluminium industry. But Toyotism has been, for a long time now, the *general* line of evolution in the process industries, even at the Cement factory at Yaqui!

References

Amadeo, E. and J.M. Camargo (1990) Capital–labour relations in Brazil, *WIDER project*.

Aoki, M. (1987) Horizontal versus vertical structures of the firm, *American Economic Review*, December.

Aoki, M. (1988) A new paradigm of work organization and coordination: Lessons from Japanese experience, *UNU/WIDER Working Paper*, published in S. Marglin and J. Schor (eds) (1990).

Bowles, S. (1985) The production process in a competitive economy: Walrasian, Marxian, and Neohobbesian models, *American Economic Review*, Vol. 75, No. 1 (March), 16–36.

Coriat, B. (1992) *Penser a l'Envers*, Paris: Bourgeois.

Duval, G. (1993) Industrie allemande: un colosse aux pieds d'argile, *Alternatives Economiques*, No. 110, September 1993.

Doeringer, P.B. and M.J. Piore (1971) *International Labour Markets and Manpower Analysis*, New York: Sharpe (revised edition 1985).

Friedman, A. (1987) *Industry and Labour*, London: MacMillan.

Glyn, A., A. Hughes, A. Lipietz and A. Singh (1988) The rise and fall of the golden age, *UNU/WIDER Working Paper*, published in S. Marglin and J. Schor (eds) (1990).

Itoh, M. (1990) *Value and Crisis*, London: Pluto Press.

Jenson, J. (1989) 'Different' but not 'exceptional': Canada's permeable Fordism, *Canadian Review of Anthropology and Sociology*, No. 26 (1).

Köllö, J. (1990) Without a Golden Age – Eastern Europe WIDER project.

Kornai, J. (1979) Resource constrained versus demand-constrained systems, *Econometrica*, Vol. 47 (July).

Lapointe, P.A. (1992) Modele de travail et democratisation. Le cas des usines de l'Alcan au Saguenay 1970–1992, *Cahiers de Recherches Sociologiques*, UQAM, No. 18-19.

Leborgne, D. and A. Lipietz (1987) New technologies, new modes of regulation: Some spatial implications, International Seminar on Changing Labour Process and New Forms of Urbanization, Samos, September, in: *Space and Society*, Vol. 6, No. 3, 1988.

Leborgne, D. and A. Lipietz (1988) Deux strategies sociales dans la production des espaces territoriaux, translated in G. Benko and M. Dunford (eds), *Industrial Change and Regional Development*, London: Pinter Publishers 1991.

Leborgne, D. and A. Lipietz (1990) Pour eviter l'Europe a deux vitesses, *Labour and Society*, Vol. 15, No. 2.

Leborgne, D. and A. Lipietz (1992) Conceptual fallacies and open questions on post–Fordism, in M. Storper and A.J. Scott (eds), *Pathways to Industrialization and Regional Development*, London: Routledge.

Lipietz, A. (1977–1983) *Le Capital et son Espace*, Paris: Maspero – La Decouverte.

Lipietz, A. (1979) *Crise et Inflation: Pourquoi?*, Paris: F. Maspero.

Lipietz, A. (1983) *Le Monde Echanté. De la Valeur à l'Envol Inflationniste*, Paris: La Decouverte.

Lipietz, A. (1985a) *Mirages et Miracles. Problemes de l'industrialisation dans le Tiers–Monde*, Paris: La Decouverte. Translated as *Mirages and Miracles – Crises in Global Fordism*, London: Verso 1987.

Lipietz, A. (1985b) Le national et le regional: quelle autonomie face a la crise mondiale du capital?, *Couverture Orange CEPREMAP No. 8521*.

Lipietz, A. (1990) Les relations capital-travail a l'aube du XXIe siecle, *WIDER project*.

Lipietz, A. (1992) *Towards a New Economic Order, Postfordism, Ecology, and Democracy*, Oxford: Polity Press.

Mahon, R. (1987) From Fordism to ?, New technologies, labor market and unions, *Economic and Industrial Democracy*, Vol. 8, 5–60.

Mahon, R. (1992) Retour sur le post-fordisme: le Canada et l'Ontario, *Cahier de Recherche Sociologique* – UQAM, No. 18–19.

Mahon, R. (1993) Lontagare and/or medarbetare? Contested identities, Ontario: Carleton University, *mimeo*.

Marglin, S. and J. Schor (eds.) (1990) *The Golden Age of Capitalism: Reinterpreting the Postwar Experience*, Oxford: Clarendon Press.

Piore, M.J. and C.F. Sabel (1984) *The Second Industrial Divide: Possibilities for Prosperity*, New York: Basic Books.

Rao, J.M. (1990) Capital–labour relations in India: Continuity and change, *WIDER Project*

Schor, J. and J.I. You (eds) (forthcoming), *Capital, the State and Labour: A Global Perspective*, Aldershot: Edward Elgar.

WIDER project, to be published in J. Schor and J.I. You (eds).

Williamson, O.E. (1985) *The Economic Institutions of Capitalism: Firms, Markets, Relational Contracting*, New York: Macmillan.

You, J.I. (1990) Is Fordism coming to Korea?, *WIDER project*.

Comment: The Many Faces of Post-Fordism

Annemieke Roobeek

Why are political economists seeking alternative models of development to replace the Fordism that has dominated the post-war period? What is the advantage of such comprehensive concepts as Fordism and post-Fordism? What do these concepts add to the analysis of changing international relations at the macro level and changing labour relations at the micro level? Is to describe dominant regulation models for countries or for regional blocs still a valid exercise?

Alain Lipietz's interesting chapter on 'The New Core-Periphery Relations – The Contrasting Examples of Europe and America' gives the reader plenty of food for thought. On the one hand Lipietz provides an elegant analysis of the crisis of Fordism and how the dominant countries have tried to find escape routes. On the other hand questions can be raised on the simplicity of the analysis and the conclusions, particularly the way in which emerging regulation models have been generalised for entire regional blocs, such as Europe and the Americas.

Although Lipietz will probably be the first to admit that categorisation of regulation models will always lead to oversimplified generalisations and leave little room for exceptions to the rule, the value of the generalisations become doubtful when the list of exceptions gets longer. It is the classical dilemma between theory and reality every researcher in the field of regulation theory is struggling with. The only excuse for rather over-simplified descriptions is that for the sake of a clear discussion of para-digmatic change one has to polarise – or even to caricaturise – to get the emerging alternatives to the Fordist mode of regulation into perspective.

Can we speak of a paradigm change in capitalism?
For the last twenty years political economists have been analysing the

151

reasons for the economic downturn since the beginning of the 1970s. But, as stated by Lipietz, no one thinks any longer of the enduring depression as being 'the final crisis of capitalism'. On the contrary, during the 1980s and into the 1990s, governments, companies and institutions have tried to develop alternatives to the Fordist mode of regulation and production. The limits to Fordism became obvious in various ways.[1] In contrast to the mass production–mass consumption concept of Fordism, other features appeared: flexibility, deregulation, liberalisation, privatisation, and social segmentation. As a result, we have witnessed drastic changes in the existing labour relations, in terms of social relations under the Welfare State, as well as in interindustrial relations. In fact the entire socio-institutional fabric of Fordism has been put under severe pressure to adapt to a quickly emerging new techno-economic paradigm. It is characteristic of the new technologies that they all contribute to energy-, material- and employment-saving innovations as a result of the miniaturisation and dematerialisation tendency. The Fordist slogan 'big is better' has been more and more replaced by the idea of 'doing more with less'. The higher degree of technological and managerial control enables producers to produce goods of a higher quality in a more compact (smaller plants, fewer suppliers), flexible, and even virtual way (in time and place due to better logistics) with less labour input. In the transformation process the new core technologies, particularly around information technology, biotechnology and new materials, can be seen as major catalysts that have sped up the conceptualisation of a post-Fordist alternative.

As I have argued elsewhere, while the new technologies can to some degree supply solutions to the techno-economic bottlenecks in the Fordist accumulation regime, at the same time they strike at the institutional roots of Fordism.[2]

The real paradigm change will occur only if a new match can be established between the new techno-economic developments and the socio-institutional fabric. During the 1980s and 1990s the dominant trend has been to combine market-driven supply-side policies with corporate strategies that stimulated technological change and economic growth. As a consequence of the introduction of new technologies, management styles have changed as well, because of the rising importance of information as a resource in contrast to physical labour.

Although with some delay, in almost all western countries we have also witnessed political attacks on the welfare-state institutions and established labour relations, often accompanied by budget cuts for education and health care. The principle of collectivism and solidarity, particularly significant for Fordism in Europe, has been more and more replaced by the principle of less state responsibility and more individualisation and privatisation. However, there are still significant differences among European countries.

Reviewing the changes in the past fifteen years, the conclusion may be that a paradigm change in capitalist development has been going on. Capitalist structures change, but the principles of capitalism remain in tact.

One of the advantages of the regulation theory is that these macro phenomena can be understood and can be put in a broader, more coherent theoretical setting. This does justice to the interrelated political, economic and socio-institutional aspects of the paradigm change in capitalist development at macro-, meso- and micro-levels. Therefore the overall concept of Fordism and post-Fordism can be seen as a theoretical construct that helps to analyse the complexity of the driving forces for change and stability of the system.

Are capital–labour relations the only determinants of post-Fordism?
In his article Lipietz states that '... we can conclude that the future of Fordism and the ways out of its crisis will once again determine the future of capital–labour relations throughout the world'. General principles of Fordism were the taylorised organisation of labour, mass production and mass consumption, long-term contractual wage relations and a guaranteed income for wage earners and social pay through the Welfare State for those who were (temporarily) unable to participate in the labour market. In short, during the rise of Fordism the focus was entirely on capital–labour relations. Around this focus a web of social and welfare institutions had come up in the decades after World War II. Characteristic of both, capital–labour relations and the institutional setting of Fordism, is the guiding principle of standardisation and uniformity for a relatively homogeneous workforce.

In many respects the social compromise under Fordism was quite simple to control and to manage. However, the socio-institutional framework of Fordism developed its own dynamics. Particularly during the late 1960s and 1970s the influence of the institutions at the macro-level on the accumulation regime (education, health care, contractual wage partners) increased considerably in relation to the capital–labour relations at the shopfloor level. The society became more complex to manage and the amount of institutions that wanted to have a say became greater and more diversified. Therefore one can put some question marks behind Lipietz's cited statement, which gives the reader the idea that the capital–labour relations are still the nucleus of the post-Fordist concept. To find out what the driving forces behind the alternatives for Fordism are we have to look not only at changes in labour organisation, technology and management, but we have to understand the role Fordist institutions are playing in defining the scope of alternative control mechanisms (direct control versus self-regulated autonomy; centralisation versus decentralisation of control), which have far-reaching consequences for capital–labour relations. This is an extremely complex matter. Moreover, because Fordism has been a concept that was filled in at the national level, the institutional set-up is very different in different countries. So, not only the heterogeneity of economies is a reality in post-Fordism, but even more the heterogeneity of institutions. This will leave room for considerable differences among countries in their attempt to find alternatives to Fordism.

Two basic doctrines for post-Fordism?
At a high abstraction level Lipietz distinguishes two extreme doctrines for advanced capitalist countries in the transformation from Fordism to post-Fordism. At the one extreme he puts 'liberal flexibility' combined with a neo-Taylorist labour organisation, which has been opted for by the US, Great Britain and to some degree also by France, and at the other extreme he puts 'negotiated involvement' combined with a 'Kalmarist' or social-democratic type of labour organisation characterised by 'responsible autonomy', which is a direction that is followed by Germany and Sweden (Scandinavia). Japan has been stamped as following a direction that is called 'Toyotism'. 'Toyotism' occupies a position in the middle of the axis, between organisational rigidity and flexibility and between direct control of Taylorism and negotiated involvement.

Having said earlier that the typology of post-Fordism is often a caricature of the actual, far more complex and diversified situation in a country, Lipietz tries to overcome the problem of simplification. He stresses the possibility that both extreme doctrines (liberal flexibility and negotiated involvement) are policies that can be combined *à la carte*. The variation of elements of the extreme doctrines is the basis for his conception of post-Fordism. At first sight this solution seems to do justice to the considerable variation of new arrangements at the firm, industry and state level. At a macro level it also helps to understand the differences between the continental blocs (Europe, America, Asia). But what it does not explain is why there is '... coexistence of countries with different wage regimes within an integrated continental bloc' as Lipietz tries to prove. However, in his argumentation he sticks too much to economic facts instead of explaining the specific contents of institutional arrangements in the different blocs that provide the necessary elements of cohesion.

What is the value added of post-Fordism à la carte at the global level?
This problem of defining the development of Fordism to post-Fordism becomes even more difficult when Lipietz tries to fill in the menus for Eastern European countries, the Newly Industrialised Countries, China and India. Here the superficial generalisations and extreme simplifications are detrimental to the very wide differences between the development trajectories of these countries. How can the concept of Fordism and post-Fordism help us to understand very different political, economic and socio-institutional developments in major parts of the world? Perhaps we should confine the conceptualisation of Fordism and post-Fordism mainly to the developed world with some room for countries like Korea.

Lipietz is right, however, when he stresses the necessity to take into account the new division of labour, which is at the global level. It is an important characteristic of post-Fordism *à la carte* in advanced countries with consequences for the development of other parts of the world, but post-Fordism is not the driving force for this new division of labour. It is rather the combination of the two aspects, the internal limits to Fordism and the internationalisation of the economy that shapes the contours of post-Fordism in the developed countries.

To conclude, post-Fordism has many faces. This makes it more and more difficult to speak of a dominant model of development or a dominant social accumulation regime. If we recognise that variety is the most characteristic element, we catch sight of the limitations of this theoretical construct.

Notes
1. Annemieke Roobeek (1987) The crisis in Fordism and the rise of a new technological paradigm, *Futures*, Vol. 19, No. 2 (April), 129–154.
2. *ibid.*, 142.

PART THREE

Post-Communist Economies in Transition

5. The Role of the State in Post-Communist Economies

Domenico Mario Nuti[1]

'Uno stato che non c'è costa a tutti molto,
molto più di uno stato che ci fosse.'[2]

The near-demise of the state in the transition

The traditional Soviet-type system, which until the end of the 1980s dominated central eastern Europe in spite of recurring attempts at reform, was totalitarian in the literal sense of the state encompassing every aspect of economic, social and political life – through dominant if not exclusive state ownership and enterprise, central planning by direct commands, the dominant indeed monopolistic role of the communist party and its interpenetration with the state apparatus. Thus it was necessary for the transition to a market economy with private ownership and political pluralism, which started in 1989–90, to involve 'the return of the state to its basic responsibilities, by relinquishing interventionism and regulations of all sorts' (IMF Managing Director Michel Camdessus, IMF Survey, 11 October 1993).

Such transition, however, was attempted at breathtaking speed, in the plausible though – as it turned out – mistaken belief that the economic and political circumstances which at last made it possible might be short-lived. There was no blueprint for changes which were qualitatively and quantitatively unprecedented, and simultaneously attempted at a time of world recession: the new leaders chose to err on the side of excess rather than caution. As a result, the transition presents us with a disconcerting paradox: the 'withering away of the state', which the Marxist–Leninist tradition had associated with the realisation of full communism in an indefinite future, now has become the deliberate or to some extent *de facto* concomitant of these countries' transition to capitalism. Not only is the state being speedily stripped of its assets, dilapidated through mass privatisation programmes designed to implement instant capitalism and to rally popular support for the project, but the aim or the facts of the transition have been the reduction of state and government roles in the management of the economy to a bare minimum, far lower than the maximum common denominator of modern capitalist countries.

These trends are reflected in a number of facile public pronouncements by government Ministers: 'All you have to do to establish currency convertibility is to announce it' (Czech Premier Vaclav Klaus in January 1991, when he was Minister of the CSFR economy); 'The best industrial policy is no industrial policy' (the former Polish Minister for Industry Tadeusz Syryjczyk); 'The purpose of privatisation is privatisation' (the Czech Minister of the Economy Vladimir Dlouhy in 1992). On the rebound from the excesses of socialist central planning the new rulers have steered the old system away from the 'convergence' to an intermediate regime originally postulated by Jan Tinbergen and others towards its 'submergence' by capitalism and then to 'overshooting' beyond it into the reaches of the proto-capitalism of the Industrial Revolution and Dickensian memory.

Unregulated private activities have activated some supply response, though to a much lesser extent to date than originally expected and primarily thanks to real wage falls so large that arguably would have eventually led to recovery and growth in any economic system – whether feudal or capitalist or centrally planned – but which could only be politically accepted during this kind of transition. The growth of private activities has been accompanied also by widespread disregard for the protection of labour legislation (safety at work, employment terms, unionisation); mass unemployment, poverty and destitution have also arisen and grown fast. Consumers are often at the mercy of monopolist producers and traders, whose idea of a market is that of spot pricing in single, non-recurring, predatory transactions in monopolistic conditions. Entrepreneurship is confused with rent-seeking. In the budding financial markets anybody can sell well printed paper for cash. Savers are subjected to fraudulent schemes long eradicated in market economies, such as 'pyramid' saving schemes offering impossible interest rates, which can only be sustainable as long as there is continuous and sufficiently fast growth of deposits.[3]

Education and health services have been cut down to the point of collapse; in the ex-USSR near extinct diseases have reappeared (including bubonic plague) and epidemics have broken out (diphtheria, whooping cough, new virulent strands of cholera and tuberculosis); morbidity and mortality rates are on the increase.[4] Long suppressed churches have reasserted their presence and undermined the state through intolerant bigotry and theocratic challenges (notably in Poland, though an early backlash occurred already with the September 1993 elections). The condition of women has deteriorated with higher unemployment incidence, social services cuts and, for instance in Poland and East Germany, with the denial of abortion. Civil disobedience and paramilitary structures have appeared; law and order have broken down or deteriorated; crime has been soaring; corruption is rife, as fragments of state powers as well as some state assets are 'privatised' by officials to their own advantage. A new mafia has arisen, quickly linked to foreign mafias thanks to the opening of European borders; Russian organised crime groups have acquired enough financial power to cause serious problems in Western Europe and the United States. There are widespread instances of acute nationalistic and ethnic strife, right down to brutal civil wars and so-called 'ethnic cleansing', i.e. genocide.

Of course the intensity of this process greatly differs in different countries: it is least strong in the so-called Visegrad countries (Poland, Hungary, the Czech and Slovak republics), Slovenia and the Baltic republics; it is slightly deeper in Bulgaria and Romania; strong in Russia, other CIS republics and Albania; very strong in the rest of ex-Yugoslavia and in some CIS areas. There has been a tendency for pre-communist traditions to reassert themselves and influence the transition: what was heralded as 'the end of history' turned out to be a return to history instead, with a vengeance. But the general drift has been well incapsulated by Jacques Nagels in the title of his recent book: *Du socialisme perverti au capitalisme sauvage* (Brussels, 1991).

Underlying reasons for de-statisation

To a very great extent this process has been the necessary consequence of the earlier interpenetration of the state and the communist party. In the Soviet-type system there was at all levels a nationwide, capillary dual structure of state and party organs, with the party firmly in control of policy decisions and moreover with state appointments – right down to the appointment of state enterprise managers – reserved to party nomenklatura. The collapse of communist parties everywhere, right down to their widespread outlawing and confiscation of assets, has involved therefore the weakening or collapse of the state and all central powers.

Even fundamental state prerogatives, such as tax collection and public expenditure or monetary issues, or military structures including nuclear weapons, have been sometimes taken over by local powers, leading to regional disintegration as well as the disintegration of larger groupings: from CMEA (June 1991) to the Soviet Union (December 1991) and now the Russian Federation itself and some of its very components, from the Yugoslav Federation (1991) to the CSFR split into the Czech and Slovak republics (1993). Such economic, monetary and political disintegration imparted severe recessionary shocks on the whole area, through the unnecessary collapse of former intra-regional trade flows; some of these developments have worrying direct implications for international security. In the former Soviet Union the disintegration of civilian aviation, with the splintering of Aeroflot into republican carriers and also some 300 regional and town-based mini-carriers, has lowered discipline and safety standards causing a number of major accidents.

Another reason for de-statisation is the time-consuming nature of institution-building, further delayed by political controversies. The central planning system was demolished but was not – and could not be – completely replaced immediately. Moreover, new institutions – including those of political democracy – take some time to establish themselves before they can function normally.[5] It was not understood that 'the state must organise its own retreat'.[6] Thus a 'systemic vacuum' was created, which was rapidly filled by *ad hoc* makeshift solutions and spontaneous developments which had nothing in common with the new target model.

Instances of such a process abound. Under central planning state enterprises were forbidden to grant credit to each other, while in a market economy they can only do so subject to their own financial constraints; in the transition they were no longer subject to such prohibition but were not yet subject to the discipline of liquidation and bankruptcy procedures, therefore they responded to the monetary squeeze by accumulating payments arrears of the order of one fifth or a quarter of GDP and destabilising the financial system. The state itself, the ultimate depository of financial credibility in any normal economy, sometimes fails to meet its contractual obligations: over-zealous Finance Minister Boris Fyodorov – hailed as a champion of the Russian transition – mistook the withholding of payments for the control of expenditure, and contributed to his own downfall by withholding the payment of wages. Enterprise managers, formerly subject to the central control of their 'founding organs' (mostly branch Ministries) and, in spite of privatisation, not yet subject to stock market discipline, can behave inefficiently or fraudulently without restraints. Trade flows, neither planned nor free, are redirected disrupting traditional supply lines and generating imbalances which can only be curbed by recessionary measures.

Often this process has been aggravated by a constitutional crisis due to demarcation disputes between state bodies whose respective powers were left overlapping or undefined in the course of transition, or were being redefined in haste through a disorderly struggle for power by any means rather than through constitutional processes. Thus the newly elected Russian President Boris Yeltsin had to contend with an old Parliament (elected or rather co-opted in 1990) no longer representing the electorate. A constitutional text made contradictory by over 340 hurried amendments made the President 'the highest official in the land' and Parliament 'the highest body in the land', empowered to dismiss government Ministers and inclined to use and abuse that power. The Russian Central Bank, which ironically in the 1988 banking reform had been made independent from the government in order to enable it to implement unpopular but necessary monetary policies of stabilisation, strong in its support by Parliament to which it was answerable, successfully countermanded and sabotaged the stabilisation and reform policies launched in January 1992 by the Russian government and presidency. The approval of a new Constitution was made a complex and long-drawn out process, dependent on the approval of all the Russian Federation's 88 components (89 at the last count, now including Chechnia), which were able to extract independence concessions in exchange for their support. In turn, both President Yeltsin's dissolution of Parliament in mid-September 1993, and parliamentary attempts at impeaching him and replacing him with a new President, were clearly unconstitutional, as were the subsequent revolt and its suppression.[7] Yeltsin's September 1993 coup was initially labelled 'democratic' (*International Herald Tribune*, 23 September 1993) but was still a coup, in spite of Gregory Yavlinsky's subtle distinction between 'legality' and 'legitimacy'.[8] It can still be considered a 'democratic coup' in spite of the October repression, in view of the relatively free elections of December 1993; but these have not resolved the Russian constitutional crisis, given the unexpected success of nationalist/populist political groupings. Elsewhere in the CIS constitutional and political disputes have been settled by coups and counter-coups.

In Poland, the fragility of the new democracy is highlighted by the frequency of general elections: three (plus a Presidential election) in four years (1989–93). State powers were weakened by the proliferation of parties in the 1991 elections, with 29 parties represented in Parliament and jostling for power, forming and reforming coalitions and opposing government policies to the point of causing the government crisis of May 1993 and the dissolution of Parliament. On that occasion President Walesa backed the government to the hilt but he has also occasionally taken constitutionally dubious initiatives interfering with government policies and of populist character (such as his often reiterated 1990 electoral promise to enrich every Pole by $10,000, standing at $15,000 in 1993, greatly at odds with government privatisation policies). Populist policies – often impossible to implement and therefore very disruptive – have been undertaken elsewhere. Under a new electoral law the September 1993 Polish elections drastically reduced the number of parties to six, at the heavy cost of disenfranchising large part of the electorate; the victory of left-wing parties, enhanced by a low poll that transformed their relative into absolute majority, prompted President Walesa to make the outrageous threat of a dissolution of Parliament *à la* Yeltsin if the new government were to reverse the transition. In Poland state powers were also weakened by a tradition of labour militancy, which had been strong enough to overthrow the old regime and maintained pressure on the government and state organs after the transition, as well as by an old national parliamentary tradition in which a single member had the power of veto ('Nie pozwalam ...').

The lack of alternatives

The questions arise of whether the transition could have had an alternative target of 'market socialism', restoring markets and political pluralism but retaining a substantial if not dominant state sector, as in China; and whether the transition to capitalism might have been more gradual and orderly avoiding at least some of the economic and social costs that have been incurred in terms of GDP, employment and inflation (see Table 5.1).[9]

In principle, it might have been possible to make state enterprises independent, operating freely at market-clearing prices rather than through central allocations of supplies and output at administrative prices lower than market-clearing, with managers subject to the rewards and penalties of markets, answerable to independent state-holding companies rather than subject to the direct commands of sectoral Ministries. In practice, an inordinately long time was wasted while the system was inconclusively directed and re-directed in this direction without ever getting there. The obtuse pursuit of price stability in the face of mounting internal and external imbalances prevented the creation of a proper market environment; avoidable shortages led to economic disruption and a goods famine – sometimes to the point of food famines. When the economic crisis deteriorated and power shifted, the market socialism option could not have been credibly resurrected. Whether or not market socialism was ever feasible, by 1989–90 the only option left was the restoration of capitalism.

Could the transition have been more orderly and less costly? Some of the costs were unavoidable: independently of the economic system selected some inappropriate capacity (heavy industry, armaments, metallurgy, chemicals, textiles, *etc.*.) would have had to be scrapped; repressed inflation and hidden unemployment had to surface in any market system. Some change would have been less costly if it had been more gradual, like the unrestricted opening of foreign trade and the introduction of convertibility; 'premature trade liberalisation' is now a widely recognized cause of the recession even in IMF circles (German instant transition is an unrepeatable exception, and even that was very costly). The dogmatic application of restrictive monetary policies, especially the credit squeeze shock that accompanied nominal monetary anchors in conditions of higher than anticipated inflation (like the astounding, unintended 50 per cent cut in real money supply perpetrated in the first quarter of 1990 in Poland) also inflicted unnecessary costs on transitional economies.

Other errors are now being recognized. In the unavoidable delays of privatisation, the state sector has been neglected, indiscriminately denied access to credit and to the reinvestment of its own profits – taxed away and subjected to punitive fiscal measures not applied to the private sector. State assets have been dissipated in mass privatisation schemes that did not provide any of the capital necessary to restructuring and did little to activate markets and establish corporate governance by new owners (Mongolia has privatised 80 per cent of state assets, without any tangible change in resource allocation). Trade liberalisation disrupted trade flows among long-standing partners, locked into a pattern of international division of labour inferior to what might have been obtained if past investments had been guided by markets but still mutually advantageous given the non-recoverability of sunk costs. Thus, while neither an alternative target model nor an alternative gradual path were available options, the mode of transition might have been improved upon with less

Table 5.1   Annual GDP growth rates, inflation rates and unemployment in Eastern Europe and the former Soviet Union, 1990–93

	Growth of GDP (% p.a.)			
	1990	1991	1992	1993
1. Albania	−10	−30	−8	3.5
2. Armenia	−12	−50	−10	
3. Azerbaijan	−2	−30	−10	
4. Belarus NMP	−3	−3	−11	−3
5. Bulgaria	−9	−12	−8	−5
6. Croatia GSP	−9	−29	−16	
7. Czech Republic	0	−14	−7	0
8. Estonia	−4	−13	−26	−10
9. Georgia	−25	−30	−10	
10. Hungary	−4	−12	−5	−2
11. Kazakhstan NMP	−2	−8	−13	−15
12. Kyrgyzstan	3	−5	−25	−16
13. Latvia	3	−8	−44	−19
14. Lithuania	−5	−13	−35	−10
15. ex-Yugoslavia				
Macedonia GSP	−11	−11	−15	−9
16. Moldova NMP	−2	−12	−21	−15
17. Poland	−12	−7	1	4
18. Romania	−7	−14	−15	−9
19. Russia	−4	−11	−19	−15
20. Slovakia	0	−16	−6	−8
21. Slovenia	−5	−9	−6	−1
22. Tajikistan	−9	−31	−18	
23. Turkmenistan	−7	−12	−9	
24. Ukraine	−14	−14	−10	
25. Uzbekistan	−1	−14	−10	
26. Eastern Europe				
(excl. ex-USSR)	−11	−4	−2	
27. Former Soviet Union	−11	−19	−13	

Source: EBRD, 1993 estimates.

Table 5.1
(continued)

	Inflation (% p.a.)				Unemployment (%)			
	1990	1991	1992	1993	1990	1991	1992	1993
1.	0	104	266	45	2	5	10	
2.	100	1350						
3.	138	1350						
4.	5	80	1076					1
5.	26	334	83	100	1.5	10	15	16
6.	610	123	664	788		15	18	18
7.	11	57	11	20	1	4	3	6
8.	23	212	1050	200			1	3
9.	81	1800						
10.	29	35	23	23	2.5	8	12	13
11.	4	91	1380	1800				
12.	3	85	855	600				
13.	11	172	952	250			2	5
14.	8	225	1021	690			1	2
15.	608	115	1691	580		18	20	
16.	4	98	1160	1000				
17.	586	70	43	39	6	12	14	16
18.	7	161	210	200		2	8	9
19.	6	93	1354	1000	0	0	1	2
20.	11	61	10	25	2	12	10	12
21.	552	115	207	45	5	8	11	14
22.	103	1450	1450					
23.	90	980	60					
24.	91	1450	1116					
25.	82	700						
26.	85	60						
27.	101	1408						

dogmatism and haste, entrusting state and government with a much greater role than they were given in the transition.

It should be recognized that the excessively *laissez faire* or rather 'free-for-all' regime *de facto* prevailing to varying degrees in the transitional economies has also had many beneficial effects, in solving many of the problems that the old ruling elite had created and had been either unwilling or unable to solve: unwilling for fear of relinquishing power until precipitously forced to do so, unable because lacking the political legitimacy necessary to implement unavoidable unpopular policies of austerity, price rises, unemployment. Nevertheless, the mode of the transition has contributed to the large scale costs incurred to date.

Mitigating factors and prospective reversals

In spite of these general trends, a number of mitigating factors have set important constraints to the demise of the state and to government policies and are now set to reverse these trends, namely: 1. a continued, if perhaps involuntary, *de facto* and large scale state presence; 2. international institutions whose much needed assistance has been made strictly conditional on the adoption of conventional policies assigning an important role to state and government; 3. the gradual filling of systemic vacuum and the consolidation of new institutions; and 4. pursuit of association with and eventual membership of the European Community.

1. Willy nilly the state has continued to exercise a large scale, dominant role; a transformation of its presence and role can be anticipated, rather than its demise. The state sector is still dominant in total production and employment (in Poland only outside agriculture). In the unavoidable technical and political delays of privatisation, transitional economies go through a necessary stage of forced market socialism, during which the state sector cannot just disappear but must be commercialised rapidly, reorganised, undergo financial restructuring and as much capacity restructuring as feasible, and be treated equally with the private sector in its fiscal burden and access to credit. State sector neglect and penalisation has been a major factor in the deep and protracted recession that has accompanied the transition and now the sector is becoming the object of increasing care and attention. A large, though minority presence of state enterprises is still the ultimate target of some of the countries (Hungary, Slovakia). Widespread disillusion about the achievements of the transition has improved the electoral fortunes of left

wing parties, including social democratic incarnations of the ex-communist parties and their allies – most spectacularly in Poland in September 1993; without drastically reversing recent policy trends, these political developments are bound to restore some of the ground taken away from government and state. The constitutional problems that marred the transition are being addressed and gradually resolved. Industrial policies are being formulated (whether *de facto*, or explicitly as recently in Hungary). With the privatisation of state enterprises their former responsibility for their employees' welfare has been transferred back to the state. The welfare traditions of these countries and deeply rooted expectations of state social support have led to a meteoric explosion of government expenditure on social security payments. In Poland expenditure on social security rose from 8.7 per cent of the budget in 1989 to 12.8 per cent in 1990 and to 36.6 per cent in 1991: the problem now is not how to restore but how to curb the welfare state.

2. To a considerable extent vanishing central government powers have been restored or replaced by external bodies, with the constraints and requests dictated by Bretton Woods institutions and other international bodies, which have made their assistance conditional on reforms steering these countries from *capitalisme sauvage* to more modern versions of capitalism, and on the adoption of detailed government policies other than those which would have been adopted otherwise, or would have not been adopted at all. Tax administration and collection are being strengthened, fiscal and monetary discipline enforced, competition enhanced, factor markets developed. The role of international institutions has been crucial in containing anarchy and chaos in Russia – though they are powerless in controlling some of the spontaneous internal developments, from illegal capital flight (estimated at between $5 bn and $15 bn in 1992, and between $1 bn and $2 bn per month at the end of 1993) to constitutional wrangles such as those that precipitated the September 1993 crisis or followed the December 1994 elections. International intervention in curbing civil wars has been ineffective to date, but the bounds of international tolerance have been overstepped and it can be reasonably hoped that such intervention may soon begin to have some effects.

3. The systemic vacuum of the earlier days of transition is gradually being filled. A mass of legislation is being passed to introduce standard capitalist institutions and replace ad hoc and spontaneous developments.

Competition from new initiatives and from increasing foreign trade erodes the monopoly power of large enterprises and their managers, restrained also by the operation of new anti-monopoly agencies. With the sheer passing of time, the new institutions establish traditions and habits, stabilise expectations and begin to operate. Outside the CIS, the transitional economies gradually begin to look increasingly like ordinary, though still somewhat undeveloped, capitalist systems.

4. If nothing else, the process of international integration of these economies, and the aspiration to join the European Community entertained by some of them, is going to enhance further rather than limit the role of the state. The *acquis communautaire* whose implementation is a condition of eventual Community membership involves the harmonisation of legislation and the 'convergence' not only of crucial economic indicators but also of institutions and policies, which will necessarily restore in central and eastern Europe the same basic role that the state and government policies have in the rest of Europe.[10] This implication is well understood: in August 1992 the then CSFR Premier Vaclav Klaus publicly aired his misgivings about the etatist nature of the European Community, in an interview reminiscent of Thatcher; he declared that his government was a conservative one and would not like a return to state interventions through the EC. The Czech republic, however, cannot afford not to seek EC membership, indeed since the CSFR split Klaus has been pressing for early accession; the new members cannot seriously expect to reduce the role of the state in Europe before or even after accession (in spite of British hopes that they might be able to do so). Moreover, Klaus has not really practised what he preaches: 1992 subsidies to state enterprises, down to 1.5 per cent of GDP in Poland, were still five per cent of GDP in Czechoslovakia; the labour market has often been heavily controlled through punitive taxation of wages in excess of statutory guidelines; in January 1994 Klaus rejected the Czech Central Bank recommendation to introduce full convertibility, favouring a more gradual approach.

The adaptation of central and eastern European countries to European institutions and policies has already begun with the so-called 'Europe' or Association Agreements of 1991 (Hungary, Poland and the Czech and Slovak Republics) and 1992 (Bulgaria and Romania), especially in view of the Community decision, at the Edinburgh summit of June 1993, that the Association Agreements countries would be prepared for eventual membership. To a smaller extent, some influence in the same direction is being exercised also by the 'Partnership and Co-operation Agreements' signed or under negotiation with a number of new independent states of the CIS (Russia, Belorus, Ukraine, Kazakhstan, Kyrgyzstan) and Georgia, and by the new Trade and Cooperation agreements with the Baltic States.

Full employment and the post-transition role of the state

With the rapprochement of institutions and policies to European standards, central and eastern European countries are also coming up against the standard failure of government policies aimed at reaching and sustaining full employment through markets, whether through greater competition and flexibility in the labour market or through higher government expenditure in goods markets (direct in public investment and consumption, indirect through transfer payments to enterprises and the population).

In the closed economy, and therefore in the world economy which is closed by definition, lower wages obtained through labour market flexibility and competition do not necessarily lead to higher employment, as:

1. They usually signal lower consumption demand out of wages, which may or may not be over-compensated by higher investment.
2. In order to induce investment, low wages must be believed to last throughout the life of investment (which is one of the reasons why monthly wages of $10 a month in Russia in early 1992 did not induce foreign investment – quite rightly, as by late 1993 they have reached $50). Experience shows that with higher employment real wages are bound to rise, and therefore investment requires a commitment to maintain low real wages over time which no market can validate but which can be obtained through a social pact, through neo-corporatist institutions, sanctioned by the state and fiscal policy.

In the open national economy, low real wages (whether achieved directly or through the manipulation of the exchange rate) may promote employment through higher net exports – if demand for and supply elasticities of imports and exports are sufficiently high (as they are in Poland but not yet in Russia). But the ensuing export of unemployment may well be – and is being forcibly today – resisted by potential trade partners: international negotiations of greater trade access are necessary before labour market flexibility and competition can promote employment.

Keynesian reflationary fiscal policies – outside a Keynesian world of infinitely elastic demand for money with respect to the interest rate, implausible today even in advanced capitalist countries, let alone transitional economies – allow higher employment at the cost of higher inflation in the short run, whether through monetary financing of deficits or through devaluations necessary to pay for the associated additional imports. Inflation crowds out private expenditure financed out of non-indexed monetary assets; crowding out also results from deficits financed out of government borrowing, and from higher interest rates necessary to avoid devaluations. The only way to pursue high and stable employment through Keynesian policies is through internationally concerted reflation; this is now well understood, as exemplified by the European Community's 'Growth Initiative' and by the IMF Board of Governors' call for a 'commitment to cooperative growth strategy' (26 September 1993, Washington).

Thus the pursuit of full or fuller employment – for both the transitional and the well established capitalist countries – demands an enhanced role for the state, not simply the enhancement of markets: internally, through the negotiation and validation of formal or informal 'social pacts'; externally, through the negotiation of improved reciprocal trade access (and the necessary temporary safeguards instead of unrestricted immediate free trade) and of internationally concerted reflation. Moreover, most transitional economies need to restructure and reduce the burden of their external debt, which cannot be left entirely to markets – not least because most of that debt is owed to public lenders.

Economic growth and the post-transition role of the state

Analogous considerations can be put forward for the role of the state in economic growth promotion in transitional economies. The investment effort required by capacity restructuring and the resumption of growth has the same scale as that of a newly industrialising country, or of post-War reconstruction. The problem is to find sources of 'primitive accumulation': paradoxically these economies, formerly plagued by endemic monetary overhangs which hastened their economic collapse, after price liberalisation suffer from a severe shortage of domestic financial capital. Hence, their reliance on foreign direct investment.

Foreign direct investment in five countries of eastern Europe totalled $2.3 bn in 1991 and about $1.3 bn in the first half of 1992; most of it went to Hungary (48 per cent) and CSFR (33 per cent), and the flow remains very small with respect to foreign direct investment in developing countries, estimated at some $28 bn in 1991 (UN-ECE, 1992). In Hungary now the growth of foreign investment has levelled out; in 1992 there has been a mini-boom of foreign investment in Poland, quadrupled with respect to 1991 but still well below Hungarian flows and Polish requirements for investment finance and balance of payments equilibrium. Other transitional economies have been much less successful. The acceleration of foreign investment flows is deterred by the lengthy nature of institutional transformation, and by the continued recession: for both reasons foreign investment flows are likely to accelerate the recovery of those transitional economies after they have been successful in institutional transformation and resumption of growth, but are most unlikely to be able to jump-start these economies before then. As a result of the shortage of domestic savings and the inadequacy of foreign investment all transitional economies have recorded large-scale de-capitalisation, which jeopardises the acceleration and sustainability of growth even in those countries where the first 'green shoots' of recovery have appeared (Poland 1992, Hungary and Romania 1993, the Czech Republic probably in 1994).

The only potential immediate source of the 'primitive accumulation' required to restructure and grow is the sale of state assets through privatisation. In Germany the net privatisation proceeds obtained by Treuhandanstalt by the end of its operation scheduled in 1994 will have been negative, but this is due to the sudden and unsustainable growth of Eastern real wages towards Western levels, unavoidable once labour mobility was established in a united Germany, not to the worthlessness of the underlying capital. Everywhere else the state, even if one quarter or one third of its enterprises were obsolete or bankrupt, still has a significant net worth, which could be realised through sales to foreign buyers and to the population. Privatisation revenues could be gradually released over a number of years and channelled into investment.

Concern about the slow pace of privatisation by standard means, and fears that the continued dominance of a state sector might encourage a reversal to a version of the old system, has led to the rapid dissipation of state assets through free or subsidised transfers to employees and to the population at large (with the exception of Germany, and to some extent Hungary where mass privatisation has been confined primarily to credit concessions). An additional reason has been the small size of savings flows relative to the stock of state assets to be privatised. But there was never a real risk of reversals, and governments could have sold state assets on credit, or used financial instruments of privatisation in lieu of wage increases. This was done in Poland for the first round of mass privatisation to take place next year: an amendment to the April 1993 law on mass privatisation, negotiated by the ex-communist party in exchange for its essential support, reserved that stage of mass privatisation to pensioners and civil servants to compensate them for the loss of indexation provisions.

Popular enrichment through mass privatisation schemes is of course illusory as there is no such a thing as a free asset: taxation (including the inflation tax) will have to be higher, and/or government expenditure lower by precisely the value of the hand-out – except that it is more difficult to claw back the gift than it would have been to use it directly to fund investment.

The state role of making room for investment finance should not cause undue concern: after all, empirical analysis does not support the neo-liberal contention that there is an inverse relation between 'Government size and economic growth'.[11] Such role of the state automatically involves choices about how best to fund investment; ultimately austerity is required, but there are many alternative ways to implement it – e.g. through taxation, inflation or a reduction of budgetary transfers, none of which can be regarded as an automatic and anonymous market process. It also involves a state role in investment allocation and some kind of industrial policy, if only by default. It would be much better to adopt an explicit industrial policy, involving not the hand-picking of winners and losers by governments but the encouragement of sectors characterised by faster productivity growth and high income elasticity of demand internationally.

Conclusion

After the initial near-demise of the state in transitional economies, the successful completion of systemic transformation is bound to restore the role that the state has in modern advanced economies. Indeed such a role is bound to be enhanced further by the need to cope with mass unemployment and to finance large scale capacity restructuring and the resumption of growth.

Notes

1. Comments by Michael Ellman, Carla Naastepad, Servaas Storm and other Conference participants are gratefully acknowledged, though responsibility for any error, omission or opinion rests solely with the author.

2. 'A state that is not there costs everyone much, much more than a state that is': Monsignor Aldo Busi (1994) *Manuale della perfetta gentildonna (con preziosi cazzeggiamenti anche per lui)*, Sperling and Kupfer Editori, Milano, p. 70.

3. See the Caritas investment scheme in Romania, a 'society for mutual help' run by Mr Ion Stoica from the Transylvanian town of Cluj, which made the *Financial Times* front page on 16/17 October 1993. The scheme was set up in April 1992 and took about $1 bn from four million Romanians by promising a sevenfold return in three months (equivalent, for the yearly rate of inflation of 300 per cent prevailing in Romania in 1993, to a yearly real rate of return of 600 per cent). In the autumn of 1993 the scheme stopped making regular payments, but Mr Stoica tried to revamp it by opening new branches around the country. It has been reported (*Financial Times*, 21 February 1994) that a new branch at Snagov collected $840,000 within four days of its opening before it was closed by the Romanian authorities solely for the lack of a legal lease on its premises. Otherwise the scheme, which enjoyed the protection of highly placed politicians and senior officials, never attracted government intervention; Mr Stoica remains free.

4. It has been reported (*Financial Times*, 14 February 1994) that in 1993 the death rate rose by 20 per cent, raising the number of deaths by 360,000 with respect to 1992. The average age of death has fallen to 66 years or lower; for male mortality it appears to have fallen to 59, i.e. far below the average in the industrialised world and the lowest in Russia since the early 1960s. According to Ms Natalia Rimashevskaya, Head of the Russian Institute for Socio-economic Studies of the population, much of the increase is due to 'killings, suicides and conflicts'. Judith Shapiro, adviser to the Russian Ministry of Finance, found that more than 25 per cent were from violent causes, but nearly 50 per cent of the extra deaths in 1993 was due to heart and circulatory failure, caused by what she calls a 'psycho-social crisis' with greatly rising insecurity rather than by rising poverty and a deteriorating health service. Infant mortality rose sharply from 17.4 per thousand in 1990 to 19.1 per thousand in 1993. The birth rate also fell sharply over the period.

5. John Gray argues that the necessary legal and institutional infrastructure of markets cannot be created quickly; such institutions are 'human practices that always come deeply embedded in matrices of cultural tradition'. They 'are like natural languages in that it is their very nature to be plural and diverse' (*Post-communist societies in transition: A social market perspective*, Social Market Foundation, 1994).

6. Martin Raiser (1993) Governing the transition to a market economy, *Kiel Working Paper No. 592* (August).

7. Zaire is the only other country that can boast two Presidents, as well as two constitutions and two Parliaments, but at least these have a temporal sequence, and Zaire does not have the size, importance and nuclear arsenal of Russia.

8. The analogous decision taken by the Peruvian President Alberto Fujimori in April 1992 was not as well received by the US and the international community.

9. For a fuller illustration of economic performance during the transition, and the causes of the recession, see D.M. Nuti (1993a), 'Lessons from stabilisation and reform in central and eastern Europe', in Laszlo Somogyi (ed.), *The political economy of the transition process in Eastern Europe*, Edward Elgar, Aldershot and Brookfield, pp.

40–66; and (1993b), 'Economic inertia in the transitional economies of central eastern Europe', in Milica Uvalic, Efisio Espa and Jochen Lorentzen (eds), *Impediments to the Transition in Eastern Europe*, European Policy Studies No. 1, EUI-EPU, Florence, pp. 25–49.

10.   The *acquis communautaire* involves a long list of obligations, including among other things: free circulation of goods, services, capital and workers; the Common Commercial Policy, and the Common Agricultural Policy; agreements with Mediterranean neighbours, Latin American, Asian and other third countries; the System of Generalised Preferences for developing countries and for ex-USSR, ex-Yugoslavia and Albania; the Lomé Conventions with African Caribbean and Pacific countries; competition policy; fiscal harmonisation.

11.   See the article bearing this title by R. Ram (1986) *American Economic Review*, Vol. 76, No. 1.

6. The State and the Market in the Planned and Post-Planned Economy: the Case of the Former Soviet Union and Russia.[1]

Serguey Braguinsky

Introduction

The conventional approach to reforming the planned economies is summarised in a recent World Bank paper as follows. 'Most researchers view the reform of former socialist economies as a process driven by exogenous policy changes (abolition of planning, privatisation, removal of price controls *etc.*). Reform is seen as a process of creative institutional destruction that is imposed by central planners in a top-down fashion. In this linear view of reform, the self-interested response of agents within the economy is expected to stimulate profit-seeking behaviour and market activity.' (Jefferson and Rawski 1994, p. 1). In China, however, the reform process 'combines rapid economic progress with an institutional and policy environment that deviates widely from standard reform prescriptions and predictions' and 'policy decisions respond to the circumstances of agents and to the impact of decentralised responses on the government's political and financial interests.' (ibid., p. 12). In another paper we find the view that 'in fact, the outcome of the Chinese process must be attributed to broader economic and political forces rather than to the will or the strategic decision making of any leader or faction. ... Certain economic forces and institutional conditions shaped a chaotic and inconsistent set of policies into a coherent process.' (Naughton 1994, pp. 472–473).

177

Looking at the realities of the reform process in Russia and other economies of the former Soviet Union, one cannot help wondering if the conventional approach really performs any better with respect to those economies than to China. In other words, the most interesting thing about the passages cited above is that they really capture not the *differences* but the *similarity* between reform processes (not outcomes) in China and other transitional economies. The real difference is not that the top-down process failed in Russia, while the bottom-up process succeeded in China, but rather that similar bottom-up gradual transformation processes have led to absolutely different outcomes.

In what follows we will present our view of those 'economic forces and institutional conditions' which in our opinion have played the most important role in shaping the reform process in Russia, adding fire to instead of mitigating the 'chaotic and inconsistent set of policies'. Generally speaking, an economist may consider his task of explaining an economic phenomenon completed if he either succeeds in deriving it from a non-economic cause (exogenous factor) or produces a coherent theoretical structure of economic interactions which explain the phenomenon in question (endogenous theories). The conventional analysis of the transitional process basically follows the former approach. Our concern here will be to develop an endogenous theory of transformation with special application to the former Soviet Union and Russia.

The planned economy revisited
The endogenous explanation of the specific phenomena observed in the economic transformation process of Russia and other countries of the former Soviet Union is deeply rooted in the historical evolution of the planned economy through its 70 years of existence. Thus we have to begin not from the year 1992 (when the communist planned economy officially passed away as the Soviet Union collapsed), nor from year 1987, when the first round of 'radical economic reform' got underway. For an adequate grasp of the endogenous approach to economic transformation and the role of the state in it, we must start from much earlier times. In this section we will try to present what we consider to be the most essential features of the planned economy in terms of a simple principal–agent game between the state and the state-owned enterprise (SOE).

The set-up
We will consider the following set-up. The principal, which is the socialist

state (the planning authorities) provides the state-owned enterprises with productive resources and wants to maximise investment by those enterprises, or the output of production, which is a function of investment. The assumption is that the output produced has no direct utility for the agent, which is the management of the enterprise in question (nor, probably, for the whole entity of the enterprise). This assumption is obviously justified if we are dealing with military production, but in the case of civilian production, too, the assumption suffices that the product cannot be sold freely on the market but should be handed over to the principal. Thus, to derive some utility from production, the SOE has to 'cheat', that is conceal some part of the produce and/or of resources provided and divert it to private use. For simplicity we ignore the possibility of double book-keeping for the output, and instead introduce the assumption that the productive resources provided by the principal have direct and immediate utility for the agent (for example can be sold on the 'black market') and that the possibility of double book-keeping exists in that sphere. Thus all the 'black revenues' in our model originate from diverting the productive resources provided by the state to private uses. This diversion of resources should be understood in the widest possible sense, and, besides simple cheating and theft, includes such various activities as workers using the facilities of the SOE to produce goods on private orders (whether carried out during working hours, or in extra time but still using materials, equipment, electricity *etc.* owned by the SOE), using working hours (also a productive resource provided by the state in the sense that the worker is still receiving his or her salary) for lining up to buy consumer goods or just working with little effort *etc..*

Since the state cannot observe the level of investment and does not know the true production of the agent it has to apply the rule of thumb when estimating how much output it will get for different amounts of resources provided to the agent. This rule of thumb we call 'the plan'. This plan in our model is represented by a linear relationship between the amount of resources provided to the SOE and the amount of output which the SOE is required to produce. Thus graphically it can be represented by a straight line, with its slope measuring the relative harshness of the plan target (the greater the slope of the line, the more produce the SOE is required to hand over to the state for a given amount of resources provided). Note that we are definitely *not* saying here that the actual path of the realisation of the plan was anything' like a linear function of the amount of resources provided. On the contrary, we will presently show that, apart from the early years ('Stalinist planned economy'), the path of actual realisation has a definitely concave shape.

We also assume here that the principal cannot devise any effective incentive scheme which will make the utility of producing the output and handing it over to the principal more attractive than diverting resources to the 'black market'. However, the plan is effective in the sense that the negative utility for the management of failing to meet the plan targets is so great as to outweigh any positive utility from diverting extra resources to private usage. For example, we may assume that the managers who fail to meet the plan targets are jailed (as they actually used to be under Stalin). This feature of our model bears similarity to the model of the financial structure of corporations developed by Grossman and Hart (Grossman and Hart 1982).

To close the model we need to specify the rule of provision of resources to SOEs. We adopt here the hypothesis that the SOE can negotiate whatever amount of resources provided to it by the state, subject to 1. the constraint of meeting the plan and 2. some well-defined upper and lower bounds.

As for the upper bound, its presence indicates that when all SOEs try to expand production and acquisition of productive resources from the state, this exacerbates overall shortages in the economy and causes the state to impose the upper limit on resources available to any individual SOE. Alternatively, we may interpret this as the rationing system, when SOEs are not allowed to procure more than a fixed amount of productive resources. As for the lower bound, it is obvious that zero and its neighbourhood do not belong to the production feasibility set of the SOE. That is, SOEs are not free to leave the business. We will find that this lower bound will never be binding.

The assumption that the SOE can negotiate the amount of productive resources it chooses might still seem a bit unrealistic, even if proper account is taken of upper and lower bounds to this freedom of choice. Actually, the amount of resources provided was the subject of bargaining between the SOE and authorities under the planned economy. So, it might be more natural to adopt the Nash bargaining solution; however, we avoid it by assigning the authorities the freedom to set the plan parameter. In practice, this parameter, too, has been the object of complicated bargaining, both at the stage of adoption of the plan and again at the stage of its final implementation. So, what we are actually doing here is to assign each of the two parameters, both of which have in reality been determined by bargaining, separately to be determined by each agent. Besides greatly simplifying the exposition, such designation has the merit that it can trace the evolution of the bargaining power of each party through time, without being concerned too much about the exact split proportion in the bargaining solution.

Let us recapitulate. In our model of the planned economy, the problem for the SOE is to maximise the utility derived from diverting resources to private use (to the 'shadow economy') while meeting the plan target. Again, for simplicity we assume that the bonus system for overfulfilment of production plans is ineffective, but the model can easily be adapted to take account of this possibility (in fact, before the black market really came to play a significant role, the bonus motivation was an important motive for the management of the SOEs; see Berliner 1957).

The production function is assumed to be of the usual S-shaped type, that is, increasing returns prevail at low levels of investment but are subsequently overtaken by decreasing returns. There is at least one point on the investment-output scale where the production function lies on or above the linear plan target function, but it does not lie above it everywhere.[2]

Graphical analysis

With the relationship between the state and the SOE in the planned economy formulated in this way, we will now follow the basic logic of the evolution of the game by employing simple graphs (technical details as well as algebraic treatment can be found in Braguinsky 1995). The following notation is used throughout the graphs:

y	for the level of output
I	for the level of investment
X	for the amount of resources procured by the agent
$x = X - I$	for the amount of resources diverted to the 'black market'
X^*	for the maximum amount of resources negotiable
$\underline{X}$	for the minimum amount of resources the agent is obliged to use.

Figure 6.1 depicts the case where the planned economy is functioning 'efficiently'. The background for the 'efficiency' is its basic feature of the growing 'frontier' economy and strict police regime imposed by the harsh ('Stalinist') government. The plan target can be attained by the agent only by fully utilising all the resources available. No resources can be diverted

to the black market, and the utility of the agent is zero. Note that liberalising the planning regime under the given resource constraint (X^* in Figure 6.1) will lead to a decrease in investment and output, as indicated by the thinner lines. Thus no incentive for liberalisation exists from the principal's side.

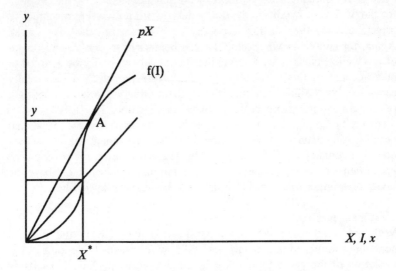

Figure 6.1 Planning in a frontier economy ('Stalinist planning regime')

Apart from the police regime, another feature of such an economy deserves special attention. To remain in the state of Figure 6.1 the growing planned economy must either match all of its growth by the growth in overall resource productivity or else have access to an infinitely elastic supply of such resources. For any particular SOE, increasing output in excess of improvement in productivity would mean entering the diminishing-returns part of the production function in Figure 6.1 and the unattainability of the harsh Stalinist plan. Thus, unless constant growth in productivity can be maintained, the other alternative for the planning authorities is to launch an ever increasing number of new projects, which would consume extra resources and alleviate the pressures of existing SOEs. Thus to maintain the 'efficient' planned economy, it has to be constantly expanding beyond its boundaries under unlimited supply of resources. Together with the police state, this was the ultimate basis on which the early planned economy was functioning.

As the planned economy matured, in order to maintain growth, the provision of resources to existing SOEs had to be increased beyond the point X^* of Figure 6.1.[3] But that would be impossible under the continued harsh ('Stalinist') planning. The planning authorities came to realise that the economy was growing slower than it could have been, and for the first time started thinking seriously about motivating the SOEs economically to increase the use of resources and its output. The political decision by Khruschev to abandon Stalinist horrors had thus as much to do with the objective task of revitalising the economy as with his political preferences.[4] However, by doing so he also signed the death sentence to the planned economy, which was finally to be executed 35 years later.

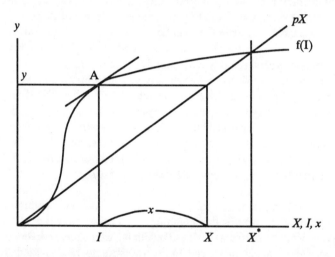

Figure 6.2 Initial effect of liberalisation

The economic essence of the new policies can be seen in Figure 6.2. Part of the authorities' bargaining power is redistributed to the SOE (the slogan of 'greater independence of socialist enterprise' originates approximately at this time); in practice this means that the authorities choose a milder plan target which in turn allows the agent to obtain some freedom of choice in the amount of productive resources employed. The result as shown in Figure 6.2, is the emergence not of a single point but of a whole lens below the graph of the production function and above the plan target line, and this range increases as the planning coefficient is further reduced. In Figure 6.2 the agent chooses the level of resources negotiated X and the corresponding amount of investment I so as to maximise the difference $X - I = x$ subject to the constraint of meeting the plan target. This point is represented by point A where the production function and the planning function have the same slope.

The peculiar feature of this stage of the game, which is not repeated in the following stages, is that this is the period of 'honeymoon' between the state and the SOE. The state, observing only the level of resources negotiated and the meeting of the plan target, is satisfied that the economy has resumed its growth and the resources are being more fully utilised, while the SOE, facing the less harsh planning, is now free to choose the amount of resources negotiated and the corresponding levels of investment and output that enable it to meet the plan target and still enjoy the surplus of resources over investment which can be diverted to the 'black market'.

This 'honeymoon' period roughly corresponds to the period of post-Stalin economic reform conducted in the former Soviet Union in the Khruschev and early Brezhnev years. As the planning regime is further liberalised, though, this initial 'honeymoon' period comes to an end as the economy hits the ceiling. This is shown in Figure 6.3, where investment and output are maximised at some 'optimum' planning regime pX, after which the agent (whose amount of resources negotiable is limited from above by X^*) resorts to a corner solution, reducing the level of investment and output in response to further liberalisation.

We can interpret this kind of solution as follows. As the bargaining power of the SOEs *vis-à-vis* the planning authorities increases, they increase investment and output as well as the amount of resources diverted, meaning that they demand more and more resources to be provided to them by the state. Also, as can easily be seen from our figures, the lower the planning coefficient, the greater is the proportion of newly acquired resources which is diverted to the black market. The authorities finally get alarmed in the face of hard evidence that the efficiency of the economy's use of resources (as officially registered) constantly declines. This in turn leads to a 'cap' imposed on the amount of resources each SOE can successfully bargain out of the state authorities.[5] If the planning coefficient is further reduced in the presence of such a 'cap', the corner solution of Figure 6.3 will prevail, and further liberalisation will lead only to the growth of the black market accompanied by a fall in investment and output.

Thus the state discovers that further liberalisation leads now to decreased instead of increased investment and output while the use of resources is not diminished. The authorities then naturally try to harden the planning constraint at some stage. This does work for some initial period, but when tightening crosses the 'optimum' level of pX in Figure 6.3, output again starts diminishing in response to further screwdriving. At the next stage the state again reverts to liberalisation *etc.*, creating the 'liberalisation-screwdriving cycle' widely observed not only in the former Soviet Union but also in other planned economies.

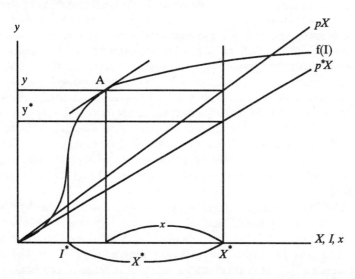

Figure 6.3 'Liberalisation cycle' and the 'optimum' level of planning intensity

As those cycles are repeated, though, some irreversible changes occur within the framework of the planned economy. The problem is that when the liberalisation is successful, it is welcomed by both the principal and the agent, since it leads to growth in both output produced for the authorities and the amount of resources available to the SOE for reselling. But when, in response to corner solutions, the authorities try screwdriving, this is fiercely resisted by the SOE whose utility suffers. And since from each period of liberalisation the SOEs emerge with increased financial strength due to accumulation of proceeds from the black market, they start using part of those proceeds to bribe the officials in periods of screwdriving.

In other words, ever since the totalitarian control regime of the Stalin years was relinquished, the vector of evolution of the planned economy has pointed to strengthening positions of SOEs together with the black-market dealers which loom behind them, and declining strength of the planning authorities. As the economy enters its mature stage, it must rely more and more on technological progress instead of simple extensive growth. But it is precisely the inability to create incentives for technological progress which is the Achilles' heel of the planned economy. So, diminishing returns are felt more and more severely and, as can be seen from our figures, the response of investment and output to liberalisation becomes weaker relative to the response of the black market as the economy travels further along the concave part of the graph of the production function. In other words, out of each increase in resources provided by the authorities, the greater portion of resources is diverted to the black market. Conversely, under retreat from the corner solution, the increase in output is relatively less in the more concave part of the graph of the production function, while the amount of resources available for diversion declines more rapidly. This implies that the authorities become easier convinced that screwdriving produces little effect and the stakes at bribing them to be so convinced are also raised.

Especially in General-Secretary Brezhnev's later years in the former Soviet Union, the number of members of the 'principal team' who were quite willing to accept bribes from the thriving black market and be not too stringent in screwdriving, had risen quite considerably. The remaining staunch communists, after Brezhnev's death tried to stage a comeback in the days of General-Secretary Andropov. They ousted many corrupt officials and politicians and launched the campaign for discipline during which, in particular, the police was brought in to capture lazy workers spending their working hours in movies, saunas and shopping lines. In the language of our model this amounted to one more desperate attempt to stop the diversion of resources to the black market and raise the *normas* of output. But the power of the senile principal, as symbolised by the death of Andropov just a year after coming into power, had already been so severely limited that this attempt produced almost no effect. The system was doomed.

In fact it was probably doomed much earlier and would have died in the early 1970s had it not been for the sharp increase in oil prices, but in the 1980s the terminal symptoms became evident to almost everybody. The control of the planning authorities over SOEs had become just a formality, and the system of actual insider control linked to organised crime – the basic characteristic feature of the present-day 'transitional' situation as we will presently see – has superseded it in many important branches of the economy. After the failure of the 'discipline campaign', the new and young General-Secretary Gorbachev tried to revitalise the system once again by a new round of liberalisation but succeeded only in producing an overall systemic crisis. Those conservatives who opposed him in the Politburo and finally tried to stage a coup had a much more sober vision of where *perestroika* was leading, but it was already too late to change the tide. Thus the conflict between the principal (the planning authorities) and the agent (SOEs) helped by the black market was finally resolved in favour of the agent following a brief showdown in August 1991. 'This was the most important economic consequence of the August revolution' (Yavlinsky and Braguinsky 1994, p. 92).[6] The socialist state was eliminated and no economic planning or centralised distribution of resources has been in force for most of the state-owned enterprises since that time. But that by no means meant the elimination of the basic elements of the old game and of its rules. This persistence of the 'invisible heritage' of the planned economy ('institutional hysteresis' in the terminology of Yavlinsky and Braguinsky 1994) is the cornerstone of our endogenous approach to economic transformation and the role of the state in it.

The state under transition
The process of evolution of the planned economy described in the previous section created a very peculiar institutional situation which continues into the current transition period. We will analyse that situation under two headings, the state and the market.

It is difficult even to count the number of 'comprehensive economic programmes of transition to market economy' which have come out in the past five years. Different in many respects, they all (with the possible exception of the first one, the '500-Day Plan') had one feature in common – being forgotten almost immediately after having been written. No attempt has been made to implement seriously any of those programmes. Moreover, the same has been true not only of programmes but of most of the Parliamentary legislature and Presidential decrees which were supposed to shape the reform process. The transformation process has basically followed its own logic which has very little or even nothing in common with economic policy decisions taken by successive governments.

This absence of effective government has very deep roots in the structure of the Russian transitional economy. The greatest problem which should be mentioned in this context is the absence of an effective system of tax collection. Needless to say, the ability to secure enough tax revenues to finance its budget is the basic ability of the government on which all the rest of its powers must rely. This has never presented any problem to the planned economy (as it does not normally present any basic problem for the developed market economy). The planned economy actually needed no taxation system in any meaningful sense of the word. The profits were calculated in advance and all the residual had to be handed over to the socialist state (subsidies were forthcoming to loss-making enterprises). The beginning of the transition to the market drastically changed this system of obtaining government revenue, but nothing even remotely resembling the effective system of taxation adapted to the conditions of the market economy has ever been established at least in the countries of the former Soviet Union. Especially, the government has no means of verifying the flows of revenues in the private sector of the economy which emerged after the freeing of economic activities. Thus, establishing a private company has become a popular means of avoiding taxes.[7]

No doubt, historians will give many reasons for the collapse of the Soviet Union. We would like to stress, however, one such reason, which probably serves as the economic basis for all the rest. This reason is the collapse of the Union budget which began in 1987 and reached its climax in 1991 when the republics, facing financial difficulties of their own, refused to meet their obligations under the tax-sharing agreement. But after the collapse of the Soviet Union, the authorities in Russia and other new independent states faced similar problems. What made the difference was the latter's decisive move to secure budget revenues by relying on the inflation tax, something which the government of the Soviet Union refused to do to the very end.

Thus the decision to free prices on January 2, 1992, hailed at the time as the most courageous step towards market reform was in fact nothing more than survival tactics employed by the state which was going bankrupt because of its inability to collect enough taxes. The truth of this view is conformed by the evidence of the following years, when despite repeated vows to the IMF and the country's own people radical reformers have done literally nothing to root out inflation. Considering that no alternative to inflationary taxation has been developed so far, it is absolutely clear that despite persistent talk about fighting inflation and sometimes, no doubt, the sincere desire to do so on the part of the authorities, nothing that can be done in terms of macroeconomic policy can ever be successful. The key to the suppression of inflation lies in establishing an effective modern taxation system, which would imply a breakthrough in the present market structure dominated by black-market dealers and criminal elements. We will discuss this problem in the next section.

Usually, the inflation tax is described as the result of the government printing money to finance its purchases, which raises the overall price level. No doubt, tax revenues of this sort played a very important role. In addition, several other aspects of the inflation tax in Russia deserve special attention. The key elements are, first, its very high level, balancing on the edge of hyperinflation (but not crossing that edge after which the money itself would completely lose all value) and, second, the almost complete absence of any effective indexation mechanisms either for the population or for industrial and other companies. Suppose, for example, that in a situation like that in the Russian economy of 1992–94, a producer in a manufacturing industry would be buying raw materials and other resources at the price of 1000 rubles expecting to produce 1500 rubles worth of output after a three-month production cycle. Under the runaway inflation observed in Russia in 1993, prices would double during that period. Assuming for simplicity that this inflationary rise had not changed the relative prices, the producer would sell his output not at 1500 but at 3000 rubles. But for tax authorities his costs are still the book cost of 1000 rubles, although it will now cost 2000 rubles to restart production. The accounting profit is 2000 rubles and profit tax is levied on that amount, which is how the effective rate of profit tax is raised high above its nominal value. No wonder then, that the high (accounting) profits of Russian industrial companies were attended by a sharp fall in production, puzzling everybody who had not understood this mechanism of inflation tax.

The same inflation tax is levied on VAT payments. The VAT included in the price paid for intermediate products is reimbursed only when the final product is sold, so if the production cycle takes some time, the real value of the reimbursement is much lower than at the time the expenses were incurred. The time lag with which fixed capital is reevaluated compels companies to count as profit what should probably be referred to as amortisation *etc.*.

It is the direct consequence of these and similar problems that inflation and the inflation tax are putting different sectors of the economy in totally unequal conditions, with most damage concentrated in heavy industry, especially those branches where the production cycle is particularly long.[8] Another very serious effect of the inflation tax is the natural reaction of self-defence by economic agents. The most dire consequence of this self-defence is the progressive expansion of the shadow economy.

The producers try to speed up the circulation of money as much as possible, so more and more resources are diverted from industrial enterprises to black-market operations where investment can be recovered fast. Moreover, since using bank settlements greatly raises the costs of inflation tax and other taxes,[9] more and more operations are being conducted on a cash basis, or with foreign currencies (US dollars and German marks) as mediums of exchange. Such settlements cannot be conducted between incorporated former SOEs, so a private commercial mediator has to act as go-between. This mediator is officially supposed to be a wholesale firm, but its only role usually is to replace non-cash settlements by cash payments. This has the net effect of retaining the tax payments (not only inflation tax but profit tax as well), due to be collected by the government, in the private sector, and might even be Pareto-improving, but clearly represents a net economic loss compared to the first-best solution.

As well as companies, the households and banks also devise ways to fight the inflation tax. The households withdraw their money from savings banks and engage in all sorts of money gambles, of which the renowned 'MMM' pyramid structure scandal is just the tip of the iceberg. As for banks, they incline more and more towards the short-term side of the market, financing mainly speculative operations which allows them to recover money in at most a few weeks or months. The share of loans extending for more than a year has been around 2–3 per cent in total commercial bank loans during the three years of reform in Russia, and even those are mostly sponsored by the government. In total, all this means that a huge and not necessarily Pareto-improving transfer of capital is taking place from the industrial sector, the sector of material production, to black-market and speculative operations promising speedy returns. This is very much the same tendency as we earlier observed for the planned economy, but on a greater scale.

The increased efficiency of self-defence by economic agents means that the type of inflationary taxation chosen by the Russian authorities is unsustainable in the long run. Though the worst scenario of tumbling into hyperinflation has so far been avoided, too prolonged reliance on too high an inflation tax has already started working itself out. In 1994 the state is finding it increasingly difficult to meet its commitments and obligations.[10] The tragedy of the situation is that during the three years of repose which the government had obtained, the modern taxation system which alone could have saved the situation now, has not been developed. This has profound and far-reaching consequences for the role of the state itself.

Stable and ample tax revenues are needed in particular to pay salaries to government officials, as well as the armed forces, the police, the prosecutor's office and the courts, all of them elements of the government's enforcement mechanism which will not function without being properly paid, to say nothing of paying for the government procurements of goods and services from the industry and agriculture. Recent years and months have seen more and more failures on the part of the government in Russia (and in other countries of the former Soviet Union) to meet its commitments and obligations. This implies, in particular, that government officials and even members of the police and armed forces are left to their own devices to find means of living and supporting their families. A portion of those government employees just left the state apparatus and made themselves available to private businesses (mainly in the black economy part of it). For example, it is well known that most assassinations which shattered Russia in the past few years have been carried out by former KGB assassins who left their government jobs. Most of those who stay (and those are mainly the professionally less qualified, who cannot find lucrative employment in the private sector), concern themselves only with rent-seeking behaviour aimed at attaining private benefits and not at all with implementing government policies. The widespread corruption and non-enforceability of most government decisions in Russia during the reform process is much better explained along those lines than by the mythical resistance of the 'old guard'. And, surely enough, no enforcement can be expected in the future unless the problems referred to are resolved in some way.

Thus by relying on inflation as its means of survival, the state in Russia as well as in other former Soviet republics has decisively downgraded its role in the economy (and the society in general) from that of the dictator, laying down the rules of the social game, as well as the ultimate arbitrator and guarantor of their implementation, to the role of just one (though significant) player in the social game. This is reflected in the severe downfall in the prestige and authority of the state and the jobs associated with government services. Although not yet in Russia, in some other countries of the former Soviet Union we can see this fact even clearer in the emergence of a whole bunch of different 'governments' at war with an another. But in Russia, too, the 'parallel' authority of the shadow economy is omnipresent and supersedes the authority of the state on too many occasions. The danger of this process of state demolition and absorption by criminals is especially great in a country which is still a member of the nuclear club. It is all but pointless to talk about any meaningful reform implementation mechanism without restoring the effectiveness of the government machine, which is in effect the problem of creating the tax and fiscal system appropriate for the transitional realities. We will return to this problem in the last section dealing with policy implications.

The transitional market

It was widely hoped that once economic activities, including the pricing mechanism, were freed, the distinction between official and black markets would disappear. This has not happened in reality. Rather to the contrary, the black market has greatly increased in its size and power, but it still remains the black market in most of its basic features. The official market, though showing unmistakable signs of dwindling, has not finally died out either, and the coexistence of the two economies inherited from the planned economy is more alive than ever. A casual observer at the micro-level of the economy might think that what had actually happened was another round of very drastic liberalisation, but by no means the abolition of the planning system with the SOE now deep in the corner solution of Figure 6.3. And yet, the planned economy and its distribution system are nowhere to be found.

In Yavlinsky and Braguinsky (1994), the reasons for the continued existence of black and official markets were brought together under the two headings of government and market failures. We have already explained what we consider to be the main characteristics of the government's failure in the previous section. Here we will examine what happened to the market by adopting a neo-institutionalist rather than the conventional neo-classical approach. In particular, we will show which features of economic and market structure inherited from the planned economy combined with the present-day institutional framework and the especially inflationary environment and the downgrading of the state have produced an economy which does not match the definition of either the planned or the market economy in any meaningful sense. Although we are dealing with the case of the former Soviet Union and Russia, we believe that the analysis itself is applicable to other transitional economies as well, once appropriate account has been taken of specific features of their economic structures (for example the degree of industrialisation and militarisation compared to Russia *etc.*).[11]

Inflation tax and the degradation of the state to direct participation in the market game on an equal footing with former SOEs and black-market dealers and with a view to private benefits of the officials, already presents a very strong reason for the continued prevalence of the shadow economy. The Russian word *bespredyel* (the term used by convicts to characterise the informal power structure and rules of the game behind the bars) which is often used to depict the current socio-economic situation, reveals more than surface analogies to criminal life. The state does not (will not) protect anybody's rights or even life, unless the officials directly responsible can be motivated to do so by those who need protection and/or enforcement. But then the same services can be obtained from informal criminal structures. Once allowed to play a major part, those structures create their own centres of power which compete with the state and with one another. The overall feeling of insecurity produced by this phenomenon has a very negative influence on the structure of the market.

There are several possible ways to describe the market failure in such an environment. One is to consider the one-shot nature of the market game played. This was the line of argument stressed in particular by Yavlinsky (1994) and Yavlinsky and Braguinsky (1994). But the matter seems to be even more complicated than that.

Even in the economy of only spot trading, inefficiencies need not necessarily result as regards at least the static allocation, if only the participation of large numbers of competitive agents and the free flow of information can be ensured. The problem with the Russian post-plan market is that these conditions are not met for reasons stated above. The collapse of the state and the conditions of *bespredyel* create a highly segmented market with a limited number of insider participants, where information flows from one segment to another are severely hindered. This is a very natural development, if we consider the fact that this market structure has been inherited from the network of insider contacts between SOEs and the segments of the black market servicing each of them. That exclusive nature of transactions in a small insider market creates ample motivation for opportunistic behaviour with hold-up problems arising in every part of the economy. The illegal nature of transactions does not allow the solution of hold-ups by formal integration into one firm, and thus the stage is set for the 'arbitration' by organised crime.[12] Even apart from the social costs of such arbitration, the reliance on the 'natural form of the game' (in professor Hurwicz's terminology) involves apparent economic losses. The segmentation of the market prevents even the law of one good–one price from operating properly.[13]

The most important among all the market institutions is, of course, the institution of ownership. The situation with ownership mirrors all the problems that Russia and CIS countries are experiencing on their ways of transition.

Ownership has been defined in recent papers as 'the power to exercise control' (Grossman and Hart 1986, p. 694). In that setting, 'the owner of an asset has the residual rights of control over that asset, that is, the right to control all aspects of the asset that have not been explicitly given away by contract' (p. 695). Also, 'in a corporation the shareholders as a group have control and delegate this control to the board of directors (i.e. management)' (p. 694). The meaning of residual control rights over an asset is further specified as the 'ability to exclude others from the use of that asset' (Hart and Moore 1990, p. 1121). This approach might work well with economies in which, as in the United States, shareholders exercise real control over management, but it leaves more questions than it answers in the context of transitional economies.

Let us then once again begin with explicitly facing the question what we mean by ownership in the planned economy. We define ownership in the planned economy as the power to exercise control acquired in accordance with the decision of the communist party and administrative bodies affiliated with it. Interpreted in this way, there is one and only one ultimate owner in the planned economy – the General-Secretary of the Communist party of the time.[14] Sometimes this single person was replaced in its function by 'collective leadership' of several members of the Politburo, but in any case this person (or a small group of people) had almost unlimited powers of control over all assets of the planned economy (including human capital during the Stalin years[15]).

However, as is well known from organisation theory, the larger the object of control, the harder it is to exercise that control effectively. Thus the planned economy was doomed to follow the path of the decline of the principal's control as it grew (those increased organisational difficulties coupled with diminishing returns described earlier). The authorities have found their answer, as we have already seen, in delegating part of their control rights to lower levels of the administrative apparatus and eventually to managers of SOEs. In the former Soviet Union, since the 1950s the slavery elements have been eliminated, at times dramatically, as happened to Gulag, and at times only gradually as happened to the peasants. The process of separation of formal ownership and control was gaining momentum, and just as the arrival of managerial (corporate) capitalism spelled qualitative changes in the institutions of the market economy, this process induced qualitative changes in the institutions of the planned economy, too. In addition, those changes, as already shown, were incompatible with the continued existence of the planned economy itself (and that was the difference from the effects the same process had on market economies), so they led to its final collapse.

If we insist on defining ownership in the post-planned economy as the power to exercise control over assets, then we really have to be very careful about what we mean because we enter very slippery grounds. According to the report by the State Property Management Committee of Russia 71 per cent of all enterprises designated to be turned into joint stock companies had completed this procedure by July 1, 1994. In the main regions of Russia this figure is 90 per cent or more. The report congratulates the Government on the successful completion of the first stage of the privatisation process and claims that 'tens of millions of people' had become owners of productive companies as the result.

But this is a very superficial way of looking at things. In fact, in the same report we can find that three quarters of all new-born joint-stock companies had chosen the so-called 'second variant of privatisation' which amounts to giving 51 per cent of shares to the employees.

Looking at this, one might be tempted to think that Russia has made a transition not to the market but to a labour-managed economy instead. But this is not true either. As persistent delays in wage payments testify, actually the country is as far away from a labour-managed economy as ever. In fact those PSOEs (post-state-owned enterprises, a term first introduced in Yavlinsky and Braguinsky 1994) are controlled by their management and the uncrowned kings of the shadow economy. The employees, very often without even seeing their shares, place them in a trust run by the management and have (with some rare exceptions) almost no say in running the business.

The net effect of this 'privatisation' has thus been the completion of the process which started much earlier, when nobody was even dreaming of dismantling the planned economy; namely the process of abolishing outside control and transferring all the control rights over enterprises to insiders (by which managers and affiliated black-market dealers are meant).

Thus ownership defined as the power to exercise control is now clearly in the hands of the insiders, that is the management of the PSOEs and those black-market dealers with whom they are affiliated. This control is quite powerful, too, since the insiders have inherited the almost unlimited (in particular not limited by law or contract) totalitarian control powers of the now dead outsider principal. The only outsiders that remain (the bureaucrats of the post-communist state and organised crime) use their powers of coercion very much similar as they did in the planned economy – to extract (extort) bribes, without checking either the efficiency or the integrity of the insiders.

But it is still not quite appropriate, in our view, to identify those insiders and coercive outsiders with owners. Although they do have immediate and exclusive control over assets, their powers are nevertheless different from the power of control and the right to receive dividends in the market economy as well as from the same powers enjoyed at the times of the planned economy. Of course, some grey zone is always present with reference to the problem of ownership, but in the transitional context this grey zone has settled down in the very centre of economic activity. Most money is now made in Russia through either criminal access to exportable resources, or through criminal *de facto* acquisition of former state property, or through diverting state budget funds, or, finally, by providing services to or extorting money from those engaged in such illegal activities. Thus the major part of those 'rights' go straight against both the old ways under the planned economy and the new ways which are to be introduced on the road to the market economy. In a sense, this is really a 'transitional' phenomenon, and its temporary nature is most apparent to the insiders profiting from it. This temporary nature of ownership, coupled with the aforementioned degradation of the state (also perceived to be of a temporary nature) create the strongest possible motivation to extract immediate profits and benefits from the power to exercise control without bothering too much about what would happen to the assets in the future.

The temporary nature of the present-day ownership 'rights' serves also as one more fundamental factor behind the continued segmentation of the market and various remaining inefficiencies. The point is that the decision to switch from the present-day segmented insider-dominated market to a competitive market may be viewed as a sort of investment decision by the firm, since it involves sunk costs of diversifying its transaction partners, collecting and providing information, developing new products and establishing an after-service network, introducing the quality-control system and retraining the working force et cetera. Of course, it also involves relinquishing tax evasion and cutting relations with organised crime (which might be the most costly thing of all). Although, on the other hand, there are apparent benefits in terms of increased efficiency, investment decisions will be carried out only if the present discounted value of those benefits outweighs costs.[16]

The problem is actually even worse than it seems at first glance. If in the spirit of Dixit (1989) and Dixit and Pindyck (1994) we think of the opportunity to shift to 'normal' behaviour as an option available to the insiders, their rational choice would involve not only the net present discounted value calculation, but also the opportunity cost of using the option (foregoing the opportunity to wait some more time). This way of looking at investment decisions is particularly relevant if there are reasons to believe that there has been a great increase in uncertainty. But that is precisely what happened when the planned economy formally died, burying the state itself with it, with all future institutional parameters, including the question of ownership still in effect to be decided.[17]

As a result, the switch from an insider to a competitive market is smooth only in such markets as the foreign-exchange market where costs are not that high and benefits very great, indeed. In most other cases, economic agents prefer to stick to old ways of effecting transactions on the segmented insider market to paying the cost of switching. The option to switch in the future is thus retained as a highly valued asset. Therefore, it is not just the high level of inflation and/or taxes which adversely affect the switch to normal market behaviour, but also the unpredictability of changes. When policies change almost daily, the option value of waiting is greatly increased and despite the best intentions of reformers creates further problems on the road to reform. In other words, even a less speedy reform might be quite a reasonable choice if it could lead to more stability and predictability of main parameters. The policy implications of this will be further examined in the concluding section.

The option theory approach also helps to explain why the shadow economy cannot take over completely, at least not immediately, and PSOEs continue to function on the official market, too, though on a reduced scale. If all resources are diverted to the black market and the enterprise is forced to cease its operations, this would also mean foregoing the value of the option presented to the insiders.[18] Thus, just as premature execution of the option right, complete running down of the enterprise's funds would be an irrational choice.

Policy implications

The above argument not only explains the failure of the comprehensive programmes of transition to the market, but also strongly suggests that no such programmes devised 'from above' can ever be successful. This is also true of specific economic policy advice. Before making any suggestions to Russian or other transitional authorities, very careful consideration should be made of whether an implementation mechanism for the policy proposals can really be designed that is based not on the good-will of the government and/or of economic agents, but on their self-interest. Especially, it is the self-interest of economic agents which is of the greatest importance.

In what follows, we try to present some such policy suggestions. The implementation of any of them is not going to be easy either, but at least it is possible to distinguish the economic and social power structures which will benefit from that implementation and thus will be cooperative to the government when it tries them in practice.

The first such suggestion, not really new, is a decisive shift in the taxation system towards less reliance on flow and greater reliance on stock and resource taxation.

The current situation in which taxes on income flows are collected from PSOEs and individuals employed therein and/or in the budgetary sector, while the large and growing shadow economy is evading the taxation almost completely has already gone far beyond the point of toleration. Unless serious measures are implemented in this sphere, the collapse of the official market and general chaos seem unavoidable in the not so distant future. The inflation tax, as we have seen, does not really solve the problem, since the shadow economy has devised effective means of evading it, too. Meanwhile, the fact that under inflation profit tax is collected not only from profits *per se*, but also from working capital and from amortisation, puts the PSOEs and other participants of the 'official' market on an even more unequal footing with the shadow economy. If the inflation cannot be stopped immediately, then at least constant indexing of fixed assets and circulating capital in order to avoid excessive taxation is absolutely necessary. This will be most vigorously supported by the management and employees of PSOEs, so such a decision by the government will be highly popular and have good chances of implementation.

Of course, if nothing else is done, this will deprive the government of most of its inflation tax revenues and lead to the collapse of the budget. Hence, the introduction of new offsetting taxes will be needed. While it is unrealistic to hope for the speedy establishing of a monitoring system designed to tax the flow of earnings in the private (shadow) sector of the economy, the difficulty can, at least in Russia, be overcome by relying heavily on fixed assets, land, property and resource extraction tax. In fact, calculations made by the Soviet econometricians in the late 1980s have shown that an oil tax alone, given the difference of domestic and world prices, could replace almost all profit tax revenues in the government budget. Soaring land and property prices in Moscow and other large cities create new opportunities of collecting taxes, if only the government has the firm will to do it. So far, the attempts have been far from successful, with the tax amount calculated on balance prices of assets and property which are tens of times lower than the actual market prices. Introduction of a serious system of taxing fixed assets and resources (which are, incidentally, much easier to capture than flow variables) could lead to overcoming the budget deficit and inflation and reduced profit taxes, which will in turn shift the balance between official and black markets decisively in favour of the former. In addition, taxing fixed assets, land property and lease rights as well as excessive inventories will also improve the circulation of those assets leading to greater market supplies, for currently too many of such assets are just hoarded by their incidental *de facto* 'owners' for speculative or rent-seeking purposes.

Certainly, the introduction of this new system of taxation will not be greeted enthusiastically by the shadow economy, which will be ultimately deprived of the greatest source of the windfall profits it has been receiving over the past years. Here, as with the reduction in other taxes, the government should move ahead gradually and cautiously, affiliating itself with those economic agents whose main operations are in the 'official' part of the market and those from the shadow economy who are prepared to relinquish the murky past and step into the limelights in response to the decisive shift of balance between costs and benefits of the two types of activities.

The implementation of the new taxation system should be accompanied by several other measures without which it will hardly be viable. One such measure of great importance is the development of effective competition. Much has been said about the necessity but almost nothing which was of real consequence has been done (except, perhaps, for opening up the economy for foreign competition which, however, has had its costs and not only merits). In our opinion, the long-term breakthrough in this matter can be achieved through stressing effectiveness rather than competition itself.

It has been an axiom of reform in Russia and other countries of the former Soviet Union that promoting competition means splitting the former state monopolies. In accordance with this axiom, the process of severing links between what used to be single entities is proceeding quite speedily, as the result of deliberate policies, as well as the collapse of the Soviet Union and the general chaotic situation. But no real competition has been introduced so far. The reason is two-fold. For one thing, many monopolies in the former Soviet Union were really of technological and not organisational origin. Once the planning authorities had been abolished, the organisational monopoly ceased to be a serious problem while lack of coordination in activities by separate production units became a new one. Second, and probably more importantly, the dissolution of state monopolies affected only the 'official' market but left the second, informal system of control by insiders on their own segments of a divided market intact or even strengthened, if only because the alternative control system has gone for good. Thus the problem faced now by the authorities in Russia is not so much how to overcome the remaining monopolistic elements (although this is very important for some technological monopolies), but how to overcome the excessive segmentation of the market and the inefficiency caused by it.

The solution to this problem is provided by the proposals for vertical integration. The former state monopolies were horizontally integrated structures and those should definitely not be revived. Vertical integration into industrial groups which will be composed of all stages of production and marketing, starting with resource extraction and ending with banking, wholesale and retail services, can help the economy to go much of the distance which now separates it from an efficient market mechanism. The desire on the part of large banks and/or PSOEs to become the centres of gravity in such groups is evident, and this desire should be encouraged and directed by conscious effort on the part of the government. Such groups, functioning on the official market and basis, will devise their own effective means of taxing the petty black-market dealers which are squandering Russia's resources in the present-day situation.

Vertical integration should provide the solution to the problem of the small-number insider market and inefficient information as well as the associated hold-up problems. It has for some time already been a common-place in the economic profession that the pure abstractions of atomistic or, on the other extreme, totally integrated economies tell us very little about the problems of real life. The real problem is which part of economic transactions it is economically justifiable to internalise (that is, conduct within the boundaries of a single firm) and which part is more efficiently carried out with the help of the market mechanism (Coase 1988). The planned economy has obviously erred on the side of too much internalisation. The present-day Russian economy errs on the other side. The problem is to attain the optimum balance of the two types of economic organisation. Moreover, as the economic history of developed market economies shows, the optimum balance itself changes from one stage of development to another. It is probably the common characteristic of the early stage of development of the market economy (especially of those economies which made a belated start and had to catch up with advanced nations) that the degree of internalisation at this stage is greater than will be required later. That observation adds strength to the belief that the tendency towards natural reintegration of separated units widely felt in Russia as well as in other CIS countries should be encouraged by the government. Although those industrial groups themselves might be the object of splitting at some stage, at this stage of the transition process, to encourage such groups and conduct economic policies in their interests is perhaps the only realistic way to reverse the tendency towards chaos and criminal anarchy in the economy and perhaps in politics as well. If democratic institutions of public control can be maintained in this process from the political side, the obvious dangers of over-domination by large industrial groups may be somewhat mitigated and at least the country will start moving with some view of the future.

One more policy proposal, which will be welcomed especially by industrialists and the larger bankers, is to implement economic policies which need not necessarily be more 'reform-oriented' than present-day policies, but which should certainly be more predictable and credible. As we have already seen, uncertainty about the future greatly hampers efficiency by attaching a higher value to the option to wait than to an immediate decision to switch to a competitive market. This applies not only to negative aspects of uncertainty which are by-products of the runaway inflation and the institutional indecision of the question of property, but also to what can be considered its positive side, for example, expectations that thanks to more pro-reform policies in the future some of the expenses of switching from the black to the official market can be reduced. Such positive expectations also end up in increasing the value of the option at hand and discourage present-day investment decisions. Thus it is vitally important for the government at this stage not just to continue its pro-reform stance, but to establish and follow some well-defined rules of the game which the agents believe not be changed in either direction.[19]

Many other specific measures can be implemented to make the self-generated transition to market economy occurring in Russia more orderly (see Yavlinsky and Braguinsky 1994, section 2). But our general message must be clear by now. The role of the state in the transitional process, at least in economies like that of Russia in which only the ruins of the former governmental machine remain, should be not to design the general direction of the transforming process and implement that design (which is impossible and leads in practice only to cataclysms and potential bloodshed), but to give selective support to those tendencies in the objective, impersonal process which could bring changes for the better in the overall situation, while putting as many obstacles as possible in the way of those tendencies that threaten to lead the process astray. This 'fine tuning' of the reform process presents a formidable task, much more difficult than to call in tanks to crush the rebellious Parliament or a tiny republic in the mountains. But it is the only way forward which is possible under the current circumstances.

Notes

1. The work on the present paper has been carried out as part of the joint research project with Mr. Grigory Yavlinsky sponsored by the Toyota Foundation. The inspiring influence of Mr. Yavlinksy's ideas will be evident to anyone familiar with his theoretical and practical work. The author would like to thank Professor Hurwicz of the University of Minnesota, Professors Kawamata and Takemori of Keio University and Professor Nagaoka from Seikei Gakuen University for important suggestions. The remaining errors as well as all the views expressed are the sole responsibility of the author.

2. When the bargaining power of the authorities is that high while they do not know the true form of the production function, it might happen that the plan will be so harsh as to become unattainable (that is, the planning line will have no common points with the graph of the production function in Figure 6.1). In that case the

management of the SOE will perhaps be eliminated (though it won't be their fault) and the necessary corrections subsequently introduced. The episode from 'Schindler's List', although not specifically dealing with the planned economy, is nevertheless a good illustration of the point in question. In that episode a Jewish woman-constructor points out a deficiency in the construction of a barrack in the concentration camp and gets shot on the spot by the SS chief of the camp. After shooting her, the chief orders the work to be redone precisely in accordance with what she had said. No doubt, this was the case under the Stalinist regime with many quite honest servants of the planned economy. According to Berliner (Berliner 1957, p. 48), 65 to 85 per cent of directors of Soviet enterprises in the 1930s held their jobs for no more than three years, and 25 to 30 per cent out of them for less than a year. The study does not distinguish between those who were promoted or just transferred from those who went into labour camps, but anecdotal evidence suggests that this was the cause of early removal in many cases. Besides, the network of *stukachi* (KGB spies) penetrating every workplace was a rather effective monitoring system, so observability by the principal can also be considered to have been quite good.

3. Thus in our setting the greater resource constraint on the macrolevel is reflected by a growth increase relative to productivity in the resources available to each single SOE which are now available on the concave parts of their production functions.

4. Those who see in Khruschev the Gorbachev of his time are thus greatly mistaken. This is substantiated by several episodes in which Khruschev did not hesitate most brutally to suppress any dissent, including ordering troops to shoot at striking miners in 1962, not to mention the bloody suppression of the Hungarian uprising in 1956. Gorbachev was the only leader of the communist planned economy who for the matter of principle refused to resort to military strength, at least explicitly. It is no chance that the system collapsed precisely under his rule, since the ultimate reliance on non-economic force was the cornerstone of the planned economy at all times.

5. The widespread shortages of basic investment goods, notably the labour force, experienced by all planned economies especially in the last two decades of their existence is the outward manifestation of the phenomenon we are referring to.

6. It is the irony of history that the most intelligent and brilliant leader that the communist system ever managed to produce became the one who oversaw the downfall of this system. It was President Gorbachev's lack of vision and very vague understanding of what he was really doing, coupled with his high intellect and good conscience that did this job for the history. In President Gorbachev's case we find one of the most striking illustrations of how impersonal forces make their way through unintentional consequences of actions taken by otherwise very brilliant and respectful leaders.

7. Tax evasion has been recognised as a major motive for establishing firms ever since the first article by R.H. Coase appeared. It is, however, in the transitional context that it becomes, indeed, one of the central motives in economic life.

8. Many 'reformist' economists have argued that the Russian industry is so uncompetitive that it might be cheaper to have it all scrapped and then rebuilt anew. This might be true and this might be not. The point is that nobody can say for sure now, because the conditions under which manufacturing industry has now to compete with other sectors of the economy are anything but fair or equal chance competition.

The too large differences in taxation and some other initial conditions which are in force now owing to inflationary environment and failures of the government tax system must be eliminated first, and only then it will become possible to judge which sectors of the Russian economy really comprise its comparative advantage. The present 'market' signals are so distorted as to make them almost as valueless as the previous planned price signals.

9. In 1991 the Central Bank of Russia ordered that all interbank settlements should go through its settlement centres established throughout the country. Those centres were absolutely inadequately equipped for the task and at the peak of 1992, with a yearly inflation rate of more than 1000 per cent, it could take up to two months before transfers could be completed from one account to another. This was an effective way of raising the inflation tax, but as could have easily been expected, undermined greatly the confidence in the banking sphere and hampered its reconstruction. The banks did not have to bother at all about the efficiency of their investment; with yearly market interest rates as high as 260–280 per cent last summer they were paying only four per cent interest on settlement accounts of industrial enterprises which constituted 40–60 per cent of their liabilities. The situation is currently improving with some major commercial banks introducing the on-line system of transfers among themselves, but it is still very far from satisfactory. This also greatly facilitated the reliance on black market cash and/or dollar settlements.

10. The increased tightness of fiscal and monetary policies in 1994 reflects the understanding of the self-defeating nature of the inflation tax on the part of the government, but as yet nothing has been done to find a really viable alternative. If anything, the government tries to increase further the burden of official taxation, resorting sometimes to coercive methods, but it is obvious that the Russian economy is already far on the right side of the peak of the Laffer curve.

11. An important conclusion of our approach is that it makes a lot of difference with what sort of industrial and market structure each country enters the stage of transition. For instance, in countries dominated by heavy and military industry (Russia, Ukraine, Belarus) the continued diversion of resources through the black market from the industry to other spheres of economic activity is the only mechanism of resource distribution in the absence of coherent industrial policies by the government. On the other hand, China, for instance, while experiencing largely similar problems with its heavy industry sector has managed to make much more progress toward a market economy owing to a large rural population which enabled the spur in TVEs ('township and village enterprises'). China was also greatly helped by a high degree of decentralisation and strong local governments. It was local governments which sponsored the TVEs, thus creating the third sector in the economy, different from both SOEs and private (black market) businesses. In Russia and other CIS countries the rural areas had been so devastated by the Stalinist regime that the remaining population is either old and sick or very low sunk indeed. Local governments have so far also enjoyed little real power, although things are gradually changing. Anyway, it is probably these differences in economic structure and the conditions of the government which really account for the differences in performance of reform processes in China and Russia. In Poland also agriculture has never been collectivised and there was initially a strong private sector in the

economy which alleviated the problems discussed here. As for the Czech republic and Hungary, those countries managed to avoid inflation tax and also conducted much more coherent privatisation policies. Thus we may conclude, that although vectors of similar directions are at work in the reform processes in all of the post-communist world, the specific features of each economy affect the relative lengths of those vectors, and that may well change the direction of their sum total. Any analysis of transition to the market thus becomes not only a theoretical but also an empirical task of evaluating the quantitative aspects of each of the opposing vectors. This alone should put an end to all discussions concerning the supposed universality of shock therapy.

12. Thus the widely reported deterioration of law and order, and the progressing 'mafiasation' of the Russian economy have objective realities of economic life behind them. Simple reliance on police force to crack down on crime would be ineffective and might even be dangerous. The only way to reverse the tendency of criminalisation is to carry through basic institutional changes. Some policy proposals which might help to go some way in this direction are listed in the final section of this paper.

13. This law is not obeyed even in the competitive sectors of the retail market, because different retailers are affiliated with different wholesalers and cannot switch them easily for fear of reprisals by gangs. From the author's personal experience – in three kiosks in a row in Moscow's main shopping area the prices of absolutely the same foreign cigarettes and liquors differed as much as 50 per cent with some items cheaper in one of the kiosks and others in another. Characteristically enough, the young wealthy people shopping there seemed to care very little how much money they were being charged and did not bother themselves with comparing the prices, which would not have taken them more than 15 seconds to accomplish. One cannot obtain more convincing evidence that the 'no-money' socialist economy is still alive in what is supposed to be the most advanced market part of the new economy.

14. It is interesting to note that the common reference to the General-Secretary among members of the Central Committee was *khasyain* (owner).

15. The Gulag was not only and even not so much a means of punishing political dissidents as a means of providing slavery working force to the planning authorities. Recent studies have revealed that the output of those slaves and especially the construction projects which they carried out in most inhuman conditions were entered into yearly and five-year economic plans. Since the death rate among slaves was quite high, each regional branch of the Ministry of the Interior had its yearly plan for detecting and sending to labour camps a certain number of 'political dissidents', with the ministry officials themselves going to those camps in case they failed to meet their *normas*. Apart from labour camps, the peasants were prohibited to move from place to place and had to work at collective farms without getting money wages, so they were almost in the same enslaved situation. Even workers and engineers in cities faced severe restrictions in changing their work-places or places of living. Thus the essence of the early stages of the planned economy was the revival of slavery in modern times. The degrees differ among the countries, but qualitatively very similar features can be observed in the Soviet Union under Stalin,

China under Mao, North Korea under Kim Il Seng, Cuba under Castro, Cambodia under Pol Pot and so on.

16. Even with full rationality it is difficult to assess whether this can really be the case in the transitional economy. Of course, the merits of the competitive market are well known and on the increase as the reform progresses, but at the same time the collapse of the state authority reduces the penalties for using the black market. Since the current position is that of the insider market, it involves more to induce the change of behaviour than would be needed to maintain it if the initial position was that of a competitive market. This is the nature of 'institutional hysteresis' (see Yavlinsky and Braguinsky 1994). Freeing the economic activity in this environment amounts to freeing the totalitarian economic monster (Yavlinsky 1994).

17. Another reason for greatly increased uncertainty is, of course, the run-away inflation analysed earlier.

18. The formal ownership of 51 per cent of shares by employees acts here as the final checking mechanism. Though usually without any say, the employees can rise in self-defence when they clearly see that the management is diverting so many resources that the existence of the enterprise is at stake. The case when the employees ousted the excessively corrupt manager occurred recently on the Moscow first watch factory.

19. At a recent conference involving Japanese and Russian top economic policy officials, a representative of the Japanese side, when comparing the investment climates in Russia and China, said that the overall degree of freedom enjoyed by foreign investors is probably greater in Russia, but the Japanese investors still prefer China because of greater stability and predictability of its environment. The Japanese official said that although he greatly appreciated the incessant drive toward implementation of reform policies on the part of Russian authorities, the investors just find it a bit hard to keep pace with daily changes. But what is true of Japanese and other foreign investors is true of Russian investors as well.

References

Baldwin, R., and P. Krugman (1989) Persistent trade effects of large exchange rate shocks, *The Quarterly Journal of Economics*, Vol. 104, No. 4, 635–654.

Berliner, J.A. (1957) *Factory and Manager in the USSR*, Harvard: Harvard University Press.

Braguinsky, Serguey (1995) Endogenous transformation – an inquiry into producer's behaviour under communist and post-communist economy, Yokohama: *unpublished*.

Coase, R.H. (1988) *The Firm, the Market, and the Law*, Chicago: University of Chicago Press.

Dixit, A. (1989) Entry and exit decisions under uncertainty, *The Journal of Political Economy*, 97 (3), 620–638.

Dixit, A. and R. Pindyck (1994) *Investment Under Uncertainty*, Princeton: Princeton University Press.

Grossman, S. and O. Hart (1982) Corporate financial structure and managerial incentives, in J. McCall (ed.), *The Economics of Information and Uncertainty* Chicago: University of Chicago Press.

Grossman, S. and O. Hart (1986) The costs and benefits of ownership: A theory of vertical and lateral integration, *The Journal of Political Economy*, Vol. 94, No. 4, 691–719.

Hart, O. and J. Moore (1990) Rights and the nature of the firm, *The Journal of Political Economy*, Vol. 98, No. 6, 1119–1158.

Jefferson, G.H. and T.G. Rawski (1994) How industrial reform worked in China: The role of innovation, in *The World Bank Annual Bank Conference on Development Economics*, April 28–29, 1994.

Kornai, J. (1980) *The Economics of Shortage*, North-Holland.

Nagaoka, S. and I. Atiyas, Tightening the soft budget constraint in reforming socialist economies, *IEN Working Paper No. 35*, The World Bank.

Naughton, B. (1994) What is distinctive about China's economic transition? State enterprise reform and overall system transformation, *The Journal of Comparative Economics*, 18, 470–490.

Williamson, O. (1975) *Markets and Hierarchies*, The Free Press.

Yavlinsky, G. (1994) *Laissez-Faire versus Policy-Led Transformation. Lessons of the Economic Reforms in Russia*, Moscow.

Yavlinsky, G. and S. Braguinsky (1994) The inefficiency of laissez-faire in Russia: Hysteresis effects and the need for policy-led transformation, *The Journal of Comparative Economics*, Vol. 19, 88–116.

Comment on Part Three

Alice H. Amsden

It is a challenge and pleasure to comment on the chapters by Serguey Braguinsky and Mario Nuti. Both contributions are complex and shoulder above most analysis of Eastern Europe's transitional problems in terms of quality. Unlike many government policies in the region and academic discourses on them – both of which tend to be outdated no sooner they appear – the essays by Braguinsky and Nuti promise to have staying power because they are thoughtful and empirically-grounded assessments of where transition policy has come from or where it is likely to go. Given the overall theme of this volume, my comments will be restricted to some 'structuralist' issues raised by the authors.

'Structuralism' has become of direct relevance in Eastern Europe insofar as all countries in the region seemingly wish to have their own political and economic structures become like those of their wealthy West European neighbours as quickly and closely as possible. Given the inordinate amount of time and energy which the East has devoted to 'privatisation' (of state-owned enterprises, or SOEs), presumably Easterners image that their greatest difference with the West lies in the forms of ownership – state property in one case, private property in the other. Insofar as Mario Nuti's paper focuses on privatisation, it gets to the heart of Eastern Europe's cardinal concern.

The presumption behind 'privatisation über alles' is that capitalism is based on private property, and the sooner state property is privatised (which is proving to be arduous, costly, and time-consuming), the sooner capitalism can emerge and Eastern Europe can catch up materially and politically with the West. This argument is so obvious or even tautological ('What is capitalism if not private property?') that Nuti does not bother to spell it out; he takes the urgency of privatisation for granted. But this argument is worth trying to clarify even briefly in order to see how much sense it makes in the current East European context. Private property may be a necessary long-term goal of capitalism, but investing time and money in achieving it in the short-term, and relying on the emergence of private property relations to trigger a dynamic process of capital accumulation, may be a political blunder and misallocation of resources compared with trying directly to make major enterprises productive and internationally competitive whoever happens to own them.

Presumably privatisation is highly desirable economically because it brings the 'hard budget constraint' that was absent under state ownership. Hard-nosed private owners, the argument runs, will act ruthlessly to cut costs, including related labour, and will have the guts to reduce employment to levels dictated by productivity (whereas political owners supposedly do not have such gumption). Of course, if this argument is correct, it also means that not just any kind of private ownership is desirable. Employee ownership that is controlling is undesirable because, as Nuti reasons, a controlling interest by workers will have a 'devastating effect on earnings, employment, efficiency, and restructuring' insofar as 'workers will be dismissed only if their wages are higher than the value of their average product, instead of the value of their marginal product', and workers 'may use their controlling power to raise earnings above the going wage rate'. Given this line of reasoning, it is unfortunate that, as Nuti notes, most privatisations in Eastern Europe to date have been employee buyouts.

Nevertheless, this may not be such a bad outcome. Employee ownership may be the best safeguard against criminality and massive de-industrialisation given the conditions of the transition in some countries – political instability and extremely short-term profit maximising time horizons to the point where non-employee owners and managers, singly or in collusion, have an incentive to strip a company's assets for personal gain rather than productive use. As Braguinsky points out in his chapter on Russia:

> The formal ownership of 51 per cent of shares by employees acts here as the final checking mechanism. Though usually without any say, the employees can rise in self-defence when they clearly see that the management is diverting so many resources that the existence of the enterprise is at stake. The case when the employees ousted the excessively corrupt manager occurred recently on the Moscow first watch factory.

In the best of times an 'agency problem' arises when there is separation of private ownership and management; the mere existence of private property does not guarantee textbook efficiency when the owner of a firm does not also manage it, as is the case for most large-scale firms. In the worst conditions of the transition, the best resolution of the agency problem and the most productive use of existing resources may occur under employee ownership. If 'excess' employment occurs, this may be relatively costless in the short-term given Eastern Europe's high rates of unemployment and extremely low wages by most international standards. If employee ownership under competitive pressures proves inferior to other forms of ownership in the long-term, it will simply not survive.

Presumably privatisation is also highly desirable economically because private owners have an incentive to maximise the value of their assets by investing long-term in organisational capabilities, physical capital, and technology. This may be true in theory and is implicit in Nuti's chapter, but the 'mass' privatisations through voucher schemes that have occurred in practice in Eastern Europe are not really capitalist transformations of ownership. Such privatisations are 'pseudo-capitalist' because the new owners of state property (adult citizens) acquire equity without providing real capital in exchange. Therefore, former state-owned firms do not acquire the physical and human resources they need to modernise (see the discussion in Amsden, Kochanowicz and Taylor, 1994). The true urgency in Eastern Europe is to relieve the technological and quality bottlenecks that are impeding the global competitiveness of state-owned firms. Yet the first five years of the transition have been spent head-scratching to devise ingenious ways to privatise state property in the absence of foreign buyers with deep pockets and local 'buyers' with no pockets at all.

Any structural analysis of the transition is beholden to explore how theories about private property, which were devised with already-capitalist economies in mind, need to be revised in order to guide behaviour in economies that are only in the process of becoming capitalist. As for the political virtues of privatisation, they may not be as widely perceived as Nuti assumes. This is perhaps suggested by recent turnouts in parliamentary elections throughout the region in which former communist party leaders were elected to top posts. The political virtues of privatisation may be especially great for the new elite that is replacing the old *nomenklatura*. If so, this new elite and the actual popularity of privatisation need further elaboration.

The Braguinsky chapter provides a good analysis of what went wrong under central planning, and then attempts to use this framework to provide a bridge to understand what is going wrong in the transition. As

Braguinsky sees it, the link lies in the inability of the government to extract revenues from state-owned enterprises. Its power to tax weakened as SOEs became more autonomous and then completely broke down during the transition. But why? Braguinsky does not really say why except to suggest that each of the republics became more independent-minded. Clearly, however, under Gorbachev the Soviet Union became fiscally unbalanced as it tried to spend more than it could extract in the form of taxes. Braguinsky then goes on to argue that price deregulation was undertaken by the Russian state in 1992 as a 'survival tactic' rather than as a reform measure. By liberalising prices and triggering inflation, an inflation tax could be exacted on the population to finance government spending.

As a consequence of this 'bottom-up' approach to reform (meaning reform as a response to endogenous social, political, and economic influences rather than a theoretic–political agenda), Braguinsky regards Soviet and Chinese reforms as similar (although generating different outcomes).

One wonders, however, if Braguinsky's interpretation of Russia's price liberalisation is entirely on the mark. Did the Russian state really liberate prices in 1992 with the foresight that freer prices would lead to inflation and hence, more resources for the state to play with? This seems unlikely given the experience and economic *naiveté* of the Russian authorities at the time. It seems more plausible that price liberalisation was theoretically driven (as a centrepiece of market reforms, much as it was throughout Eastern Europe), and that price liberalisation was then responsible for runaway inflation and a plunge in real incomes, which, in turn, depressed demand for the output of state-owned enterprises, which, in turn, made such enterprises unable to pay their taxes (see the discussion by Lance Taylor in Chapter 2, Amsden, Kochanowicz and Taylor, 1994).

From this perspective, the reform paths as well as reform outcomes of China and Russia have been very different. The Chinese authorities deliberately and explicitly resisted swift price liberalisation ('shock therapy') on the ground that it was too inflationary and hence politically de-stabilising. They reformed the price system step-by-step and still administer key prices when necessary. They also deliberately invested resources in state-owned enterprises to restructure them; unlike Eastern Europe they emphasised enterprise modernisation rather than privatisation. The small and medium-size enterprises that arose alongside the state-owned sector tended to be collectively-owned; even now only a small share of national firms are entirely private.

There has been heated debate among economists about whether fast-growing China can act as a model for stagnating Eastern Europe. Advisers like Jeffrey Sachs have hotly denied the possibility arguing that because China is mainly agrarian, its appropriateness as a model is limited. China, of course, is relatively more agrarian, but this is irrelevant to the argument, that given the disparate performance of Russia and China, Russia would probably be much better off if price liberalisation had been gradual and if efforts had been made to restructure rather than privatise the best state-owned firms. Braguinsky belittles the differences in the Chinese and Russian reforms by comparing them only along the dimension of 'bottom-up'/'top-down'.

Braguinsky's main policy point is that 'the role of the state in economies like that of Russia, in which only the ruins of the former governmental machine remain, should be not in designing the general direction of the transformation process but in selectively supporting those tendencies which could bring changes for the better and putting as many obstacles as possible in the way of those tendencies that threaten to lead the process astray'. This seems highly sensible, and is backed with several good suggestions in which the government might lend a helping hand. One is in forming large, vertically integrated business groups that have a chance of reaching efficient scale in Russia's large domestic market and in exporting to world markets. There has been so much talk in the transition of busting up old monopolies that it is forgotten that much of world trade is dominated by large oligopolies. That Braguinsky suggests ways to increase competition among these groups is also welcome. It might be worth thinking further of how the government might stimulate the growth of *diversified* business groups. Although these groups challenge conventional economist's wisdom of specialisation, they have thrived in almost all successful late-industrialising countries – Japan (*zaibatsu, keiretsu*), Korea (*chaebol*), India (business houses) and now China (see Amsden and Hikino, 1994)

References

Amsden, Alice H., Jacek Kochanowicz and Lance Taylor (1994) *The Market Meets Its Match: Restructuring the Economies of Eastern Europe*, Cambridge, Ma.: Harvard University Press.

Amsden, Alice H. and Takashi Hikino (1994) Project execution capability, organizational know-how and conglomerate corporate growth in late industrialization, *Industrial and Corporate Change*, Vol. 3, No. 1.

PART FOUR

A Sustainable World System

7. Environmental Feedbacks in Macroeconomics

Lance Taylor

This paper discusses how macroeconomic events may (or may not) affect and be affected by other broad areas of human concern – environmental interactions of people with nature is an example of great current interest. Before taking up these questions, it makes sense to review the main themes of macroeconomic discourse.

There are phenomena (for example, national output flows, rates of inflation, financial booms and crashes, and trade and financial movements on the external account) which are generally agreed to be macroeconomic. They are created at the politicoeconomic level of the world or nation state by many actors operating within a constantly changing structure of environmental influences and social, political, and economic institutions; like all human individuals and groups, the actors are not completely sure of their own motivations and do not fully comprehend the situations in which they live.

This behavioural uncertainty and the complications of economic life make it impossible to analyse macro level events in terms of what the actors do in their multitudes. In the jargon of complexity theory, macroeconomics is an 'emergent' consequence of the micro and meso level actions that the actors undertake and of the relationships among them. In contrast to other complex systems, macroeconomics is not intellectually difficult to grasp. Multiplier spillovers, the fallacy of composition, and the paradox of thrift are typical macro phenomena – messy to quantify but easy to understand. All emerge from economy-wide adding up or aggregation conditions that individuals' actions have to satisfy.

Its emergent properties suggest that macroeconomics can and should be pursued on its own terms. Practitioners naturally work with aggregate indicators – typically constructed on the basis of accounting schemes

217

which purport to add up what statistically accessible actors such as enterprises and households are doing economically – and attempt to formulate the laws according to which they affect one another. The examples just mentioned show that these 'laws' follow from accounting identities implicit in the construction of the aggregates and rules of thumb about how they make each other move about.

When set up mathematically, the rules are usually linear (or linearised from general-looking formulas with little precise content), and simplistic. When not formalised, they take the form of a macroeconomic 'vision' (in the usage of Schumpeter 1954) which is not always easy to transmit. In either form, the rules are rationalised in different ways by different sorts of economists – neoclassicists prefer stylised optimisation exercises performed by representative actors while some structuralists still like to think in terms of technological relationships, institutions, and social classes – but all boil down to statements based on intuitive perceptions about how the aggregates interact.

In practice, these ideas are often expressed in terms of stylised laws and facts: a stable saving, investment, or portfolio balance function exists; money velocity, the capital–output ratio, or the labour share is almost constant over time; 'Say's Law' that all resources are fully employed and that an increase in one sort of spending will necessarily squeeze out some other either is valid or it is not. Even demolitionist macroeconomists who assert that such relationships shift as people learn to outsmart the government when it tries to intervene in the market system (see Barro 1974, for example) postulate a stable underlying macroeconomic model and perfect private sector acuity in grasping its implications.

As is well-known, some economists think that Barro's and similar models postulating economic actors' super-rationality have great verisimilitude; others find them bizarre. More generally, despite a consensus that they exist, there is no professional agreement about the form and content of the stylised macroeconomic laws and facts. Within the mainstream, Phelps (1990) distinguishes seven schools of thought and there are numerous dissident gangs as well. However, there *is* a fairly well-defined realm of discourse, and agreement about admissible subjects and objects of macroeconomic debate.

With due trepidation, one could also assume that there are admissible subjects and objects of environmental debate. The questions at hand are about relationships among these and their macroeconomic analogs. This interface will be assessed here from a macroeconomic perspective. Given the author's competence, this approach is unavoidable but it may be of more general import as well. People who practice macroeconomics – heads of state, central bankers, ministers of finance, large scale currency speculators – wield much more power than environmentalists. Are the latters' concerns interesting, let alone substantive, from the formers' points of view? If not, given the way that the world is presently organised, ecological concerns will continue to be given short shrift by the capitalist system.

Are there comparable objects of debate?

Macroeconomists concentrate on a short list of variables and ask how they interact as a system (the entries in the list and the nature of the interactions will of course depend on which of the seven or seventeen schools of macroeconomics one adheres to). They distinguish between 'fast' and 'slow' variables according to how rapidly they change in time. The former are often expressed as flows per unit of time (gross domestic product or net fixed capital formation per year) and the latter as stocks (total productive capacity or the physical capital stock) which cumulate relevant flows gradually. Finally, there are policy and/or exogenous variables which influence the flows and changes of stocks, e.g. monetary rules, fiscal interventions *etc.*. Herein, we will assume that all these variables are quantified according to currently accepted methods, i.e. we do not discuss extensions of macroeconomic accounting to incorporate environmental concerns.

To be specific, assume that a short vector X of macroeconomic variables exists. At any point in time (measured continuously), X can change in response to changes in stock variables K_x and policy variables Z_x. It is also interesting to ask whether X will react to K_x and Z_x in a muted (stable) or extreme (unstable) fashion, but in either case the adjustment will be 'fast', e.g. largely taking place within a short period. By contrast only the time derivative of the 'slow' vector K_x (dK_x/dt or $\dot{K}_x$) will be affected by changes in X or Z_x so that K_x evolves over the years. For later reference, define the stock of people (or population) as N, and let k_x stand for the vector with elements made up of the stock variables K_x expressed in per capita terms, or divided by N.

Is it reasonable to impose a similar structure on the non-macroeconomic systems? If such aggregation is possible, then there is a short vector of environmental flow variables Y, with a stock vector K_y (k_y in per capita terms) and a policy vector Z_y. As discussed presently, the Y-system might interact with the macroeconomic X-system as illustrated in spreadsheet form in Table 7.1.

There seem to be no agreed-upon emergent environmental properties which can be quantified *à la* GDP. Are there other aggregates which can be constructed to capture essential concerns? If not, a spreadsheet like the one in Table 7.1 makes no sense; to environmentalise macroeconomics one would have to switch to 'thick description' or similar modes of discourse. Since it puts them on unfamiliar ground, economists resist such a step, and try to assign monetary values to indicators from the other fields.

For example, instead of working with flow environmental variables such as the volume of logging per year and stocks such as the percent of national forest cover they will look at the value of logging sales or the capitalised valuation of the trees. At the micro level, attempts at evaluation of non-economic objects at times satisfy criteria of common sense, at other times not. The dollar value of a tree at least has a market basis, but economists' attempts to assign 'contingent valuations' to environmental amenities such as clean air over the Grand Canyon strike most people as epistemological nonsense (Sagoff 1988). This is one reason why economists' pronouncements about the environment often go unheeded.

For sensible discussion, then, environmental variables will have to be expressed in quite *ad hoc* fashion. Tree cover as a proxy for K_y becomes a metaphor for the health of entire ecosystems, and the estimable cost of reaching certain ambient standards has to be treated simultaneously as a (positive) benefit flow Y and the macroeconomic cost Z_y of getting the associated environmental gain. Policy costs could be quantified in standard fashion. Economists like to ponder how such indicators trade off with one another according to some sort of 'welfare function' $W(X, Y; k_x, k_y, N)$, but such an exercise will not be pursued here.

Are there feedbacks or not?

Turn to the spreadsheet in Table 7.1. The 'result' variables listed down the left-most column are affected by 'inputs' arrayed along the top. The first task is to discuss the signs of responses (magnitudes are a much more complex matter!) that have been assigned. The following observations implicitly treat the vectors X, Y etc. as having only one component, i.e. as scalars. Generalisations to slightly higher dimensionality (two, or maybe three) are not impossible to work out.

Entries 1-A and 2-B in the spreadsheet represent feedback effects of X and Y upon themselves. The macroeconomic variable X is usually assumed to be self-stabilising, in the sense that if it has a small upward blip then there is an offsetting negative adjustment $\Delta \dot{X}$ in the (fast) time derivative of the variable itself, signalled by the 'minus' sign in cell 1-A. However, such stable adjustment may not apply for X or the environmental indicator Y (by convention measured so that a bigger value means an improvement) under some circumstances – for example if increasingly tight environmental restrictions on output increases are encountered. If the own-feedbacks in cells 1-A and/or 2-B become positive, then a drop in X or Y will make the induced change in its time-derivative negative as well. As discussed later, enforced decumulation of the stock variable K_y may follow in a frequently noted environmental peril.

Table 7.1. Stylised interactions

	Inputs					
	A.	B.	C.	D.	E.	F.
Results	X	Y	K_x	K_y	Z_x	Z_y
1. $\Delta \dot{X}$	$-/+$	$+/-$	$-/+$	$+$	$+$	$+/-$
2. $\Delta \dot{Y}$	$-/+$	$-/+$	$-$	$+$	$+/-$	$+$
3. $\Delta \dot{K}_x$	$+$	$+/-$	$-$	$+/0$	$+$	$+/-$
4. $\Delta \dot{K}_y$	$-/+$	$+$	$-/+$	$-$	$+/-$	$+$
5. $\Delta \dot{N}$		$-$	$-$			

Next look at cross-effects. Does an increase in X help or harm Y? A negative entry in cell 2-A signals harm in the near term, as many environmentalists fear. In the other direction, does a change in Y have *any* impact on X? If so, in which direction does it go?

A general rule of thumb is that shocks exceeding one or two percent of GDP can notably perturb the macroeconomic system. The underfunded expenses of Lyndon Johnson's wars on poverty and in Vietnam amounted to 2–3 per cent of US GDP and upset the economy for years. The profits from the two oil shocks and the American 'twin deficits' of the 1980s amounted to a percent or so of world GDP and had strong effects on global macroeconomics. Whether in the short run plausible shifts in large scale environmental indicators will move a national or world GDP level by 1–2 per cent appears to be an open question. Nor do we have much feeling for the signs of such influences.

Similar observations apply to the policy variables Z_x and Z_y, but here quantifications may be on firmer ground. For example, in Brazil mid-range estimates of the costs of global warming control/biodiversity protection and attacking domestic poverty and environmental degradation amount to 1.2 per cent and 2.6 per cent of GDP respectively (Abreu, Carneiro and Werneck 1994). Even if the former outlays were financed from abroad, in an economy subject to tight fiscal limits these programs could crowd out 'productive' public and private investment to such an extent that output growth might be slowed by two to three per cent per year – a big reduction. Using a model postulating full employment of all resources, Jorgenson and Wilcoxen (1990) similarly assert that environmental protection expenditures in the United States squeeze out capital formation via Say's Law, and substantially retard economic growth.

In Zimbabwe, in another example, an environmentally friendly land reform package would entail increased investment outlays and a bigger trade deficit due to a decline in agro-exports; after a lag, food production would probably rise (Davies and Rattsø 1994). The reform would be viable only if the government could obtain compensating external finance. Both these results and the ones for the U.S. and Brazil come from macroeconomic models with causal structures which, as always, are open to debate. Nonetheless, the models' predictions would give the greenest imaginable finance minister considerable pause.

For X and Y, the final question is how they react to changes in the slow or stock variables K_x and K_y. Columns C and D in Table 7.1 illustrate possibilities. In cell 2-C, it is assumed that if X has a detrimental effect on Y, perhaps through adverse 'scale' effects or tightening environmental restrictions (Daly 1991), then the same is true of the associated stock. By contrast, more K_y helps Y recuperate in cell 2-D. Similar stories apply in the first row, with decreasing returns for X from more K_x as a possibility in cell 1-C.

Turning to the accumulation process itself, cells 3-C and 4-D postulate directly self-stabilising behaviour for K_x and K_y, as part of a bald summary of highly complex interactions. For example, the environment may self-regenerate unless overwhelmingly assaulted by X or K_x, while system-wide destabilisation can occur via shifts in X and Y induced by the evolving stock variables, as in Figure 7.5 below. Thus in cell 3-D, more environmental capital is assumed to help accumulation of K_x, while in 4-C a higher level of K_x may crowd-out or crowd-in the growth of K_y. Crowding-out can reflect scale effects stemming from the fact that the environment is a resource that deteriorates as economic activity and/or the human population rises. By contrast, crowding-in of $\dot{K}_y$ by K_x coupled with a positive effect of K_y on $\dot{K}_x$ (cell 3-D) is a 'win–win' situation of the sort stressed by technological and/or market optimists such as the World Bank (1992).

In row 5, more of either sort of capital slows population growth $\dot{N}$. The rationale for the negative effect of K_x on $\dot{N}$ in cell 5-C is the demographic transition – wealthier households are less pressed to have children. Presumably the same logic applies to better environmental conditions in cell 5-D as well. These population linkages also influence accumulation of stock variables per head, since $\dot{k}_i = d(K_i/N)/dt = (1/N)[\dot{K}_i - k_i\dot{N}]$. Higher K_i values will reduce $\dot{N}$ and speed up $\dot{k}_i$ through slower population growth, in a potentially important long-term feedback. In cells 3-A and 4-B there could be similar repercussions through the fast variables X and Y, with crowding-out or -in of accumulation in the off-diagonal cells 3-B and 4-A.

'Fast' scenarios

The implications of some of the hypothesised responses in Table 7.1 can be illustrated with two-dimensional phase diagrams in standard fashion. For the 'fast' variables the curves in Figures 7.1 to 7.3 represent loci of points along which X and Y are constant, or $\dot{X} = 0$ and $\dot{Y} = 0$ respectively. Local directions of adjustment when the variables do not lie on the schedules are shown by the small arrows nearby. At a point where the two curves cross, X and Y are in a dynamic equilibrium ($\dot{X} = \dot{Y} = 0$) which may or may not be stable. By the Poincaré-Bendixson Theorem, with only two planar dimensions in continuous time there is no possibility of chaotic dynamics, although such trajectories would be of great interest to explore.

Figure 7.1 illustrates cases in which Y does not affect X. In the simplest situation, X has only one equilibrium value which holds for all Y; $\dot{X} = 0$ is the coresponding vertical line in the (X, Y) plane. By contrast, a higher (better) macroeconomic level X may well reduce the environmental indicator Y. When Y is self-stabilising (a negative response in cell 2-B of Table 7.1), the $\dot{Y} = 0$ schedule has a negative slope, as in the top diagram. The small arrows signal that both variables have stable own-adjustments.

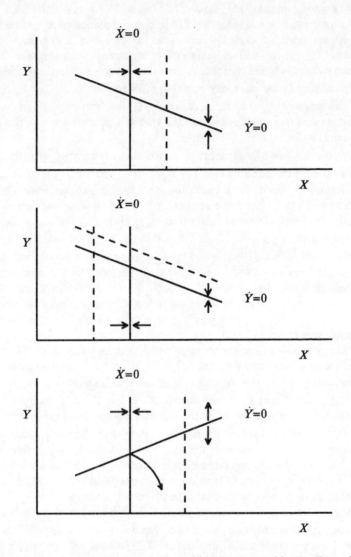

Figure 7.1 Short-term adjustment when the macro variable X affects the environmental variable Y adversely, and Y does not affect X. Upper diagram: an increase in X hurts Y. Middle diagram: a policy that improves Y has a negative effect on X. Bottom diagram: Y is self-destabilising

The top diagram shows how a policy improving X (or shifting the $\dot{X} = 0$ curve to the right) reduces Y. As noted above, such an outcome is a familiar and valid environmentalist critique of many economic initiatives. With no feedbacks from Y to X, however, the upper diagram is unlikely to trouble people whose attention is riveted on macro performance. They are more prone to be worried by the middle graph, where a policy that improves Y (the upward shift of $\dot{Y} = 0$) affects X adversely by shifting the $\dot{X} = 0$ schedule to the left. The movement of the equilibrium point toward the northwest summarises the model results of Abreu *et al.* (1994) and Jorgenson and Wilcoxen (1990) discussed previously.

Finally, the bottom phase diagram illustrates a case in which Y is self-*de*stabilising. The intuition is that if Y becomes more weakly self-stabilising, then the $\dot{Y} = 0$ schedule in the top two diagrams rotates clockwise as the same change in X leads to a bigger shift in Y. If the process continues until $\delta \dot{Y}/\delta Y$ passes through zero from an absolutely small negative to a positive (destabilising) value, then $\dot{Y} = 0$ takes a positive slope as in the lower diagram. An initial reduction in the environmental variable then leads to further deterioration of the status of the environment, as shown by the dynamic responses of X and Y (solid arrow) to a policy which shifts the schedule along which $\dot{X} = 0$ to the right. As discussed later, the deterioration of Y could lead to decumulation of the environmental stock variable K_y as well.

Figure 7.2 illustrates the same thought experiments as in Figure 7.1 when Y affects X positively. Better environmental conditions aid economic performance in the short to medium run – a response which many orthodox economists believe has yet to be established. Its potential importance is demonstrated by the middle diagram showing the implications of a policy that directly raises Y and reduces X. For the macroeconomic variable, there is an ambiguous final outcome due to the positive influence of Y on X. The top diagram is very similar to the one in Figure 7.1, where an improvement in X unambiguously makes Y decline.

The bottom diagram illustrates the case where Y is weakly self-destabilising so that the $\dot{Y}=0$ locus has a steep positive slope. The policy aimed at improving macro performance now leads the equilibrium to shift to the left with *lower* X and Y values which are approached cyclically (solid spiral arrow). Just after the policy is initiated, an initial rise in X causes $\dot{Y}$ to turn negative; the environmental variable's positive own-feedback makes Y fall further and ultimately reduces X since $\delta \dot{X}/\delta Y > 0$. This potentially harmful

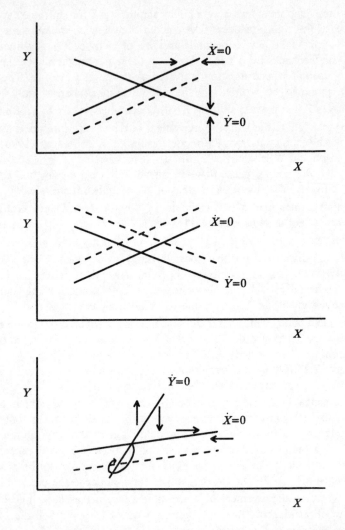

Figure 7.2 Short-term adjustment when the macro variable X affects the environmental variable Y adversely, and Y affects X favourably. Upper diagram: an increase in X hurts Y. Middle diagram: a policy that improves Y has a negative effect on X; in the new equilibrium the final change in X is ambiguous. Bottom diagram: Y is self-destabilising and a policy aimed at improving X can worsen the situation overall

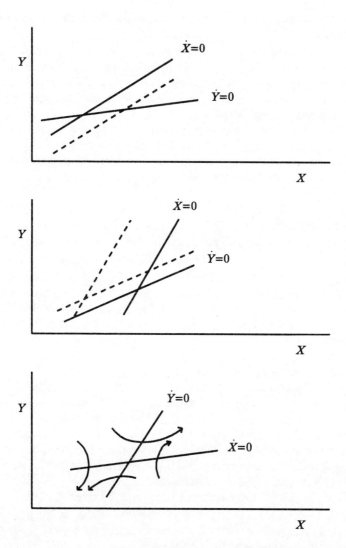

Figure 7.3 A 'win–win' situation in which X and Y influence each other favourably. Upper diagram: an improvement in X raises Y. Middle diagram: a policy that raises Y also reduces X; in the new equilibrium, both variables can decline if the effect on X is strong. Bottom diagram: strong cross effects lead to an unstable (saddlepoint) equilibrium

effect of environmental deterioration on economic performance is precisely what many activists stress.

Figure 7.3 illustrates a 'win–win' situation in which $\delta \dot{X}/\delta Y$ and $\delta \dot{Y}/\delta X$ both are positive – the two variables crowd each other in. In the top diagram, for example, a policy aimed at improving X will lead to a higher value of the environmental variable also. In the middle diagram, a policy raising environmental standards can fail if it strongly reduces X and thereby pulls down Y. Bhagwati (1993) argues against environmentally based restrictions on international trade along such lines. In his view, getting rid of green impediments to trade will stimulate economic performance so strongly that environmental improvements will follow in train.

The bottom diagram in Figure 7.3 illustrates an unstable 'win–win' situation in which X and Y stimulate each other very strongly (a shallow $\dot{X} = 0$ curve means that a small change in Y induces a big change in X and a steep slope of $\dot{Y} = 0$ says the same about the effect of X on Y). As illustrated by the solid arrows, the $\dot{X} = \dot{Y} = 0$ position is a saddlepoint – an upward (downward) perturbation from equilibrium leads both variables to diverge toward infinity (zero). If X and Y really could grow unboundedly, creation of this dynamic configuration would be a policy goal worth aiming for.

A global portrait of 'slow' dynamics

The foregoing themes can be combined in a representative global dynamic portrait of the per capita stock variables k_x and k_y in Figure 7.4. Phase planes based on these variables are used in the literature on sustainable growth (Karshenas 1992; Pezzey 1992). The interpretation is that when environmental capital k_y falls toward a low value, there is a grave risk of unsustainability; a low capital level k_x suggests an unviable economic system. For simplicity, we assume that k_x behaves in self-stabilising fashion and that its accumulation is facilitated by more k_y. The locus of points along which $\dot{k}_x = 0$ thus has a positive slope in Figure 7.4. It represents macroeconomic steady states in which the capital stock K_x is growing at the same reate as population N.

As Karshenas emphasises, the Y-reducing scenarios of Figure 7.1 could easily lead to decumulation of environmental capital. He is concerned about '... an economy with stagnant technology, low investment and capital stock and a growing population which eats into the natural capital stock in order to survive'. Such unfavourable dynamics could be worsened by negative effects of K_x and K_y on the growth of N as discussed in connection with Table 7.1.

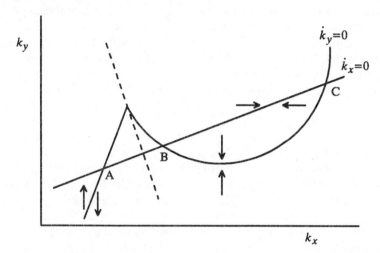

Figure 7.4 Phase diagram for the productive capital per capita k_x and environmental capital per capita k_y in which k_y is self-destabilising at equilibrium A and self-stabilising at B with more available k_x. Equilibrium C is an unstable 'win–win' position with unbounded growth of both k_x and k_y to its northeast

Point A in Figure 7.4 represents this low level equilibrium trap, of the sort previously illustrated in the bottom diagram of Figure 7.2. An economic optimist might assume that it could be overcome by injection of physical capital so that as k_x rises the destabilising effect of k_y upon itself would be reversed: $\delta \dot{k}_y / \delta k_y$ would change sign from positive to negative. Such a transformation is assumed to occur along the dashed ridge line in Figure 7.4. Both the low level equilibrium A and the higher level point B (with dynamic properties of the sort illustrated in the upper two diagrams of Figure 7.2) are stable attractors with 'basins' separated by the ridge.

Policy-driven accumulation of physical capital could in principle push an economy over the ridge from point A toward B. Empirically based environmental 'Kuznets curves' of the sort discussed by the World Bank (1992) imply that such transformations occur naturally as per capita income rises. However, it is not immediately obvious that capital accumulation alone would be sufficient to overcome the trapping forces around point A. Sociopolitical and other factors enforce ongoing exploitation of the environment by the poor.

Figure 7.4 has a third point at which $\dot{k}_y = \dot{k}_x = 0$. The equilibrium at C presupposes that when k_x is high it crowds in accumulation of k_y as opposed to crowding it out. This is a saddlepoint 'win–win' situation of the sort illustrated in the bottom diagram of Figure 7.3. Ultimate bliss would involve ever-growing levels of k_x and k_y to the northeast of C. For believers, the policy riddle is how to steer the system to get there.

'Slow' and 'fast' dynamics

A more realistic case, perhaps, is one in which slow degradation of environmental capital can lead the macroeconomic system to crash. This possibility, the last to be considered here, can be illustrated by the familiar concept of bistability or hysteresis. The basic idea is that a certain level of k_y is needed to support a 'high' level of macroeconomic activity X. The fast equilibrium system takes the form shown in Figure 7.5, and it is assumed that X is initially on the upper solid branch of the S-shaped curve (or 'equation of state' $X = g(k_y)$ along which $\dot{X} = 0$).

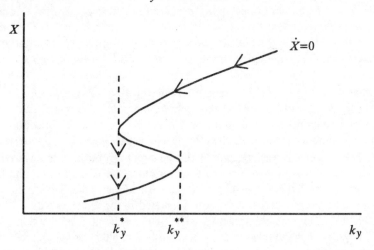

Figure 7.5 A bistable situation in which gradual decumulation of k_y along the upper branch of the $\dot{X} = 0$ locus leads X to crash to the lower branch as k_y falls to the critical level k_y^*

Over time, the high X leads to gradual decumulation of k_y, and this variable moves toward a critical level k_y^* at which dg/dk_y suddenly becomes positive along the dashed line, for example as X changes from a self-stabilising to a self-destabilising regime. The level of economic activity drops suddenly to the lower branch of the curve. Perhaps a reverse jump to the upward schedule would be possible if at lower values of X, k_y regenerates toward a second critical point k_y^{**} where dg/dk_y also changes sign, but such a transition is by no means assured. The bottom line is that environmental catastrophes can last forever.

References

Abreu, Marcelo de P., Dionisio D. Carneiro and Rogerio L.F. Werneck (1994) Growth and environment trade-offs: three-gap simulations for Brazil, Helsinki: World Institute for Development Economics Research, *mimeo*.

Barro, Robert J. (1974) Are government bonds net wealth?, *Journal of Political Economy*, 82, 1095–1117.

Bhagwati, Jagdish (1993) The case for free trade, *Scientific American*, 269 (No. 5), 42–49.

Daly, Herman E. (1991) Elements of environmental macroeconomics, in Robert Costanza (ed.), *Ecological Economics*, New York: Columbia University Press.

Davies, Rob, and Jørn Rattsø (1994) Land reform as a response to environmental degradation in Zimbabwe: Some economic issues, Helsinki: World Institute for Development Economics Research, *mimeo*.

Jorgenson, Dale, and Peter J. Wilcoxen (1990) Environmental regulation and U.S. economic growth, *Rand Journal of Economics*, 21, 314–340.

Karshenas, Massoud (1992) Environment, employment, and technology: towards a new definition of sustainable development, London: School of Oriental and African Studies, *mimeo*.

Pezzey, John (1992) Sustainable development concepts: an economic analysis, *World Bank Environmental Paper No. 2*, Washington D.C.: The World Bank.

Phelps, Edmund S. (1990) *Seven Schools of Macroeconomic Thought*, Oxford: Clarendon Press.

Sagoff, Mark (1988) *The Economy of the Earth*, New York: Cambridge University Press.

Schumpeter, Joseph A. (1954) *History of Economic Analysis*, New York: Oxford University Press.

World Bank (1992) *Development and the Environment: World Development Report 1992*, New York: Oxford University Press.

Comment

Abhijit Sen

This chapter provides a fairly exhaustive menu of the possibilities that may arise when macroeconomic variables interact with environmental variables, treating both of these at a high level of aggregation. The chapter is 'environmentalist' in the sense that it assumes that a better environment is generally good for the macroeconomy. However, the analysis is agnostic in that it does not presuppose the nature of the feedback from the macroeconomy to the environment. Various specifications are considered and the outcome is examined in each case. The purpose is to sign the likely effects, on both the macroeconomy and the environment, of policies addressed primarily to one or the other of these objectives.

Because the analysis is aggregative, general and agnostic, its structure is not detailed enough to offer macroeconomists any real insight into how their actions might actually affect the environment. For this reason, the title of this chapter may be a bit misleading. Its real value seems to lie not so much in its elucidation of how the environment and economy might *in fact* interact with each other, but, rather, in its ability to pinpoint those possibilities where the environmentalist argument might be heard with greater effect by those concerned primarily with macroeconomic issues. As the author notes, final decisions on the matter are likely to be made by those for whom immediate macroeconomic considerations are more important than purely environmental concerns. In this sense, the chapter is more about how macroeconomics and environmentalists might interact on policy matters: it is an outline of how the intelligent macroeconomist is likely to evaluate environmental arguments. If this is accepted, it is easy to see why the generality of the chapter, and the author's unwillingness to give more definite structure to the precise economy–environment interaction, is not a weakness but a strength.

The most important point that the chapter raises analytically, is that, from the point of view of dynamics, the issue of macroeconomy–environment

232

interaction involves far more than whether the feedbacks from the one to the other are positive or negative. Two other features are of crucial importance. First, the time dimension, or the economists' traditional distinction between stock and flow variables. Are we interested in the 'fast dynamics' where only the effect on short-run flow outcomes (immediate income and environmental quality) are considered, holding constant the stocks of economic and environmental capital; or is it the 'slow dynamics' where we may be less interested in changes of immediate flows but more concerned about how stocks (of physical and environmental capital) may change over time? This matters because macroeconomists are generally more interested in 'fast dynamics' than environmentalists who have longer-run concerns. Second, since each type of variable (economic or environmental) would have its own dynamics even if the other was somehow held constant, it is important to specify whether the variables are self-stabilising (i.e. robust to small perturbations) or self-destabilising (i.e. perturbations persist or magnify). Economists prefer to think in terms of models where the economy is ultimately self-stabilising, but they also know that this takes time and that even fairly small shocks (of one or two percentage of GNP) can cause large medium-run perturbations in the macroeconomy. On the other hand, economists have few priors about the stability properties of environmental variables, so that this needs to be specified.

Consider the 'fast dynamics' first. If the feedback from the macroeconomy to the environment is negative, as environmentalists in the West usually argue, any policy which improves the macroeconomy will worsen the environment. On the other hand, pro-environment policies will always improve the immediate environment, but, because these are likely to involve economic costs, are likely to have some adverse effect on immediate macroeconomic indicators. A trade-off between these two desirable goals can be ruled out in a self-stabilising environment only if the positive feedback from the environment to the macroeconomy is very strong. Unless environmentalists can show evidence of this, macroeconomists are unlikely to be convinced of the short-run merits of any large environmental outlay, particularly because they know that even small macroeconomic shocks can have large medium-run perturbations on the economy. The case for large environmental outlays is, of course, even weaker if the feedback from the macroeconomy to the environment is positive, as some economists would argue is the case in developing countries. Here purely environmental interventions would definitely worsen the macroeconomy and, because of the positive feedback, lead only to small (and maybe even negative) environmental gains. The really strong case for environmental intervention, in terms of 'fast dynamics' arises if the environment is self-destabilising and there is a large negative feedback from the macroeconomy to the environment. Here, attempts to improve macroeconomic variables alone may cause both the economy and the environment to suffer so that there is really no trade-off and thus no real alternative to putting the environment first. A lack of any trade-off is also likely in the case where there is a positive feedback from the macroeconomy to a self-destabilising environment, but now policies which improve (worsen) either the environment or the macroeconomy would also improve (worsen) the other, so that a purely environmental concern is unnecessary. Thus, one important (though unstated) conclusion of this chapter seems to be that, if interest focuses on 'fast dynamics' alone, as is the wont among macroeconomic decision makers in contrast to environmentalists, proponents of environment-first policies would have greater persuasive power if they argued in terms of extreme cases. Therefore, it is perhaps not surprising that most environmentalists end up arguing either the *doomsday* case (of an unstable environment on which economic growth can have large adverse effects) or, though less often, the *rosy green* one (of a stable environment, improvements in which can have large economic benefits), rather than anything in between.

Interestingly, the analysis in the chapter suggests that, if anything, advocacy of a pure environment policy is more difficult when only the 'slow dynamics' (outcomes in terms of underlying *stocks* of economic and environmental capital) are considered. This is because the worst degradation of environmental stock is likely to occur not where economic capital is very high but where it is very low, so that the *doomsday* case does not really apply. And nor does the *rosy green* possibility seem very likely because that would require the not so justifiable characterisation that any positive feedback from the environment to the economy be greater for more wealthy economies. Among the possibilities considered in the chapter, there are only two situations of real concern with 'slow dynamics'. First, when a very poor economy is in (or risks falling into) a low environment–low income trap. Second, when a very rich economy is in risk of falling off a win–win trajectory where both the economy and the environment improve over time without negative feedbacks from the economy to the environment. In both of these cases there are strong reasons why more economic capital may be desirable, and in neither is the environment-first argument likely to move decision makers strongly.

The really strong case from the environmentalist point of view arises when 'fast' dynamics in the macroeconomy interacts with 'slow' dynamics of the environment. If the feedback from economic activity to environmental capital is negative, and the self-stabilisation of the latter is low, high economic activity will lead to environmental degradation. This can lead eventually to a macroeconomic crash if the positive feedback from environmental capital to economic activity operates only above some environmental threshold so that it is impossible to sustain the high level of activity by simply running down such capital any further. This is the classic environmentalists' *doomsday* story, which works best in this form because the negative feedback argument, that the environment is not sufficiently stable and that economic activity can degrade it, is more plausible for the environmental stock than for environmental flows. Also, the consideration of macroeconomic flows rather than stocks permits neglect of the positive feedback that might arise if economic capital could substitute for the degradation of environmental stock. But even here, for there to be a catastrophe rather than some sort of equilibrium, the story requires that there be no environmentally sustainable positive rate of economic growth because otherwise low economic activity would regenerate the environment again. Most macroeconomists would probably argue that there is some such positive sustainable rate of growth, because of natural regeneration and possibilities of substituting environmental capital by economic capital, and that, in any case, one need not worry too much until that threshold level of environmental capital gets very near and that may be a fairly long way away.

The important point to note about the above is that when economists do start to consider environmental problems seriously, they usually begin with the third type of interaction and discuss issues such as 'sustainability' and the economic valuation of environmental resources in this *doomsday* context. But, normally, their habits of thought lead them to think implicitly in terms of the other two types of interaction where the case for a purely environmental policy is weaker. From a short run perspective, an immediate concern for purely environmental issues seems to have mileage only in extreme situations. And, in the very long run, the presumption is that building up economic capital may actually be good for the environment or, at least, that the two could substitute for each other so that some sort of equilibrium will not be difficult to sustain. As a result, environmental concerns seldom enter into the routine preoccupations of macroeconomists. When they do, they relate to particular environmental problems, almost inevitably dressed up in the *doomsday* garb, which economists reduce quite quickly to microeconomic exercises of the cost–benefit variety, with macroeconomic modelling added primarily to identify the costs rather than benefits. Although there have been attempts, e.g. by Daly (1977, 1987, 1991) and Perrings (1987), to formalise a distinctive 'environmental macroeconomics', this is still a minority taste.

The real problem lies perhaps in the fact that environmentalists do find advocacy easier when they put their case in *doomsday* terms, pitting consumption of present generations against the possibility of a catastrophe facing future generations. This flavours arguments with some traditional macroeconomic concerns, such as the sustainability of growth in the presence of natural resource constraints and the choice of appropriate discount rates in the presence of uncertainty, so that dialogue can proceed. But, matters remain unsatisfactory because growth-mongers can always point to the possibility of future technological fixes. Further, with the issue discussed essentially in inter-generational terms where the obvious constituency is missing, the environmentalists' arguments unavoidably acquire a moral undertone. In practice, environmental policies predominantly take the form of setting standards. This had the apparent virtue that environmentalists feel they have achieved something concrete, government budgets are less affected than if public expenditures were required, and growth-mongers can be mollified that such standard-setting is only sector specific and the implicit costs can eventually be reduced through technological progress. But, of course, such standards have macroeconomic consequences and, as is evident with the issue of global warming, macroeconomists are reduced to quantifying the costs of different standards when the moral pressure mounts to impose some standards. The debate then acquires a spurious precision where economists and environmentalists can display their respective prowess confronting physical environmental indicators against calculated economic costs to ultimately fudge a political compromise. But, as economists know all too well, the main result of such calculations is simply that the same standards can have very different macroeconomic consequences in different economic environments.

An immediate consequence of this is that global environmental issues, such as that of global warming, get bogged down with the environmentally reasonable but economically impossible task of setting uniform global standards in a world where individual macroeconomics differ considerably in their characteristics. The demand for such global standards, in fact, gets stretched beyond global environmental issues because, in an integrated world economy, the local macroeconomic side-effects of even local environmental regulations can be mitigated by requiring that others follow the same standards. Such conflicts between the search for global environmental standards and local macroeconomic consequences are usually highlighted when nations confront one another to set international standards, but it should be obvious that the same problem can exist within each nation if, as a result of the standards, different segments of the population have to pay different macroeconomic costs. An apparently inter-generational problem is thereby converted quite naturally into an issue of redistribution between members of the current generation – something which neither environmentalists nor mainstream macroeconomists are unduly concerned with.

This would not be a serious problem if it were simply a redistributive issue with no dynamic consequences. But, unfortunately, it is not. As the chapter under discussion points out, there are environment–macroeconomic interactions where a worsening of the immediate macroeconomic indicators leads also to a worsening of the environment. The final effect of seemingly 'green' standards can be distinctly non-green if the redistributive impact is adverse for groups subject to such interactions. The situation is worse because today's macroeconomics is itself concerned with arbitrary standards such as fiscal deficits, which are usually sought to be achieved by cutting payments to the poor. In such a setting, it is possible that grandiose plans to save tomorrow's environment by invoking *doomsday* scenarios to impose standards may have the effect of impoverishing the poor and driving them into activities which degrade the environment today. It would, therefore, perhaps serve the 'greens' better if they eschewed this narrowly inter-generational outlook and realised that there are also win–win situations where future generations may be saved not by forcing unspecified macroeconomic cuts today but by redistributing from today's rich to today's poor. That agenda would also force macroeconomists to look more closely to the links between today's distribution of resources and the chances of a better environment tomorrow. This may not solve all environmental problems but is likely to be less full of uncertainties and zero-sum outcomes of today's practice.

References
Daly, H.E. (1977) *Steady-State Economics*, San Francisco: Freeman.

Daly, H.E. (1991) Towards an environmental macroeconomics, *Land Economics*, 67, 255–259.
Perrings, C. (1987) *Economy and Environment*, Cambridge: Cambridge University Press.

8. A Problem Common to the Three Worlds: Promoting Economic and Social Democracy

Ignacy Sachs

1. The 1992 Earth Summit emphasised the inseparability of the social, environmental and economic dimensions of development. The 1993 UN Conference on Human Rights highlighted the assymetry at present existing between the instruments to protect the political and civil rights and those to guarantee the effective implementation of economic and social rights. Although the situation with respect to political and civil rights is far from satisfactory, the picture is even more dismal as far as economic and social rights are concerned. Yet, the strong version of democracy encompasses all these rights. The challenge before the forthcoming March 1995 Summit on Social Development is to formulate a concrete agenda to start reverting the present trend.

2. The three groups of countries – South, East, North in shorthand – are at present affected, in different forms and with varying degrees of intensity, by structural unemployment and underemployment and the ensuing phenomena of social marginalisation, exclusion and segregation. In addition, they have all paid a high environmental price for their unprecedented economic growth in the second half of the twentieth century.

In the South, the historical record of the peripheric late capitalism has been, on the whole, rather negative when assessed by means of political, social and environmental criteria. Even the performance of the South-East Dragons, not speaking of their historical exceptionality, is questionable from these points of view, however enriching may be the study of the experience of these developmental States in governing the market economy.

In the East, the so-called countries in transition face the daunting task of stabilising and restructuring their economies, while building almost from scratch the political, social and economic institutions required for a democratic regulation of a mixed economy governed by the three principles of social equity, environmental prudence and economic efficiency. The mirage of instant capitalism, of a relatively painless transformation and of a rapid competitive insertion in the global economy did not work. The prospect now is one of gradual transformation. Its success will ultimately depend on the ability to use the present unique political configuration for inventing (the word is not too strong) new institutional solutions while deeply restructuring the whole economic fabric. The chances of a happy ending do not look too bright, however, to judge by the performance of the last four years.

Lastly, all the Welfare States of the North experience a crisis, as if they were not prepared to withstand the compound effect of slow growth (or even recession) and of the prevailing pattern of labour-displacing technical progress leading to growth with little or no employment generation.

Seventeen million registered unemployed in the European Community alone, not counting several million more being at present retrained and those who have given up looking for jobs, is a measure of the severity of the social crisis in the North. The more so as work continues to be the main form of socialisation and, conversely, protracted unemployment leads to social marginalisation. The poor are less and less necessary to the rest of the society even as a workforce. Exclusion is taking precedence on exploitation in advanced economies, while the deteriorating condition on the labour market intensifies, at the same time, the rate of exploitation and the shift from wages to profits in the distribution of national income.

The prospect for the productive inclusion of the excluded is bleak given the dominating technological trends, the segmentation of labour markets, the lack of spatial mobility of the workers *etc.*. The few relatively successful reconversion programmes in depressed regions have required massive public investment; even so they have helped the ailing enterprises more than the marginalised people.

The lessons that the South and the East can draw from the Northern performance are not encouraging indeed. The possible exception is the experience of Japan which follows a policy of protecting low-productivity jobs in the services. The prevailing paradigm is one of growth through increases of productivity at the enterprise level and of search for competitiveness on the global markets with little regard, if any, to the externalised social and environmental costs. Unbridled social darwinism becomes the dominating ideology. The strong are the celebrated victors while the victimised weak are blamed for their pretended lack of skills and entrepreneurship. As a result of growing inequalities between the successful minority and the rest, within as well as between nations, social fragmentation becomes a universal phenomenon. The concept of dual (or plural) societies, elaborated initially in the specific context of post-colonial countries, is nowadays currently utilised to describe the situations prevailing in the industrialised countries and in the former Soviet empire. Making a virtue of pretended necessity, some ideologies present in a positive light the 'multi-gear society' oblivious of the fact that *apartheid* is the asymptote of growth through inequality and even more so of the slow growth through inequality now prevailing.

3. At the international level a corollary of this situation is the return to more or less covert forms of protectionism and discrimination against the exports from South and East, notwithstanding the free-trade rhetorics of GATT. The philosophy of international solidarity, on which UNCTAD was built, implying in economic relations between unequal partners rules of the game favouring the weaker one, is giving way to the arbitrary invocation of 'social dumping' an ill-defined and ahistorical concept. The least one can say is that the attitude of the North is contradictory.

On the one hand, to increase their exports, the South and the East are advised to open their borders wide to foreign direct investment attracted by low wages and cheap materials. On the other hand, whenever the mix of advanced imported technology with low wages gives them a competitive edge, they are accused of perpetrating social dumping.

Preventing delocation of industries is a matter for internal policies in the Northern countries so long as they continue to pay lip service to free trade. The accusation of social dumping branded in an arbitrary way on Southern and Eastern countries can only deepen the present divide between them and the North.

What will be in this context the effect of an indiscriminate opening of the economies prescribed to the South and East alike by the so-called Washington consensus? What criteria ought to be used to distinguish genuine from spurious competitiveness? What priority should be given to improving systemic competitiveness at the national level as distinct from the micro-level competitiveness? While even the most advanced industrial-ised countries find it difficult to keep pace with the present rate of technological change, how to prevent the 'creative destructiveness' postulated by Schumpeter from becoming destructiveness *tout court*? What place should be given in the development strategies to the widening of the internal market and to the non-tradables?

Whatever the theoretical merits of export-led growth, more inward-looking and self-reliant strategies (which should not be mistaken for autarky) have a better chance of succeeding in the present international environment, in particular in large countries. Many countries in the South and, lately, in the East, have learned by experience that the gap between the rethorics of foreign assistance and the harsh reality of international economic relations is very wide indeed.

At a more general level, how to deal with the consequences of the three 'decouplings' analysed by Peter Drucker, between output and employment, between output and the demand for raw materials, between the real and the financial economy?

Before going into the central issue of how to manage the increases in productivity of labour for the benefit of the entire society, let us briefly comment on the second and third decouplings.

The sluggish demand for raw materials produced by the developing countries is the main economic factor behind the structural deterioration of the international economic environment, as viewed from the southern point of view. In consequence, the commodity producers in the South cannot rely on an export-led growth unless they modify substantially their export mix through an overall diversification of their economy. A steady expansion of the internal market by means of employment-intensive growth, leading to a more equitable income distribution, becomes the cornerstone of a development strategy and a precondition for a successful export-drive.

The effects of the dissociation between the financial sphere and the real economy are much more difficult to cope with at the national level, given the globalisation of the financial markets and the level of speculative profits achieved in this 'great casino' so far escaping a reasonable regulation. One trillion dollars are traded daily on the foreign-exchange markets alone, about fifty times more than the volume required by the foreign trade. These huge sums yield financial profits but do not generate material wealth and, to a considerable extent, are sterilised from the point of view of gross fixed-capital formation. Robert Triffin has wisely suggested a modest tax on speculative profits, but, as was to be expected, this move is being fiercely resisted by the powerful financial lobbies and, so far, by governments of industrialised countries.

Clearly, the Bretton Woods institutions, set up half a century ago, do not seem in their present form capable of ensuring the governance of the international economic system to the benefit of all the partners.

4. In certain circumstances, the return of economic growth, unless it is exceptionally fast (a rather unlikely assumption), will not by itself solve the plight of the victims of unemployment and exclusion either in the OECD countries, or *a fortiori*, in the rest of the world. According to UNDP estimates, between 1975 and the year 2000 the output of the world economy will more than double, while total employment will increase by less than half.

The pressure of market forces induces the enterprises to improve their competitiveness by a combination of increases in labour productivity, wage flexibilisation, sharing of work and reduction of social overheads.

Economic progress and the progressive freeing of human-kind from painful work depend, in the last instance, on the increments of productivity of labour. However, the final impact depends on the ways in which these increments are used and to whom they accrue. Growth through inequality may bring spectacular increases in wealth per capita and yet result in misdevelopment in terms of income distribution, access to resources and basic amenities of life and, above all, denial of the right to work – not only a source of livelihood but also a key element of social integration and human dignity.

Behind the postulate of wage flexibilisation looms the danger of undermining the very principle of minimum legal wage, already depressed in many countries both for structural reasons and on account of endemic inflation. To transfer to the workers the burden of the necessary adjustment is often an expedient to forego other, politically more difficult ways of reducing the costs of production, for instance by lowering the cost of borrowed money.

The concept of work sharing is central to the futuristic vision of a non-acquisitive society capable of self-limiting its material needs and of equitably distributing the socially necessary heteronomous work among all the citizens, who will use most of their life-time for autonomous, non-market oriented activities.[2] But this vision has little to do with current practices of transforming full-time jobs into part-time employment to weather the impact of the recession.

As for the reduction of social overheads, two attitudes most be distinguished. One favours the reduction of social protection on the pretext that Welfare States have gone too far in their generosity and should be dismantled, at least partly. The other offers a constructive criticism of the mechanisms to finance social protection.

Part of the problem arises from the fact that the social overheads paid by the enterprise are calculated in proportion to the wage bill. In some cases the total cost of labour thus exceeds by fifty or even a hundred per cent the amount paid in wages. Both social partners are dissatisfied: workers complain about low wages and employers about the high total lost of labour. Yet the social overheads could be financed in a different way, for instance through a fixed–capital tax or the value-added tax.

5. To preserve and universalise the social advances achieved in the last century, national and international public policies ought to be thoroughly revised and strengthened. The very concept of Welfare State must be saved from the onslaught on the part of neoliberal extremists.

Profound reforms may be needed to curb the excesses of 'statism', to improve the systems of democratic governance, to debureaucratise public administrations and to overhaul the service delivery systems, but too often their urgency is used as a pretext further to undermine the capacity of the States to design and carry out consistent sectoral public policies inspired by a long-term strategic vision of development (a 'national project').

Efficient macroeconomic controls are, of course, a necessary but by no means a sufficient condition. Entrepreneurship at the micro level should be strongly encouraged. But, it is the meso level which requires the most urgent attention.

The tasks ahead include, on the one hand, institutional transformation, reform or adjustment and, on the other hand, design and coordination of synergic public policies to foster a socially responsible ecologically viable and economically efficient development. Increments in productivity ought to be primarily used to generate employment and/or occupation opportunities. As the finality of development is social, high 'social value-adding' jobs should be carefully considered, alongside the prior effort to promote a productive integration of those hitherto economically and, therefore, socially and politically excluded.

The challenge before the forthcoming 1995 UN Conference on Social Development will be to prevent a 'social Munich' by reverting the present trend toward economic and social polarisation within nations and between nations, which in turn exacerbates all other forms of racial, ethnic and minority discrimination. Economic *apartheid* should not become our legacy to the next century.

6. To establish or consolidate democratic systems of governance guaranteeing the universal and effective implementation of economic and social rights may require close (re)examination of the four institutional questions outlined below:

a) Modes of articulation between the public and private spheres of action, going beyond the simplistic dichotomy State versus Market and exploring diverse *modi operandi* with the participation of public, cooperative, community-based, market profit-oriented and private, individual and collective non-profit forms of organisation and property. While the ideological discussion centres on two extreme forms of property – public and private profit-oriented – a diversity of successful intermediate forms has evolved in many countries, starting with producer and consumer cooperatives, citizen non-profit organisations active in education, health and social care, culture and sports, mutual financial and insurance companies which apply rules of conduct different from profit-oriented companies while competing with them on the market, community owned enterprises of urban services using the profit generated to finance social activities. Examples abound in Western Europe, in North America and, in less sophisticated forms, in the South, in some cases rooted in the age-old traditions of mutual aid. Regrettably, obnubilated by the neo-liberal gospel the so-called countries in transition have not up to now explored these possibilities in depth.

b) Search for innovative forms of partnership between the social partners of development, with special reference to the cooperation between public authorities, enterprises and citizen organisations giving concrete contents to the postulate of popular participation in development processes; exploring for this purpose the variety of societal experiences – past and present – in self-organisation, mutual aid and collective action aiming at a synergy between citizen actions and public policies.

c) In that context, emphasis on efforts to make possible local development bottom-up initiatives and peoples' empowerment, while recognising the paramount importance of the linkages between the local, regional, national and transnational loci and mechanisms of decision-making, as well as of the distribution of power and balancing of rights and duties between the different 'spaces of development'.[3]

d) Drawing up, on the basis of a reformed UN organisation, a system of global governance geared to the following three objectives:

- To ensure peace and security.
- To create a favourable international environment for the development endeavours in the South and for the structural transition and socio-economic rehabilitation in the East.
- To establish along the lines suggested by the Earth Summit, held in Rio de Janeiro in 1992, an effective prudential management of the international commons and life-supporting systems, acceptable to all three groups of countries and implemented through mutually agreed and synergistic national transition strategies towards sustainable development. For reasons amply discussed in Rio, the North must assume the bulk of the required adjustment both in terms of financial costs and, what is more important, of efforts aimed at modifying its development styles and consumption patterns.

Given the recent setbacks of the UN system in the handling of international crises (Somalia, Bosnia, Rwanda) and the probable neo-liberal orientation of the World Trade Organisation which will succeed to GATT, the prospect is one of a long and harsh struggle. The more so, as two and half years after the Rio Summit, little concrete progress has been achieved in implementing its Agenda 21 and that, up to now, the fiftieth anniversary of the Bretton Woods Conference has not generated a momentum towards the much needed reform of the institutions then created – the International Monetary Fund and the World Bank.

7. A global long-term strategic vision of the development process in the form of a national project and of regional programmes introducing the territorial dimension[4] provides the framework to test the mutual consistency of sectoral policies and properly to evaluate the social, environmental and economic impacts of single large scale projects and their cumulative (often irreversible) effects.

A national project requires both a vision – the collective invention of a desirable future informed by a set of consensual values – and a strong sense of realism about the feasibility and the time sequencing of the proposed goals. The main variables of the harmonisation game between social goals, ecological constraints and economically viable solutions are:

a) At the *demand level*, patterns of consumption and lifestyles, hard but not impossible to change[5] under the combined pressure of ethical considerations and of the realisation that the *status quo* is likely to bring about violence, anomy and ecological disasters.

b) At the *supply level*:

- patterns of resource-use with special reference to the potential for energy and resource-conservation and substitution by renewable resources of fossil fuels and scarce or polluting materials;
- choice of technologies responding to the criteria of social and environmental sustainability and of economic efficiency evaluated at the social level[6] with special reference to positive-sum games, the so-called 'win–win opportunities' in which socio-economic gains go hand in hand with environmental gains;
- the locational choices already mentioned.

Public policies belong to two categories. Reactive policies respond *ex post* to the arising situations. Proactive policies are anticipatory. They aim at new configurations. The difference between the two is particularly clear in the realm of social policies.

Reactive social policies redress the wrong done to those excluded or marginalised from the productive process. They 'alleviate' poverty treated as an unavoidable cost of the technical and economic progress. They also provide a minimum income for surviving, while keeping the survivors in their statute of excluded from the productive process and thereby deprived of their citizenry. By contrast, pro-active social policies attack the roots of exclusion and marginalisation by seeking a productive insertion for all those whose right to earn a decent livelihood is not respected.

8. The accumulated backlog of deprivation and dire poverty requires, both at national and international levels, the intensification of policies establishing and/or improving social safety-nets. Provision of adequate social protection[7] is a fundamental obligation of the states.

The more so as much can be done with marginal changes in the allocation of resources in the 25-trillion dollar world economy. The 1995 Social Summit should consider in that respect the possibility of establishing an automatically financed Fund for Relief Action and Poverty Alleviation (say by a value-added tax of one thousandth on the Gross World Product or the tax on speculative gains proposed by Robert Triffin).

However, an ever greater attention should be given to pro-active social policies. Provision of gainful employment on the labour markets and/or of opportunities for autonomous economic occupation ought to become the central piece of such policies all over the world to counter the trend towards structural unemployment.

Higher rates of economic growth are, of course, necessary. But going back to previous patterns of growth will not solve the unemployment problem in the absence of fine-tuned employment policies, challenging the employment/growth elasticities estimated from the experience of last decades. This should be done by means other than wage flexibility, already referred to, and keeping in mind the limited scope for work sharing in the short run.

Six entry points are suggested below to explore the labour-augmenting components of sustainable development strategies. Most of them require little if any additional investment. Of course, the scope for such modifications in development strategy will vary from country to country. As for the time-span necessary to introduce and disseminate the innovative approaches here discussed, it will depend on the ability of governments to redirect their public policies and of the international community to build an effective cooperative framework:

a) Notwithstanding the messages sent by environmentalists, fossil energy is still being used in a profligate way even in industrialised countries. The scope to improve the efficiency of its end-uses is considerable, not to speak of the potential modifications in lifestyles. In the South and in the East the degree of wastefulness observed in the prevailing patterns of resource-use is far greater. Paradoxically, this constitutes a reason for some guarded optimism for the future, as reducing these inefficiencies would be tantamount to releasing resources for development.

This 'reserve for development' could be evaluated by identifying the opportunities to improve waste management and recycling, to use productively agricultural residues, to cut down post harvest losses, to promote energy and water conservation and to forego future capital outlays by a more careful maintenance of fixed equipment, vehicles, infrastructures and built environment.

Three powerful reasons speak in favour of a systematic 'war against wastefulness':

- It is labour-intensive; moreover, many jobs finance themselves by the savings achieved in energy and resource-consumption.
- It belongs to the realm of 'win–win opportunities' combining socioeconomic and environmental gains.
- Insofar as it results in a longer life-cycle for the existing productive capacities (reducing thus the real depreciation) and allows for their fuller use (by 'transforming waste into wealth') it brings about a higher rate of growth at a given rate of investment and overall capital–output ratio. Yet, little attention has been paid up to now to this question.

b) The second green revolution, based on recent progress in biological knowledge and ecological awareness, calls for reconsidering the prospect for modern small-scale farming, a crucial question indeed for countries in the South and in the East where small peasants are a significant social group and where conditions for democratising access to land prevail. Blending of *techne* and *episteme* (peasant know-how and advanced science) allows designing highly productive, yet labour-intensive, integrated food and energy producing agrosylvopastoral systems using natural ecosystems as models. The condition is to provide small farmers organised in 'biovillages' with packages of biotechnologies scaled down to their needs, and to grant them access to credit and to markets.

Unfortunately, the present trends work in the opposite direction. A handful of large multinational enterprises pratically control the research on biotechnologies and the recent GATT agreement makes the access to them for developing countries more difficult, not to speak of the fact that the multinationals are not interested in strengthening the independent small farmers, but, on the contrary, making them dependent on their supplies of hybrid seeds requiring massive doses of specific pesticides. In the circumstances, much will depend on the ability of the Southern governments to foster public research oriented to the needs of their small farmers.

If properly handled at the socio-economic and political levels, the second green revolution will diversify the modernisation paths in the countryside and help to slow down the rural exodus in those countries which have not as yet gone through hyperurbanisation. By contrast, modern labour-displacing agriculture and the prospect of becoming urban archipelagos in a rural quasi-desert constitute for the developing countries a 'lose–lose' option compounding high economic, social and environmental costs.

c) Biotechnology holds a high potential not only for increasing the productivity of biomass but also for widening the range of biofuels and other products derived from biomass by 'green chemistry'.

The combination of these two applications of biotechnology opens a new direction for the industrialisation of countries enjoying favourable natural conditions for the production of biomass and endowed with extensive reserves of agricultural land and forested areas.

At what point of time biomass-derived industrial products will become competitive on the world markets is open to discussion and will depend on the evolution of the oil prices. Yet, their immediate use within national and/or regional markets may be envisaged for a variety of reasons such as security of fuel supply, insurance against the risk of a new oil shock, reasonable import substitution, environmental considerations, finding new uses for idle agricultural land, provisioning of local remote markets, prospect of rapid reduction of production costs *etc.*.

Biomass-based industrialisation and the substitution of biofuels for fossil fuels should offer many 'win–win' opportunities on the condition of following the prudential rules of ecological sustainability. It can lead, however, to environmental disasters if this condition is not strictly respected.

Whenever oil, used as fuel or feedstock, is replaced by biomass, an upstream employment multiplier is set in motion generating additional agricultural occupation and non-agricultural rural jobs in the production and transformation of biomass.[8]

d) More generally, the prospect for the industrialisation of rural areas[9] has considerably improved with the progress of telecommunication and the shift to flexible specialisation, which in certain cases renders obsolete the concepts of economies of scale and concentration inherited from the previous industrial revolution.

The example of North-East Italy (the so-called 'terza Italia') shows the potentiality to foster modern and highly competitive small-scale decentralised industries clustered in specialised Marshallian districts. To what extent and under what conditions the Italian experience could be emulated should be analysed on a case-by-case basis. Some evidence suggests that 'diffuse industrialisation' might prove less investment-intensive, more labour-absorbing and less income-concentrating than the classical highly concentrating model. However, the case of Italy also points to some kind of complementarity between the two models of industrialisation.

At the other end of the spectrum of small-scale industries, large countries with a deficient transportation system have much to gain from encouraging the development of labour-intensive industries working for the local markets. Instead of tolerating or even actively promoting the destruction of cottage industries, they should manage technological pluralism as part of their employment policies, in particular in the sphere of non-tradables where the question of competitiveness on an international scale does not arise. The paramount consideration in establishing the bottom for labour productivity should be the minimum acceptable level of earnings for the worker.

The items b, c and d taken together lead to a revision of the conventional views of the rural/urban configurations and on the unavoidability of the trend toward hyperurbanisation.

e) Public works constitute a domain *par excellence* of employment policies. There are good and well-known reasons for it, even in the industrialised countries where civilian spending on the overhauling of infrastructures should take the place of military spending as an engine of growth. Only three observations will be made here.

Firstly, as far as their financing is concerned, the strict rules of budgetary equilibrium enforced by the Washington consensus act as a straightjacket. Deficit financing within reasonable limits should be admitted for works conducted through highly labour-intensive methods to the extent to which the supply of wage goods is elastic.

Secondly, a bias in favour of labour-intensive techniques can be imposed to the contractors whenever such a choice does not entail a significant increase in cost. Alternative ways of organising public works through workers' cooperatives or associations may be explored.

Thirdly, the argument for the priority for public works is the need to improve first the systemic competitiveness through the modernisation of infrastructures rather than allocating public investment and foreign assistance to the improvement of competitiveness within single enterprises.

f) Social services by definition provide jobs with high social value added. Their expansion, as in the case of public works, is constrained, however, by financial limitations.

The costs of such services could be reduced by conceiving innovative service delivery systems based on a partnership between the State, the citizen, non profit and voluntary organisations and the users expected to pay modest users' fees. Even so, expenditure on social services will tend to increase through a combination of demographic, economic and technical factors (aging of the population, increased cost of personnel and of technical equipment for the health sector). The rate at which additional social workers are recruited will, therefore, depend on the political priority attached to the expansion of social services.

Countries in the South and East with a low general level of wages enjoy in this respect a special situation. They have an absolute comparative advantage in loading their goal function with social services that can be delivered through fairly labour-intensive methods. In fact, a primary school teacher or a social assistant in those countries has the same 'productivity' as in the North. Yet their wages are several times lower. The ratio of 'social value added' (hardly quantifiable) to the cost (consisting predominantly of wages) is very high indeed even if a provision is made to improve the excessively depressed level of wages in social professions whose status and prestige should be enhanced.

A small change at the margin in the allocation of resources would make an enormous change in the quality of life. Instead of treating the welfare state as a luxury only accessible to rich countries, developing countries could reverse the historical sequence followed by the industrialised countries. Where poverty, exclusion and unemployment are widespread, the welfare state is an immediate necessity.

9. Employment policies intersect, as we have seen, with many other policies -- social, environmental, scientific and technological, economic, financial *etc.*. Starting from the employment policies it should be, therefore, possible to identify the necessary contributions of other sectors to attack social exclusion and poverty at their roots. Hopefully, such an exercise will be performed as part of the preparation of the 1995 UN Conference on Social Development by the concerted efforts of UN agencies, governments, citizen organisations and scientific community.

10. Conferences are not important as events. Their success or failure depends on whether or not they generate a process and a movement of public opinion strong enough to influence the decision-makers. The stakes are very high indeed. Social and economic democracy is yet to be instituted within countries and to become also the cornerstone of the international system of governance. A social compact to this effect must be evolved establishing contractual links between all the actors of development. Such a compact ought to be supplemented by a natural compact for which the Rio de Janeiro Summit laid the foundation.

The world cannot afford to continue on the present track nor pretend to ignore the impending moral and social disaster.

Notes

1. Revised and enlarged version of a paper read before the Committee on International Affairs of the Brazilian Senate in August 1993.
2. In this model which is far advanced with respect to the cultural and political realities of our time, the increments in labour productivity arising from technical progress are essentially used to shorten the length of heteronomous work, the per capita output of the market economy being kept constant after having reached a level deemed satisfactory.
3. The principle of subsidiarity is ambiguous insofar as it does not state who in the last instance decides about its application, the lower or the higher echelon.
4. The territorial distribution of human activities is a key variable in planning for sustainable development, both as a goal (for instance the opening of new settlement frontiers) and an instrument to reduce the environmental impacts of certain projects.
5. The required changes in consumption patterns do not imply at all a generalised austerity or the imposition of Spartan lifestyles. If they go hand in hand with a more equitable distribution of income and access to resources, the end result might be a reduction of global consumption combined with an improvement of the living conditions of the majority.
6. The task of public policies in a mixed economy is to create such an environment for the enterprise as to make overlap as much as possible the motive of reasonable profit with these criteria.
7. The word 'protection' should perhaps be substituted by a less paternalistic term.
8. The working of the agro-industrial complexes of the kind described here will further induce additional upstream employment in the management of life-supporting systems – soils, water, forests. Their absence could jeopardise the very existence of such industries. Their expansion might yet prove the best way of forming the economic decision-makers to internalise the environmental dimension.
9. The word 'rural' is used here by contrast with 'large urban'. Rural development includes small towns.

Comment

Piet Terhal

The rich chapter of Ignacy Sachs can be subdivided into three main parts:

1. a concise description and short analysis of the worldwide emergence of
   – what Sachs calls – 'unbridled social darwinism';
2. a defence of the (concept of the) welfare state which should be
   institutionally transformed to 'foster a socially responsible, ecologically
   viable and economically efficient development'; and finally
3. a concrete description of policies and programmes which could be
   undertaken.

In the first part of the chapter the emphasis is strongly on the situation
in the Northern welfare states which would imply discouraging lessons for
the South and the East. Particularly for the large countries of the East and
South there seems to emerge a strategy of self-reliance – without too much
reliance on export-led growth. In the rest of the chapter – and particularly
its last part – the emphasis is indeed on 'national projects' (apparently
located in the South). The aim of saving the concept of the welfare state
binds the chapter together. It is not an easy task. The initially successful
performance of the welfare state in Northern countries is under severe
attack and even in crisis. At the least, important institutional changes are
needed to adapt the concept to the reality of the international situation.
Some hope can apparently be derived from the opportunities opened by
new technologies, which would permit win–win strategies with respect to
employment and environment provided that they are sufficiently under the
control of public authorities.

My short comment will follow the above tripartite sub-division of the
chapter. In sections 1–4 Sachs elaborates on various aspects of worldwide

254

social and economic exclusion as a consequence of present patterns of 'development'. The main emphasis is on un(der)employment, social marginalisation and ecological destruction. These together form, according to Sachs, the 'externalised social and environmental costs' accompanying 'the prevailing paradigms of growth through increases of productivity at the enterprise level and of search for competitiveness on the global markets'. The picture becomes even worse because growth is slow.

The diagnosis is sweeping. Does it reflect adequately the empirical evidence? As far as the slowness of growth in the Northern welfare states is concerned, the picture may be considered too gloomy, now that growth rates are rising again. However, the other aspects, in particular the labour displacement and low level of labour absorption, the social marginalisation, as well as the ecological costs accompanying growth are certainly manifest today. That economic growth guarantees economic, social and ecological protection for societies at large has often proved to be an illusion. Despite growth, the institutional mechanism through which such protection could be approximated in certain Western societies, namely the welfare state, is under severe attack.

It would be instructive to delve somewhat deeper into the factors which undermine the welfare state. For this we may use the analysis of the sociologist Nico Wilterdink (1993) of the secular shifts in the income distribution in the welfare states. Wilterdink in his turn goes back to some fundamental notions developed by Norbert Elias. According to the latter, relations of interdependence between people are the fundamental matrix, in which economic interaction is embedded. Interdependence implies power relations. People are seldom equally dependent on each other. Different degrees of mutual dependence result in differences in power, which in their turn lead to differences in privileges and rewards, and – in the economic sphere – to income inequality. The narrowing down of income levels in welfare states which took place during the last century can be traced back to growing mutual interdependence – within individual nations – between labour, capital and the government. As long as there is sufficient demand for labour, wage earners have bargaining power *vis-à-vis* capital. Moreover, the ensuing levelling down of power and income differences was essentially promoted through the political process of democratisation and public redistribution. More social cohesiveness within states, however, was accompanied by fierce competition between states, leading even to two world wars. After the Second War this process of income equalisation in Western states essentially continued until the 1970s, when the global economic power relations shifted in a direction which was unfavourable to Western societies. Since then the inequalities of income within these states are growing because international dependencies are increasingly eroding the domestic interdependence. The concomitant shift in power relations results in a shifting income distribution. Capital and management income is determined by international competition and standards, while labour income – particularly in the lowest skill categories – is subject to the international competition of very low-priced labour, both through trade and through (illegal) migration. Public authorities of individual welfare states gradually lose their equalising leverage on the domestic income distribution, unable as they are to control the process of growing economic international dependence.

If his diagnosis were correct, then what is there to say about Sachs's line of defence of the concept of the welfare state, which he formulates in sections 5 and 6 of his chapter? While Sachs underlines the need 'to save the Welfare State ... from the onslaught on the part of neoliberal extremists', he is also strongly emphasising the need for institutional transformation.

The weakening of the national state provides opportunities for a stronger role for other actors, which would blur the dichotomy 'state versus market' and may indeed give birth to 'innovative forms of partnership between the social partners of development' (see 6.a; 6.b; 6.c). In the context of growing global interdependencies, however, the last point (6.d) would deserve special attention, namely a system of global governance based on a reformed United Nations System. This special attention would follow from the brief analysis above of the erosion process of national social security systems.

Along the lines proposed by Jan Tinbergen we should distinguish here goals, instruments and institutions. The goal can be formulated as the safeguarding of socio-economic human rights worldwide. The prevailing institutions today, including Western welfare states, are only partially able to cope with the task. In particular the new worldwide economic interdependencies call for some countervailing transnational public power which would intervene in the global income distribution in favour of the marginalised sections of the world population, and in that way essentially supplement the efforts of national governments. A basic reason is that – given the labour-saving and skill-demanding nature of modern technologies – the free operation of international markets tends to exclude a certain section of the population of all countries from formal employment. The fact that their labour is not in demand makes these people rather powerless in front of the rest of society. Given the transnational nature of the economic system they are confronted with, the protection of their socio-economic rights should also, at least in part, be organised transnationally. The set of institutions needed for this would gradually evolve into an integrated system which would deserve the name given to it by Jan Tinbergen in his short contribution for the Human Development Report 1994, namely a World Government. In the area of global economic governance Tinbergen mentions a World Central Bank, of which IMF would be the forerunner, a World Investment Bank (the present World Bank reformed) and a World Treasury. The latter institution is needed to give the performance of transnational public tasks a firm and reliable financial basis. A World Treasury would be empowered to raise international taxes and to allocate them according to agreed objectives, one of which would be the universal public protection of socio-economic rights.

However, such protection should not wait until a world government has been put in place. There is a growing consensus that while economies are pressed through structural adjustment programmes to adapt to the rules of world markets, governments should be supported to alleviate poverty and expand socially necessary expenditure for that purpose. So called publicly supported safety nets are bound to grow in importance in many developing countries. Particularly in sub-Sahara Africa, sizeable external funds are needed to enable governments to perform their social role. The question is how to mobilise the finance needed for transnational public social security, even in the absence of a full-fledged World Treasury.

Coming now to the third part of Sachs's chapter (sections 7–10) we will concentrate and elaborate on one particular instrument which is twice mentioned by Sachs and which would appear attractive and feasible for strengthening social policy worldwide, namely an international tax on foreign exchange transactions. Sachs ascribes this policy instrument to Robert Triffin, but it is James Tobin who first advocated it in 1978 in his presidential address to the Eastern Economics Association. Tobin has returned to it recently, for example in his short contribution to the Human Development Report 1994. There are basically two objectives in such a proposal. The first objective is to 'throw some sand in the wheels of international finance'. As the recent technologies which promote mobility of financial capital greatly exceed the span of control of present public institutions, the autonomy of national decision making in matters of monetary and macro-economic policy is at stake. A small tax of – let us say – 0.5 per cent on foreign-exchange transactions would be an important disincentive for the destabilising speculative short-term round tripping on a foreign money market, without affecting long-term portfolio or investment decisions, or ordinary commercial transactions in trade and transportation. The potential gains of such an internationally agreed tax would be enormous, given the size of foreign exchange transactions. A tax of 0.5 per cent would yield about $1.5 trillion a year.

The second objective of this tax would be that part of the fund could be used to support public social security policies worldwide, broadening a bit the related proposal of Sachs. The logic behind such use would be that the international mobility of financial capital is basically undermining not only monetary and macroeconomic policies of governments, but also social-security policies. This does not negate that capital mobility as such may promote allocational efficiency with respect to international investment. However, international efficiency should not be separated from equity considerations. Essentially, public authorities have to avail themselves of the means to protect those whose economic rights are not secured by market processes. To link the generation (of part) of such means to the operation of international financial markets seems to be a perfectly logical proposition.

It is in this context that another element which Sachs mentions may be underlined, namely public works. These offer an opportunity to generate public demand for labour which can lead to large-scale investment in infrastructure, both social and economic, and to environmental protection. One preferable form of social security financed through the international fund could be that public authorities give an employment guarantee on public works, as has been done with a measure of success by the state government of the Indian State of Maharahstra.

Particularly in those poverty stricken backward rural areas in the South ruled by vicious circles of poverty, environmental degradation and demographic growth, public works employment guaranteed at minimum wages would establish a floor in the labour market, effectively increase the bargaining strength of rural labour households and channel surplus labour resources in a systematic way into productive investment, provided that such works are well integrated in the overall development strategy and planned, implemented and monitored in a decentralised way with the essential participation of local people, and NGOs (see Hirway and Terhal 1994).

Three other preferable forms of social security which could be supported out of the fund are a guaranteed income support to those who owing to age, sickness or handicap are not able to work (including for example a worldwide old-age pension), subsidised credit for self-employment (including training), and finally a more general support of public expenditure for health and education, especially in backward areas and for underprivileged groups. The exact shape of each country's social-security policy should be determined by its own polity. The international allocation of the fund should follow objective criteria in which the economic strength of a country (autonomous capacity for social security policy), the need for social protection and the actual shape of national policies are evaluated. While by far the major proportion would flow to the majority of the poor living in the South, there is no reason for excluding financial support to Northern welfare states wanting to maintain and strengthen their social security.

References

Hirway, I. and P. Terhal (1994) *Towards Employment Guarantee in India. Indian and International Experiences in Rural Public Works Programmes, Indo Dutch Studies on Development Alternatives,* No. 14, New Delhi: Sage.

Wilterdink, N. (1993) Ongelijkheid en interdependentie. Ontwikkelingen in welstandsverhoudingen (Inequality and interdependence. Development in welfare relations), in: *Amsterdams Sociologisch Tijdschrift,* Vol. 20, No. 2, October.

Author's index